Applied Statistics
with SPSS

Eelko Huizingh

Applied Statistics
with SPSS

S SAGE Publications

London ● Thousand Oaks ● New Delhi

First published 2007

 SAGE Publications Ltd
1 Oliver's Yard
55 City Road
London EC1Y 1SP

SAGE Publications Inc.
2455 Teller Road
Thousand Oaks, California 91320

SAGE Publications India Pvt Ltd
B-42, Panchsheel Enclave
Post Box 4109
New Delhi 110 017

British Library Cataloguing in Publication data

A catalogue record for this book is available
from the British Library

ISBN-10 1-4129-1930-4   ISBN-13 978-1-4129-1930-2
ISBN-10 1-4129-1931-2   ISBN-13 978-1-4129-1931-9

Library of Congress Control Number: 2006928332

Typeset by C&M Digitals (P) Ltd, Chennai, India
Printed on paper from sustainable resources
Printed in Great Britain at the Alden Press, Witney

Contents

Preface

Statistical analysis nowadays is not just a matter of the scientific world. In any newspaper you can find the results of statistical research. Television programmes present their own surveys and when election time approaches, new predictions are published on a daily basis. The advent of statistical software has significantly contributed to this development.

For several decades now, SPSS has been one of the most widely used statistical software packages. Over time, the package has continually been adapted to meet the changing needs of its users and the ever expanding technical possibilities. The most important difference between SPSS for Windows and all preceding SPSS versions is its ease of operation. Carrying out statistical analyses has never been this simple.

There is, however, a downside as well. With SPSS, anyone can do a t-test, but does every user fully understand what conclusions may be drawn from the results, or whether the t-test may be applied at all in the first place? As statistical analysis has become increasingly easy to perform thanks to modern computer technology, more and more users with a limited background in statistics are performing analyses that were previously left to statisticians. In practically oriented treatises of statistics the emphasis is therefore shifting to questions involving the assumptions analytical techniques make and the interpretation of the outcomes. The trouble of doing all the 'mechanical' calculations may be well left to the computer.

The aim of this book

A good book on SPSS should do more than teach the user how to 'press the buttons': it should offer a wider perspective on the uses of SPSS. The aim of this book is therefore:

Teaching students how to reap full benefit from the SPSS features in order to perform sound statistical research.

With this aim in mind, the book has been organised into two parts. The first part, titled 'Learning to work with SPSS', outlines the purposes for which the program can be used in each phase of the research process. In addition, Part I contains three tutorial sessions. The sessions simulate a small research project, implying that you have to perform the same tasks that you will have to do when carrying out your own research. You can study these chapters while seated at your computer desk. All mouse clicks and keystrokes are explicitly noted, with further explanations where necessary. This proven concept makes the book eminently suitable for self-study.

Part II, 'Working with SPSS and Data Entry', has been designed more as a reference guide. Suppose you have collected data and want to analyse them. You are now facing the question of how to realise your research objectives by using SPSS. For conducting interviews and data entry, SPSS uses a specific module called Data Entry. The features and options of this module are discussed and illustrated at the beginning of Part II. The remainder of Part II deals with the many analytical techniques that SPSS contains. In each case, the dialogue boxes are shown and the full SPSS output is presented, discussed and interpreted in lay terms. To help ensure that your statistical research is sound, each chapter starts with a discussion of the assumptions a technique makes, and also refers to comparable techniques. In order to enhance the accessibility of Part II, the inside cover shows an overview of the available statistical techniques in relation to the measurement level of your data.

How to use this book

For over twenty years now, I have been teaching courses at the University of Groningen in which we use SPSS. Years ago, based on my teaching experience, I developed this book, which has now seen more than ten editions. In these successive versions the book was constantly adapted to further improve its use and to cover new SPSS features.

It is my personal experience that learning to work with SPSS and using SPSS in statistical research are two different things. That is the reason for organising this book into two parts. The basic point in learning to work with SPSS is that the best way of familiarising yourself with software is by working with the software. Long treatises on software packages are of little use – no better teacher than hands-on experience. That is why Part I includes three tutorial sessions in which the most important features of SPSS are discussed by using them.

Sound statistical analysis requires an easily accessible reference manual in which the analyses are discussed step by step and the output is explained in a way that is easy to understand. Additionally, it should be clear what conclusions can be drawn from what results. These ideas form the basis for the organisation of the chapters in Part II.

Acknowledgements

While preparing this book I have been fortunate to receive important contributions from a number of people. First of all, I would like to express my gratitude to SPSS Inc. for our excellent collaboration, which I have been enjoying for over fifteen years. Time and again, my contacts with SPSS staff turn out to be friendly and efficient experiences, forming a pleasant stimulus for the continued re-editing of this book.

Finally, I would like to mention Gea, Ilse and Evelien; thanks to them I live in the happy circumstance of being able to alternate between the joys of family life and productive work. I really appreciate your patience, impatience and love.

Groningen, October 2006
Eelko Huizingh

Selecting a chart

1. Selecting a type of chart: see Section 13.1 and the table below.
2. Creating a chart: see section in table below.
3. Changing a chart: see Section 13.11.

Goal chart	Measurement level of your variable(s)		
	Nominal	Ordinal	Interval/ratio
Describing a variable or group	Bar chart (5.3, 13.2) Pie chart (13.5)		Boxplot (13.8) Histogram (13.9)
Describing a trend		Bar chart (5.3, 13.2)	Bar chart (5.3, 13.2) Line chart (13.3) Area chart (13.4)
Presenting differences between variables or groups			High-low-close chart (13.7.1) Range barchart (13.7.2) Difference line chart (13.7.3)
Analysing association between variables		Scatterplot (13.6)	
Comparing observed distribution with normal distribution		Histogram with normal curve (13.9) Normal quantile plot (13.10) Normal probability plot (13.10)	

Selecting a statistical method

The table below helps you to select the most appropriate statistical method based on (1) the goal of your analysis and (2) the measurement level of your variables. Of course, other considerations are also important; see the section in which the selected method is discussed for the assumptions you have to meet.

Goal analysis	Measurement level of your variable(s)		
	Nominal	**Ordinal**	**Interval/ratio**
Describing a variable	Frequency table (4.7, 12.1) Multiple response analysis (15)	Statistics (12.1.1, 12.2, 12.3.1)	
Determining the average	Mode (12.1.1)	Median (12.1.1)	Mean (12.1.1)
Testing sample average to another average	Binomial test (19.2)	Sign test (19.7.2)	One-sample t-test (16.2)
Analysing distribution	Chi-square test (19.1);	Kolmogorov-Smirnov (19.4)	
Describing groups of cases	Crosstable (14)		Statistics (16.1)
Comparing two independent groups	Chi-square test (14.3)	Mann-Whit ney (19.5.1) Kolmogorov-Smirnov (19.5.2)	t-test (16.3)
Comparing more than two independent groups	Chi-square test (14.3) Median test (19.6.2)	Kruskal-Wallis (19.6.1) Analysis of variance (17)	F-test
Comparing related groups		Wilcoxon Signed Ranks (19.7.1) Sign test (19.7.2) Friedman (19.8.1)	Paired t-test (16.4)
Analysing the association between two variables	Chi-square test (14.3)	Spearman rank correlation (14.4, 18.1)	Correlation (18.1, 18.2)
Explaining a variable: - linear relation - non-linear relation			Regression (18.3) Curve estimation (18.4)

Part I

Learning to work with SPSS

The first part of this book consists of three introductory and three do-it-yourself chapters. The first three chapters explain the background and applications of SPSS, while the other three, in the form of tutorials, show the way SPSS works.

Chapter 1 presents the history and features of the SPSS data analysis system. Chapter 2 discusses the question of how you can use SPSS in your own research. Seven stages are distinguished in the research process and we explain how SPSS and the module Data Entry can be of help in each of these stages. In each case the discussion includes an overview of the relevant SPSS commands.

Before any statistical analysis can be performed, a database needs to be made available. This usually involves 'translating' the measurements or survey questions into variables, and, after coding the data, entering the data into a computer file. This process is summarised in the form of a code book, which is the subject of Chapter 3.

The last three chapters of Part I are of a practical nature. Each consists of a session which takes a simple example to show all essential topics that one encounters in working with SPSS. The three sessions have been written in a way to enable you to study them while using your computer, that is, all mouse clicks and keystrokes are explicitly noted, with further explanations where necessary. In these sessions we simulate a small research project. During this guided tour you will perform the same tasks that you have to do in your own research.

What is the purpose of the sessions?

For experienced SPSS users, the sessions are a means of quickly getting acquainted with the most recent version of the software. For those who have no prior knowledge of the program (in SPSS parlance they are new friends, as distinguished from the experienced old friends), the sessions provide an overview of the structure, the operational aspects and the features of SPSS.

1 Background to SPSS for Windows

In a world in which the pace of change is constantly accelerating, SPSS is one of the oldest, yet still widely used, statistical software packages. The first version of SPSS appeared on the market way back in 1968! Section 1.1 summarises the development that the package has seen since that time. The SPSS software consists of a base module needed for all applications, plus a number of add-on modules for additional purposes that are briefly discussed in Section 1.2.

1.1 SPSS: history and development

Many statistical computations involve sequences of simple arithmetic operations repeated many times over. Consider, for example, the computation of a common statistic such as the standard deviation. This is done as follows:

- determine the number of cases;
- compute the sum of all observed values;
- divide this sum by the number of cases: this gives the mean;
- for each case, compute the observed value minus the mean;
- compute the squares of these differences;
- determine the sum of all squares;
- divide this sum by the number of observations minus 1;
- find the root of the division result.

Although the detailed recipe thus involves quite a number of steps, clearly the knowledge required to execute each individual step barely exceeds the level of primary education. It is a useful exercise to perform this computation by hand once or twice, to get some feel for statistics. But doing the arithmetic in situations involving a hundred cases would be a formidable task, not to mention the likely errors. It is not surprising, therefore, that from the very beginning of the computer age statisticians have been eagerly using electronic technology as an aid to arithmetic. Equally understandably, it was the advent of computers that marked the true take-off of applied statistics.

Ever since 1968 when SPSS was introduced as a statistical analysis program for the social sciences, the package has been part of this development. The original meaning of the abbreviation SPSS is Statistical Package for the Social Sciences, but in its present form SPSS is much more than that. It has grown into a comprehensive modular package that handles data, data processing and format. The target group has long included users from disciplines other than the social sciences. SPSS can be used wherever data are collected, analysed and presented in the form of tables and charts.

One of its strong points is that SPSS is capable of performing almost all common types of analysis. This makes the software particularly suitable for analysing data obtained by questionnaires. Such research projects usually include variables at different measurement levels, that is, ratio or interval data occur together with nominal or ordinal variables. The broad applicability of the program is also evidenced by the number of users, which SPSS claims to exceed 3 million worldwide.

1.1.1 Evolutions in statistics and technology

Over the many years since 1968 the SPSS package has gone through many adaptations to match the ongoing developments, both in statistics and in technology. Many of the statistical methods that have been developed or improved over the last three decades have been included. Additionally, SPSS has seen the development from computing centres dedicated to operating large *mainframes*, to *notebook computers* the size of a writing pad. In the past, users had to prepare sets of instructions and deliver them, at first in the form of stacks of punch cards at the desk of a computing centre, and in later years as electronic files via a computer terminal. At some later time the SPSS user would then pick up the printed output from the service desk. Subsequent program versions were increasingly user-friendly, a development that took place by many modest steps in addition to two major advances. The first major step was the introduction, in 1983, of an SPSS version for personal computers (SPSS/PC). The second major step came nine years later, with the introduction of SPSS for Windows in 1992. This version was still easier to use, as it was the first that did not require knowledge of the special SPSS command language. Since then, SPSS has continued to become ever easier to learn and use.

1.1.2 The users

Thus, over time, the SPSS software has gone through a far-reaching evolution process. In addition, the user profile has significantly changed as well. The 'first' SPSS user, towards the end of the 1960s, was used to carrying out many of the techniques by hand. As a result, this user was thoroughly familiar with the assumptions, the computation methods and the interpretation of the outcomes. Many present-day SPSS users are much less familiar with these fundamentals, which carries the risk of incorrectly performing or interpreting analyses. The increased ease of use enhances that risk: with SPSS, any layperson nowadays can perform advanced statistical analyses, but a full grasp of what this entails is another matter. SPSS offers little protection against such risks and therefore a good basic understanding of statistics remains a prerequisite for properly applying these techniques.

1.2   The SPSS data analysis system

SPSS offers a very broad range of statistical methods. As such, this has the potential disadvantage that users have options at their disposal that many will never use. That is why SPSS has been organised into modules that together form the *SPSS data analysis* system. Users can decide which of these special modules they need in addition to the base module; these modules can be bought separately.

This book deals only with the various features of the base module and the module Data Entry. All applications of SPSS require the base module. It contains commands for creating and transforming data files, plus the most widely used methods of analysis. Examples of these include frequency tables, crosstables, many types of charts, t-tests, analysis of variance, correlation analysis and regression analysis (see Section 2.5 for a more detailed overview).

Besides the base module, SPSS contains a constantly growing set of add-on modules. One of these is Data Entry, a module used for questionnaire design, conducting structured interviews and entering collected data.

This book is based on SPSS for Windows, version 14.0.1, which came onto the market in the autumn of 2005. For reasons of convenience, the book refers to this version as 'SPSS'. Only in cases where there is risk of confusion is the full name and version used. The version of Data Entry described is Data Entry Builder Release 4.0.0.

2 The use of SPSS in statistical research

This chapter gives an overview of the purposes for which SPSS can be used. The various phases of the overall research process are used to structure this overview. We start the research process at the stage where the data are collected and proceed to the end when all analyses have been done and the research report can be written. For each phase we explain how SPSS can support the user. We also specify the relevant SPSS commands. References are included to the sections that deal with these commands, making this chapter a useful source, also for research in progress.

The research process as discussed in this chapter consists of a preparatory phase followed by six phases oriented at performing statistical analyses. Section 2.1 briefly describes all of these. Next, Sections 2.2–2.7 deal with the six phases involving the statistical analysis, one at a time. Creating the data file is the subject of Section 2.2, followed by checking the data in Section 2.3. The next step is that of data transformation, which is required when not all of the original data are to be used in the analysis (Section 2.4). Data analysis, Section 2.5, is the core substance of SPSS, which explains why this is the longest section. After the analyses comes the interpretation of the results (Section 2.6). Finally, Section 2.7 is concerned with writing the research report.

2.1 The research process

Although many scientists have devised all sorts of schemes for better structuring the process of statistical research, most studies are quite similar. A project starts with the formulation of the problem (the general research question), from which one or more testable hypotheses are derived (specific questions). In order to test the hypotheses one has to collect data that can be subjected to statistical analysis. The process ends with writing the research report which includes the outcomes, conclusions and often also the recommendations. The part of the research process for which SPSS and Data Entry can be used consists of seven phases (see Figure 2.1). These are briefly discussed below.

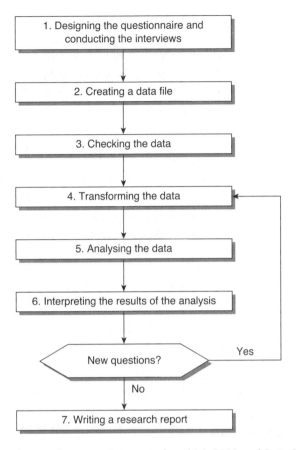

Figure 2.1   The phases of a research process for which SPSS and Data Entry can be used

1. Designing the questionnaire and conducting the interviews – After defining the issues on which the field study is to provide information, a questionnaire is developed and conducted. The module Data Entry, described in Chapter 7, enables you to present questions and answers in a neat, well-organised form. In case you need paper forms the questionnaire can be printed, but Data Entry is mostly used for telephone interviews. An option is to convert the questionnaire to a web page format enabling data collection via the internet. During the interviews Data Entry automatically presents the questions and shows the possible answers. Furthermore, Data Entry can automatically check the data while they are being entered (to detect typing errors), skip questions that are not relevant for a respondent and, where needed, recode the data. In other words, Data Entry offers comprehensive computer-assisted telephone interviewing (CATI).

This initial phase is of course relevant only when you have to collect data specifically for your own research project (primary data). When using existing data sources (secondary data) this phase is skipped.

2. Creating a data file – After data collection by questionnaires, paper forms or measuring equipment (e.g. scanning), the next phase involves the creation of a data file capable of being analysed by SPSS. The variables have to be defined and the data coded, typed and saved in a data file. If the data are already in a computer file, for instance if Data Entry or scanning were used, this file can either be imported by SPSS or converted into SPSS format.

3. Checking the data – Next, the database must be checked. Only after you have verified that the data have been entered and/or converted free of error can you proceed to the analysis phase. If the data file contains errors, the process returns to the previous phase. The erroneous data are corrected, and the data are checked again.

4. Transforming the data – In many cases some form of data transformation is required before the actual analyses can be performed. Examples of data transformation include grouping values into categories and selecting a group of cases (e.g. male respondents, or people older than sixty years). This phase is optional: if you want to include all of the original data in the analysis, there is no need for data transformation.

5. Analysing the data – The actual data analysis does not take place until we come to phase five. For each research question you have to determine the most appropriate method of analysis. This choice depends on the goal of the analysis and the extent to which the data meet the assumptions underlying various analysis methods. Once you have selected a method, you have to execute the corresponding SPSS command by determining all relevant specifications like the names of the variables and the table and charts you want to be included in the output.

6. Interpreting the results of the analysis – SPSS presents the outcomes of an analysis as tables or charts containing various statistics like means, significance levels and correlation coefficients. It is the task of the researcher to interpret this information and to decide whether the analysis has satisfactorily answered the research question. It frequently happens that the interpretation leads to additional questions, requiring another round of transformation and analysis.

7. Writing a research report – When the data have exhaustively been analysed, that is, all research questions have been answered, the research report can be written. Among other things, the report will contain the interpretation of the results together with the relevant SPSS output (charts and tables). Normally, the main text contains only a limited part of the output: detailed results often go into the appendices.

The remaining sections of this chapter each deal with a separate phase (excluding the first, preparatory, phase). For each phase we will show how you can benefit from using SSPS.

2.2   Creating the data file

After gathering the data, the next step is to create a *data file* in which the data are stored in such a way that SPSS can handle them. The data may represent characteristics, opinions or aspects of individuals, businesses, homes, production series, subsidies, etc. SPSS refers to the objects or subjects possessing these properties as *cases*. The properties that have been measured are the *variables*. The SPSS data file is a matrix in which the cases are organised as rows and the variables as columns.

Creating a data file is a two-step process. First, the measurements are converted into variables, and then they are entered into the data file. Both steps are briefly discussed below. It is also possible that the data are already available in a computer file (such as an Excel or Access file). How to retrieve data files from other software in SPSS is discussed at the end of this section.

2.2.1 From measurements to variables

Because SPSS deals with variables, you will have to 'translate' the measurements into variables and to determine the valid values for each variable. In the case of a survey this means that each question must be converted into one or more variables, and that we have to assign a code to every possible answer (e.g. 'disagree' is coded as 0 and 'agree' as 1; see Section 3.1). The rules for converting measurements into variables are laid down in an overview called *code book*. Among other things, the code book contains the names and definitions of all relevant variables and their coding schemes (see Section 3.2 for more details). When the SPSS module Data Entry is used for collecting the data, the code book is designed in the previous step of designing the questionnaires and conducting the interviews.

The Variable View of the Data Editor is used to *define variables* in SPSS. This is a matrix in which you can enter the variables and their properties. Basically, this amounts to specifying the contents of the code book in SPSS (see Section 4.4).

2.2.2 Entering the data

The following step is to fill the data file with data. The easiest and most reliable way of entering the data is by using the module *Data Entry* (see chapter 7). If you do not have Data Entry, you can use the Data View, a tab in the Data Editor. The Data View is a matrix in which the rows correspond to cases and the columns to variables. The procedure for entering the data is explained in Sections 3.3 and

4.5. Section 8.2 deals with a number of other useful functions of the Data Editor for inserting and changing the order of variables and cases.

2.2.3 Reading data from other software

Sometimes the data are already available in a different software format. In these cases SPSS can convert the data to its own format for a number of software packages. SPSS can import data files created with various database (e.g. Access) and spreadsheet packages (e.g. Excel and Lotus 1-2-3). In addition, SPSS can import ASCII files and, of course, also data files made with other versions of SPSS (see Sections 8.4–8.6).

2.3   Checking the data

After the data have been entered or converted, we have to check them for any errors. Using the module Data Entry you have the option to automatically check the data during the input process (see Section 7.3 in particular). With Data Entry you can define rules that determine whether answers are valid or logically consistent (e.g. the combination 8 years old and high school education is improbable) and rules for skipping questions or automatically returning values.

In case you used the Data View to enter the data, checking them has to be done manually. This can be a time-consuming step, but it may well pay off if you can avoid having to repeat the analysis because of errors in the data file. Using the Data Editor you can check the data by systematically going through the cells one by one. Another possibility is to print this window and then compare the contents with the source (for example the filled-out questionnaires).

Furthermore, it is advisable to make frequency tables for all variables before proceeding to the analysis stage (with the Frequencies command; see Sections 4.7 and 12.1). Inspection of the tables will reveal whether non-valid codes have been entered for a variable (e.g. the value 2 for a variable with the valid codes 0 and 1). Moreover, the frequency tables provide you with a useful overview of the collected data.

In case the data file contains any errors, the Data Editor contains a number of useful functions to locate quickly the errors in the data file (see Section 8.3).

2.4   Transforming the data

The next step in the research process is the transformation of the data. This step is only needed when not all original data are to be used in the analysis. When you want to use classifications, analyse a specific group of cases or merge data files, the data must be transformed before the analysis can begin.

Transforming may involve the following operations:

- *variables*: for example, grouping values into categories, or computing new variables;
- *cases*: for example, selecting a group of cases or sorting the data;
- *entire data file*: for example, merging multiple data files or transposing a data file.

Each type of operation is separately discussed in one of the subsections below. The corresponding sections in Part II of this book are indicated in parentheses.

2.4.1 Transforming variables
The transformation commands in this category allow you to:

1. Perform computations with variables
2. Count the number of times a certain value occurs for different variables
3. Group values into categories
4. Determine ranking numbers
5. Convert string variables to numeric variables
6. Replace missing values with valid values (for time series data only).

1. Computing with variables: Compute (9.1). The Compute command defines a new variable as the result of a computation using one or more existing variables. The computation may include several functions, e.g. for rounding, square roots and logarithms. It is possible to execute the command for a specific group of cases.

If you have asked a respondent about the expenditures for court rental, tennis clothing and a tennis racket, you can use Compute to define a new variable called TennisExpenses, being the sum of the other three variables.

2. Counting the number of times a certain value is found: Count (9.2). With the Count command you can define a new variable that indicates the number of times a certain value occurs for a number of variables. The command can be executed for a specific group of cases.

Suppose that you have formulated five propositions relating to the importance of certain aspects of the environment and asked whether respondents agree or disagree with these. This will give you five answers (five variables) per person. Using Count you can define a new variable Environment that indicates the number of propositions supported by a respondents. Accordingly, Environment can take values between 0 and 5.

3. Grouping values into categories: Visual Bander and Recode (9.3). Grouping values into a limited number of distinct categories is often used to make a frequency table or a crosstable for a continuous variable. Recoding the variable reduces the many different values to a much smaller number of categories.

If you have measured people's ages in years and want to summarise the results in a frequency table with a limited number of rows, you first have to define age categories using the Visual Bander (or Recode) command, for example, younger than 20, between 20 and 40, and over 40.

4. Determining ranking numbers: Rank Cases (9.4). The Rank Cases command is used to define a variable that reflects the ranking order of the cases based on one of more variables.

If you want to rank a hundred persons according to their ages, for example, you can use the Rank Cases command to define a new variable that runs from 1 to 100, the value 1 being assigned to the youngest person and the value 100 to the oldest (or the other way round).

5. Converting string variables into numeric variables: Automatic Recode (9.5). The Automatic Recode command automatically converts a string variable into a numeric variable.

Suppose that a number of people have been asked to name their favourite tennis player and that the data file contains a string variable with the full names of the players, for example 'Federer', 'Nadal', and 'Roddick'. With Automatic Recode you can convert this variable into a numeric variable with the values 1, 2 and 3. SPSS will then automatically assign the label 'Federer' to code 1, etc.

6. Replacing missing values for time series data: (9.6). For time series data, the Replace Missing Values command computes the likely values of missing values, and completes the time series by replacing the missing values.

Suppose that a child's height is recorded once each month over a period of a year and that the value for May is missing. By replacing this missing value with the average of the values for April and June you obtain a value for May that will usually be acceptable.

2.4.2 Transforming cases

Using the transformation commands for cases you can:

1. Split the observations into groups, if you need the same analyses for each group
2. Select cases
3. Assign different weights to cases
4. Sort cases.

1. Split the observations into groups: Split File (10.1). The Split File command divides the total set of cases into groups of cases. SPSS will then automatically carry out all subsequent analyses for each of these groups separately.

Suppose that you want to have similar crosstables, bar charts and correlation analyses for all-male and all-female groups. With Split File you define two gender groups, and SPSS will then perform all analyses for each of the groups separately.

2. Selecting cases: Select Cases (10.2). The Select Cases command enables you to select a certain group of cases, and the subsequent analyses are performed for that group only. Cases can be selected based on a condition, their case numbers or at random.

If the gender of each individual respondent is known, Select Cases can, for instance, select the group of all women. If the data file contains a large number of names and addresses, you can use Select Cases to obtain a random sample. Select Cases also be used to restrict the analysis to, say, the first fifty respondents.

3. Assigning different weights to cases: Weight Cases (10.3). By default, SPSS assigns equal weights to all cases. The Weight Cases command makes it possible to change these weights. Weight Cases is also useful when you do not have the original data, but only their distribution (see example in Section 10.3).

Suppose that in a study men are overrepresented with respect to women. This means that, relatively speaking, there are more men in the sample than in the population. To redress the correct proportions of men and women, one could assign a lower weight to each man in the data set.

4. Sorting cases: (10.4). Normally, the data file contains the cases in the order in which you entered them. With the Sort Cases command you can sort them, that is, arrange them in a different order. Sort Cases is useful in combination with the command to select cases based on case numbers (see Select Cases).

If you want to include only the fifty youngest respondents in the analysis, you first sort all cases based on the age of the respondent, then select the first fifty cases.

2.4.3 Transforming the data file

In contrast to the other transformation commands, the commands that operate on the entire data file create a *new data file*. Using this category of commands you can:

1. Merge data files
2. Combine (aggregate) cases
3. Restructure (transpose) the data file.

1. Merging data files: Merge Files (11.1). Sometimes different data files each contain part of the total body of data. Using the Merge Files command you can merge these files by adding cases or variables to a data file.

Suppose that two persons enter the survey answers into a data file, each using their own PC. That way, two files are created, containing the same variables but different respondents. With Merge Files you can add the cases from one file to the other file.

Suppose you study voting behaviour and have carried out two identical surveys at different times, before and after an election, and that the answers were stored in two different data files (a 'pre-election' file and a 'post-election' file). The two data files now contain the same cases but different variables. With Merge Files you can add the variables from one file to the other file.

2. Aggregating cases: Aggregate (11.2). Using the instruction Aggregate you can change (i.e. lower) the level of detail of your analyses by aggregating cases. For each variable separately, you can specify how to aggregate the cases (e.g. by using the sum of the cases, the mean of the cases or the value of the first case in the group).

Suppose that a shop keeps daily records of how many washing machines it sells and their average price. You can then aggregate these daily records into weekly records, by taking the sums of the daily sales and computing the week price as the average of the day prices.

3. Restructuring the data file: Restructure Data Wizard(11.3). The SPSS data file is a matrix composed of rows and columns, where cases should go in the rows and variables in the columns. In practise, however, the structure of the available data file may be different. The Restructure Data Wizard enables SPSS to cope with such situations.

Suppose you have a data file containing the monthly sales of several varieties of jelly (apricot, strawberry, cherry and so on). If we are to test whether the average monthly sales of apricot jelly exceed those of cherry, we need a data file with the varieties of jelly as variables and the months as cases. But in order to test whether average sales of jelly in January were higher than those in June, we need a data file with the months as variables and the varieties of jelly as cases. The Restructure Data Wizard is able to make the necessary switch of cases and variables.

2.5   Analysing the data

The fifth step in the research process is performing the actual statistical analyses. As explained in the previous chapter, SPSS consists of a base module plus a number of add-on modules. While the latter offer a wide spectrum of advanced techniques, this book only deals with the analytical techniques in the base module.

The analytical techniques detailed in this book can be categorised into the following six groups:

1. Description of variables
2. Description of groups of cases
3. Testing differences between independent groups
4. Testing differences between related groups
5. Determining the relationship between two variables
6. Estimating a variable by means of one or more other variables.

Each of these groups is discussed in a separate subsection. On the inside cover there is an overview of these analyses in relation to the measurement levels of the variables involved.

Because each method of analysis imposes specific requirements on the measurement level of the variables, we start by briefly describing the four measurement levels, before proceeding to a discussion of the various techniques. If you are already familiar with the concept of measurement levels, you may skip the next subsection.

2.5.1 The measurement level of a variable

The remainder of this section is dedicated to a discussion of many different statistical techniques. For almost any goal of an analysis, such as describing groups or determining the relationship between two variables, there are multiple techniques available. It is the researcher who has to select the most appropriate technique. Most techniques assume a certain *measurement level* of the variables; accordingly, this is one of the most important criteria in selecting a statistical technique. Only if the variables meet the measurement level requirements may the technique be applied. Of course, statistical techniques often make additional assumptions, so that meeting the measurement level requirements may not be sufficient for a valid analysis. Part II of this book, which discusses each statistical technique in greater detail, also provides additional clarification on any other assumptions made.

Statistics is about the analysis of the measured properties of phenomena. Generally speaking, there are differences in the extent to which these properties (the variables) can be quantified. In order of increasing level of measurement, four types of variable are distinguished: nominal, ordinal, interval and ratio variables. Each of these measurement levels is now briefly described and illustrated with examples.

1. Nominal scale. Nominal variables are assigned unique but arbitrary values. A nominal scale applies when a property is not quantifiable but can only be identified. Examples include properties like hair colour, brand of tennis racket, gender, blood group. For each property one distinguishes certain categories and each category is assigned a number. The numbers only serve as labels: they do not represent magnitudes of any kind. The hair colours red, fair and black may be assigned the numbers 1, 2 and 3, respectively, but any other order of the values would have served our purpose just as well. A larger number for hair colour does not mean darker hair, longer hair or more hair.

In the example above, numbers are assigned to a property. It also happens that the property itself is a number while the scaling level is nominal nevertheless. Examples include properties like telephone numbers, bank account numbers and the numbers football players have on their shirts. Again, the magnitude of such numbers does not reflect the value of properly.

2. Ordinal scale. One step up, on an ordinal scale the value of a property is not entirely arbitrary; instead, the values refer to a ranking. A higher value on the scale indicates that a property is larger, longer, higher, more important, better or more attractive. However, the only information conveyed is whether a property is present to a higher or a lower degree, the magnitude of the difference being left undecided. This is typical of the ordinal measurement level.

One can test how well people like different sweets, using a five-point scale where 1 means 'definitely not nice' and 5 means 'very nice'. A sweet with a score of 4 is liked better than a sweet with score 2, but one cannot say that it is twice as nice as the other. Moreover, the difference between the scores 1 and 2 need not be equal to the difference between the scores 4 and 5. Another example is ranks in an army. The higher the rank, the more important is the officer, but there is no way of quantifying how much more important. Ordinal scales are often used to measure people's opinions (perceptions or attitudes).

Thus, the value of a property gives information about that property. In principle you are free to decide which of the two extremes of a property will correspond to the highest score. For example, if you use a five-point scale when measuring the extent to which people agree with a proposition, you can code the answer 'totally agree' as 5 or as 1. However, it is customary to use *ascending scales*, which means that if the scale represents the 'extent of agreement', a lower score means less agreement with the proposition. In other words, it is preferable to choose a score of 1 for 'totally disagree' and 5 for 'totally agree'.

3. Interval scale. The interval scale also represents a ranking order, but now the difference between values is a meaningful quantity. At any point on the scale a difference of one unit between two values corresponds to the same absolute difference. However, the zero point on the scale is arbitrary. An example of an interval scale is the Celsius temperature scale. The temperature difference between 5 and 10°C is just as large as the difference between 30 and 35°C. The zero point on the scale is defined by arbitrary convention, which means that 0°C is not the lowest possible temperature. Consequently we cannot say that 20°C is twice as warm as 10°C. This becomes obvious when we realise that temperature can be expressed in degrees Fahrenheit just as well as in degrees Celsius, and that 10°C and 20°C correspond to 50°F and 68°F, respectively.

Another example is that of calendar years. The period between the years 800 and 1000 took as long as the period between the years 1800 and 2000. However, since the zero point is arbitrary, one cannot say that the year 2000 occurred twice as late as the year 1000.

4. Ratio scale. The ratio scale possesses all the properties of the interval scale and in addition has a natural zero point. Consequently, not only the differences between the numbers on the scale have a real and consistent meaning, but this also applies to the ratio between two numbers. Examples of this type of yardstick are lengths, widths, distances, sums of money and numbers. Suppose that town A lies at a distance of 20 kilometres from town X, and B at 100 kilometres. We can then say that town B lies 80 kilometres farther from X than town A, but also that B is removed five times as far from X than A.

Many techniques that apply to ratio variables may also be used for interval variables. This explains why these groups are sometimes collectively called *continuous variables* (SPSS sometimes uses the term scale variables).

2.5.2 Describing variables

Gaining insight in the distribution of a variable is often one of the first analyses a researcher performs. These analyses help the researcher understand the nature of the data, which is useful for determining the subsequent analyses. A variable may be described in terms of the following:

1. The frequency of each value
2. The central tendency
3. The dispersion (the extent of variation)
4. The fit with a theoretical distribution
5. The trend in the data (time series).

1. The frequency of each value. In essence, determining the frequencies of the values is nothing more than counting their occurrence. The frequencies can be summarised in a table, a *frequency table* for which SPSS has the Frequencies command (see Sections 4.7 and 12.1). There is no basic restriction on the measurement level, but for continuous variables with many distinct values, frequency tables become very large and cluttered. In such cases it helps to first group the values of the variable into a limited number of categories (with Visual Bander; Section 9.3). When dealing with a large number of similar nominal or ordinal variables (having the same range of values and the same value labels), *multiple response analysis* can be a useful approach to make the frequency tables (see Chapter 15).

Frequencies can also be presented in the form of charts. The frequency of nominal and ordinal variables can be represented in *bar charts* (Sections 5.2

and 13.2). In the case of continuous variables, a *histogram* (13.9) is a good alternative for a bar chart, but they can also be summarised graphically in the form of a *stem-and-leaf plot* (Section 12.3) or a *boxplot* (Section 13.8).

2. Central tendency. The central tendency refers to the average for a group of cases. The following three statistics are used:

1. The *mode*: the value with the highest frequency. Used for nominal variables in particular.
2. The *median*: the value corresponding to the middlemost case when the cases are sorted in ascending or descending order. Used for ordinal variables in particular.
3. The *mean*: the sum of all cases, divided by the number of cases. Used for interval variables and ratio variables in particular.

All three measures of the central tendency can be requested with the Frequencies command (button Statistics; see Section 12.1.1).

You can also test whether the average for a variable differs from another average (e.g. the national average, or some norm):

• For dichotomous variables (variables with two categories) the mode can be compared with a specified probability by using the *binomial test* (see Section 19.2).
• For ordinal variables, the median may be tested using the *sign test* (Section 19.7.2).
• For interval variables and ratio variables, a *one-sample t-test* can be performed with the One-Sample T Test command (Section 16.2).

3. The dispersion. Various statistics indicate the amount of variation or spread in the data. Useful statistics for variables at the ordinal level or higher are *percentiles*, the *minimum* and the *maximum*. For interval variables and ratio variables some additional dispersion statistics are available, such as the *range* (the difference between minimum and maximum), the *standard deviation* and the *variance*.

SPSS has three comparable commands to request these dispersion statistics: the button Statistics of the commands Frequencies (Section 12.1) and Explore (Section 12.3), and the button Options of the Descriptives command (Section 12.2).

4. Fit with a theoretical distribution. There are multiple ways to study the fit between the observed distribution of a variable and a theoretical distribution (such as the normal distribution). You can do this by using statistics, graphs or a statistical test.

Statistics that give information about the fit with the normal distribution are skewness and kurtosis. The *skewness* measures the type and degree of asymmetry of a distribution. The normal distribution is symmetric, that is, the two halves of the curve on either side of the average (the mode) are each other's mirror images. Being perfectly symmetric, the normal distribution has zero skewness. One speaks of positive skewness when the distribution has a 'tail' to the right (higher values), and vice versa. Positive skewness means that there are more cases exceeding the mode than cases with a value lower than the mode. The *kurtosis* is a measure of the type and degree to which the observations cluster around a central point relative to the normal distribution. The normal distribution has zero kurtosis. Distributions that are relatively more pointed (more observations around the mode) or, instead, flatter compared with the normal distribution have positive and negative kurtosis, respectively; furthermore, the higher the peak, the more positive the kurtosis, and vice versa. Both skewness and kurtosis require that the variable is at least ordinal. Both statistics can be requested with the commands Frequencies, Descriptives and Explore (see Chapter 12).

Various graphs provide insight into the fit between an observed distribution and the normal distribution. Examples include *boxplots* (Section 13.8) and *histograms* with a normal curve superimposed (Section 13.9). More specialised graphs used to compare an observed distribution with various theoretical distributions are the *(normal) quantile plots* and *(normal) probability plots* (Section 13.10).

The analyses described above provide insight into the fit between the observed distribution and a theoretical distribution. It is also possible to test for this fit. One test is the *Kolmogorov–Smirnov test* (Section 19.4), if the variable is at least ordinally scaled. The observed distribution of a nominal variable can be tested against a theoretical (or expected) distribution with the *chi-square test* (Section 19.1). SPSS allows you to specify the expected frequencies. For example, you can verify whether the numbers of men and of women interviewed are equal, by specifying the theoretical distribution as 1-to-1. Another application of the chi-square test is when the distribution (the frequencies) of the population is known, e.g. the percentage of men and women in the population. Using the chi-square test you can then determine whether your sample is, with respect to gender, representative of the population. This will be the case if the ratio of men to women in the sample is comparable to that in the population.

5. The trend in the data (time series). When the cases represent measurements made at successive moments in time, i.e. time series or longitudinal data, it may be meaningful to investigate the trend in the data. Useful graphs include *bar charts* (Sections 5.2 and 13.2), *line charts* (Section 13.3) and *area charts* (Section 13.4).

2.5.3 Describing groups of cases

To describe groups of cases one can, depending on the measurement level of the variable, apply one of the following techniques:

- A *crosstable* (or two-way table) contains information on the number or percentage of cases in the various groups and can be made with the Crosstabs command (Chapter 14). Crosstables are mainly used for nominal or ordinal variables.
- For interval variables or ratio variables the Means command (Section 16.1) is used to *request statistics for each group*, such as the mean, the dispersion and the number of cases.

Useful charts for the description of groups are the following:

- *Grouped and stacked bar charts* (Section 13.2) for nominal and ordinal variables.
- *Line charts* (Section 13.3) and *area charts* (Section 13.4) for analysing the trends within various groups.

An alternative option is to split the data file into different groups with the *Split File* command (Section 10.1) and then analyse the distribution of variables (e.g. with frequency tables, statistics or charts). SPSS will then perform each analysis for each group separately.

2.5.4 Testing differences between independent groups

SPSS can do several tests to determine whether independent groups differ significantly from each other. It is customary to distinguish between situations with two groups and with three or more groups.

With two independent groups the following tests are available:

- The *chi-square test* for nominal variables, using the button Statistics of the Crosstabs command (Section 14.3).
- The *Mann–Whitney test* (Section 19.5.1) or the *Kolmogorov–Smirnov test* (Section 19.5.2) for ordinal variables.
- The *t-test* for interval variables and ratio variables, using the Independent Samples T Test command (Section 16.3).

When there are more than two independent groups, the following tests are used:

- The *chi-square test* for nominal variables, using the button Statistics of the Crosstabs command (Section 14.3).
- The *Kruskal–Wallis test* (Section 19.6.1) and the median test (Section 19.6.2) for ordinal variables.
- *Analysis of variance* (the F-test) for interval variables and ratio variables. The SPSS software has two commands for analysis of variance: One-Way ANOVA (Section 17.2) if the groups are distinguished based on a single variable, and GLM Univariate (Section 17.3) which allows groupings based on multiple variables.

2.5.5 Testing differences between related groups

Sometimes the cases in the different groups are not independent but in some way related to each other. This situation occurs, for example, when you did not interview just men and women, but couples; or when the same people are interviewed before and after a certain event. SPSS offers the following tests that enable you to determine whether related groups differ significantly from each other:

- The *Wilcoxon Signed Ranks test* (Section 19.7.1) and the *sign test* (Section 19.7.2) for two related groups and ordinal variables.
- The *Friedman test* (Section 19.8.1) for more than two related groups and ordinal variables.
- The *paired t-test* for interval variables and ratio variables, using the Paired-Samples T Test command (Section 16.4).

2.5.6 Determining the relationship between two variables

To determine whether and how two variables are related, you can use:

- a *crosstable* for nominal and ordinal variables, requested with the Crosstabs command (Section 14);
- a *scatterplot*, in which one variable is plotted on the horizontal axis and the other on the vertical axis, and where each case is shown as a point in the plot. Scatterplots are made with the Graphs Chart Builder command (Sections 6.2 and 6.5) and are only meaningful for ordinal variables and higher. Scatterplots not only provide insight into the strength of the relation between two variables, but also in the type of relation (e.g. linear or non-linear).

The extent to which two variables are related can also be expressed in the form of a statistic. There are several options:

- The *chi-square test* for nominal variables, to determine whether or not two variables are independent of each other (Section 14.3).
- The *phi coefficient* for nominal variables, to determine the degree of relation between two variables (Section 14.4).
- The *Spearman correlation coefficient* and *Kendall's tau*, for ordinal variables (both discussed in Sections 14.4 and 18.1).
- The *Pearson correlation coefficient* for interval variables and ratio variables. The corresponding SPSS command is Bivariate Correlations (Section 18.1) and, if you need to control for the effect of a third variable, Partial Correlations (Section 18.2).

2.5.7 Explaining a variable (regression)

Regression analysis is used to test for a linear relation between a dependent variable and one or more independent variables. The result of a regression analysis is an equation that numerically describes the dependent variable in terms of the independent variable(s). Important assumptions are that there is a causal relation between the dependent and the independent variables, that the variables are interval or ratio and that the relation between the variables is either linear (a straight line) or can be linearised (by using some kind of transformation). The corresponding SPSS command is Linear Regression (Section 18.3). If the relation is non-linear (curvilinear) and can be expressed in the form of a mathematical formula, you can use the Curve Estimation command (see Section 18.4).

2.6   Interpreting the output of an analysis

The output of an analysis consists of tables or charts showing numbers, percentages, averages, significance levels, coefficients, etc. But numbers are just that – numbers. To reach a conclusion, that is, to answer your research questions, you have to interpret those numbers. The help you can get from SPSS has its limits: interpretation is, and will remain, the task of the researcher.

However, SPSS makes interpretation easier in a number of ways. The program automatically shows all output in the Viewer where you can evaluate it and, insert comments, make changes, and save interesting parts. SPSS highlights interesting results: it marks a significant correlation coefficient with asterisks, or shades cells of special interest. Moreover, for statistical tests, e.g. the chi-square test, the t-test or the F-test, SPSS shows the significance level (the p value). In a few cases it is possible to let SPSS apply interpretation criteria during the analyses. One example is regression analysis, where you can specify the criteria that a variable must meet in order to be included in the equation. SPSS then checks whether a variable satisfies the conditions and acts accordingly.

To facilitate the interpretation of the SPSS output, Part II of this book offers detailed examples of all techniques, carefully specifying and explaining the corresponding SPSS commands. In addition, these examples show the actual SPSS output as it appears on your screen, going into great detail to discuss and interpret the results.

2.7   Preparing the research report

Almost without exception, research reports are prepared in word processors and not in SPSS. Nevertheless, the Viewer has facilities for composing simple reports. Using the Viewer you can select output, add comments, save and print the output. If you prepare your report with a word processor, such as MS Word, you can select parts of the output in the Viewer and copy them to your word processor. This way you can insert tables and charts in your report (see Section 6.9 for an example).

3 From data source to data file

A common application of SPSS is the analysis of data collected by means of questionnaires, such as surveys, warranty forms, visit reports, and regular assessments. In this chapter we describe the steps from a questionnaire to an SPSS data file. The first step is to 'translate' the questions into variables to be used in the data file, and to determine the coding for the answers (see Section 3.1).

To facilitate the transformation from data source to data file one makes use of an overview with the variable and the coding that correspond to each of the questions (see Section 3.2). This overview is called the code book. Following these preparations, the next step is the process of actually entering the data, using either Data Entry or the Data Editor. Section 3.3 contains practical tips to help you minimise the time needed for this chore, while keeping the risk of errors down.

By way of illustration, we go through all stages of an imaginary survey among tennis players. The questionnaire and the code book used in this survey can be found in Section 3.4.

3.1 From questions to variables

Before SPSS can be put to work, the data collected via questionnaires must be transferred into an SPSS data file. As SPSS operations involve variables, the questions first need to be *translated* into variables. For every question one has to decide what variables, how many of them and what codes are required. In this section we discuss three types of questions:

- closed questions;
- open questions;
- questions with multiple answers for each respondent.

Each of these is discussed in a separate subsection.

3.1.1 Closed questions
Closed questions are those allowing a limited number of valid answers only, and all possible answers are known in advance. Often the number of answers is limited simply because no other answers are possible, as in simple Yes/No questions.

Closed questions also include those that address continuous properties which are grouped into categories, like questions about people's incomes requiring answers in terms of predefined income brackets. Closed questions usually are simple to deal with: each question is translated into one variable, while the coding is implicit in the question.

An example can be found in the survey among tennis players (see Table 3.1). The question about new tennis shoes is a closed question, because there is only one answer possible that can take two possible values which are known in advance (yes and no). Thus, in this situation one variable suffices, for which there are two coding options:

1. *A string variable (also called alphanumeric or text variable),* coded *Y (= Yes)* and *N (= No).* This offers the advantage that you do not have to first code the answers: they may be copied from the questionnaire straight away. However, string variables have serious disadvantages as well, which is why, generally speaking, their use is not recommended (see Section 3.2.3).
2. *A numeric variable, coded 1 (= Yes) and 0 (= No).* The reverse coding (0 = Yes and 1 = No) might also be used, but ascending scales are usually preferred (Section 2.5.1).

Table 3.1   An example of a closed question where each respondent can provide only one answer.

Did you buy new tennis shoes last year?
☐   Yes
☐   No

3.1.2 Open questions

Open questions are those for which the possible answers have not been specified beforehand. We distinguish between quantitative and qualitative open questions. A *quantitative question* is one that asks for a number representing some property. Cases in point are sums of money (number of dollars), distances (number of miles or kilometres) or temperature (number of degrees Celsius or Fahrenheit). The translation from question into variable is straightforward: for each question there is only one variable (which is usually an interval or ratio variable), and the numeric answer to the question is the value of the variable. There is no need for coding such variables. Also refer to Table 3.2 for an example (age expressed as number of years).

A *qualitative question* is one that asks about a non-numeric property, that is, a property not naturally expressed as a number. Examples include colours, cities, brands, titles of books; referring to our fictitious survey, the second question, about the favourite tennis player, is a qualitative question (see Table 3.2). Because

Table 3.2   Two examples of an open question.

Quantitative question
What is your age? _____ years
Qualitative question
Who is your favourite tennis player? _____ (name)

each respondent may name only one tennis player, one variable suffices. As for the coding, there are two possibilities:

1. *Numeric variable*, with the coding from 1 to the total number of players named in the survey, and each code is labelled with the name of the player. Because it is not known which players, and how many, will be named until all interviews have been completed, this solution has the disadvantage that coding can only be done afterwards. In mail surveys with a small number of respondents that is not a serious problem, but when dealing with many respondents or in telephone and personal interviews this may be not be acceptable. Of course, the coding could also be done simultaneously with entering the data, by assigning to each next new player the next higher number. This method, however, can easily lead to coding or data entry errors. Besides, it is only possible if all data are entered by a single person.
2. *String variable*, with the players' names as values, either in full or in part (e.g. the first three letters of the name). This has the advantage that it is not necessary to postpone coding until after all interviews have been conducted. On the other hand, string variables in SPSS have considerable disadvantages compared to numeric variables (see Section 3.2.3). When using shortened names one may run into difficulties if some players have similar or identical names.

Closed or open questions? When designing the questionnaire you may have a choice between a closed and an open quantitative question. In that case, open questions are usually preferred because they result in variables at the highest possible measurement level (interval or ratio). Other phenomena cannot be expressed in numbers and call for qualitative questions, in which case closed questions are to be preferred. The reason is that the coding of open qualitative questions is more difficult. In practise, we observe an increasing use of closed questions which is due in large part to the advent of computer-aided interviewing (e.g. by means of Data Entry; see Chapter 7), which usually requires prior coding.

Still, there are many situations where open qualitative questions are used. Sometimes the reason is that not all possible answers can be known in advance; sometimes it may be undesirable to state possible answers. An example of the latter is a study to determine the familiarity of a detergent brand: when answering a closed question the respondent needs only to recognise a brand, while in the case of an open question he or she has to recall the brand names. A closed question will lead to a considerably higher brand familiarity score.

Partially open questions. If not all possible answers can be known in advance, one often uses *partially open questions* with the aim of making coding and data entry easier. Table 3.3 asks respondents to name their favourite tennis player in the form of a partially open question. Several predetermined players are given (closed qualitative question), while in addition the respondent has the option of supplying another players' name (open question).

Table 3.3   An example of a partially open question.

Who is your favourite tennis player?

☐   Roger Federer
☐   Rafael Nadal
☐   Andy Roddick
☐   Someone else, namely: _____

This example, too, allows two possibilities for coding. If the survey is conducted in printed form and the number of questionnaires is not too large, the answers entered under 'Other player, namely:' may be listed and coded as 4, 5, etc. In that situation the question is translated into a single variable. The usual way, however, is to define two variables, a numeric variable for the closed part of the question and a string variable (or a numeric variable if desired) for the open part. If needed the two variables can be combined into one at a later stage with the Compute command, and the players' names that occur less frequently can be grouped into the category 'Other', with the Recode command (see Chapter 9).

3.1.3 Questions with multiple responses for each respondent

Translating questions into variables is more difficult when each respondent can give more than one answer (response) to a question. This situation is referred to as a *multiple response question*. Chapter 15 discusses how to analyse such answers; in this section we focus on the translation of such questions into variables.

Table 3.4 contains an example of a closed question allowing multiple responses for each respondent. It is possible that someone plays singles as well as doubles. There are two ways to translate this question into variables:

1. *A single variable with all possible combinations of answers*. In this case there are four possible situations: someone plays neither singles nor doubles, singles only, doubles only, or both. We may therefore define a single variable with codes 1, 2, 3 and 4 corresponding to these different situations.

2. *A separate variable for each sub-question*. In this case, the question is regarded as consisting of two sub-questions, namely: 'Do you play singles?' and 'Do you play doubles?'. Both can be answered by either Yes or No. We now define two variables, each with the coding 0 = No and 1 = Yes (or N and Y, see Section 3.1.1).

Table 3.4   An example of a closed question where each respondent can provide multiple responses.

Which type of play do you practice?
☐   Singles
☐   Doubles

The first solution may appear to be the natural one since it requires only a single variable, thus minimising the amount of typing. However, it is often not the most practical solution. It may be used if the four groups are analysed as four different groups. However, if you intend to study singles players and consider it irrelevant whether they also play doubles, the second solution is preferred. This is all the more true when there are several sub-questions, because the number of combinations of answers then increases steeply and soon becomes impracticable to handle. Two yes/no sub-questions lead to four combinations of answers, three sub-questions to eight combinations, and with four questions there are already 16 different possible combinations. Coding the answers is then much easier (and quicker and less likely to result in errors) when using a separate variable for each sub-question. You can then still analyse the responses as a group by defining the variables as a *multiple response set* (see Chapter 15). Note that, if it turns out later that you did not make the proper choice, you can still convert one coding scheme into another with the Compute and Recode commands (see Chapter 9).

3.2   The code book

The code book is a useful aid, both in the process of entering the data and in analysing them. It can be used to look up the meaning of a given code, or the question to which a given variable refers ('What was the exact wording of that question?'). The code book is a table showing which variables correspond to which questions, and the way each of the variables has been coded. A code book consists of four columns (see Table 3.5). All except the first column, which contains the number of the question, are described in the separate subsections below. Section 3.4 contains an example of a code book.

Table 3.5   The structure of a code book.

Column	Contents
1	Question number in the questionnaire
2	Variable name
3	Variable description (variable label)
4	Coding (value labels)

3.2.1 Naming of variables

Each variable must have a unique name (see Section 8.1 for an overview of restrictions); these names are listed in the second column of the code book. For practical reasons, a name should be both clear and short. Often it is not easy to find self-explanatory variable names; therefore a label is assigned to each variable (see the next subsection).

We recommend to always begin with a variable that contains the number of the respondent or the case number. If the cases (e.g. survey forms) are not numbered, then number them yourself, consecutively and starting at 1. A case number will help you to trace quickly any data entry errors or extreme values back to the original questionnaires. SPSS also assigns each case a sequential number (to be found in the margin of the data sheet), but these row numbers change when you sort or select cases. It is therefore better to include a separate variable containing the respondent numbers.

3.2.2 Describing the variables (variable labels)

The third column in the code book contains a brief description of the variable. In SPSS parlance: this description is the *variable label*. Because it is not always easy to find a name that is both clear and short, longer descriptions are often essential. Particularly when the number of variables is large, or when it is difficult to find succinct keywords that summarise the variables, the variable names usually sound rather cryptic: abbreviations tend to be much clearer to their intellectual parents than to others. Hence the separate column for the label to explain the name.

3.2.3 The coding

The fourth column of the code book displays how the answers are coded. For the question whether someone has bought new tennis shoes last year, we fill in 0 = No, 1 = Yes (or N = No, Y = Yes). For uncoded variables, like age, price, number of employees, this column specifies the units used (e.g. age in years, number of employees in hundreds). Sometimes special codes are used for incorrect or missing answers (e.g. code 0 might be used in case a respondent did not fill in his or her age). In that case you have to specify the code used for missing values when defining the variable in SPSS (see Section 6.4 for further details).

It is not advisable to introduce group classifications (e.g. age groups) during the coding step if the data were originally collected without group classification (e.g. age in years). Leave the classifications to some later stage. Classifying data into groups before entering the data precludes a different group classification that one might wish to make later on. It also unnecessarily lowers the measurement level of the variable: age in years is a ratio variable, age groups represent ordinal data. Consequently, some types of analysis may no longer be possible because the data may no longer meet the required measurement level (see also Section 2.5). For example, age group data cannot be used for correlation analysis or regression analysis.

String variables versus numeric variables. Coding a variable also includes choosing between numeric variables and string variables. As a rule, it is best to avoid string variables. Disadvantages of string variables include:

- *The difference between upper case and lower case*. String variables in SPSS are case sensitive. In other words y and Y refer to different values even if they are not meant to. You therefore need to be careful and use either upper case or lower case throughout.
- *Some commands only accept numeric variables*. Determining the group classification for analysis of variance (One-Way ANOVA) is one example; in that case string variables first need to be converted into numeric variables with the command Automatic Recode (see Section 9.5).
- *The need to use quotation marks*. When referring to the value of a string variable you have to place the value between quotation marks. Thus, compare NewShoe = 'Y' with NewShoe = 1. Clearly, this means more typing work and a larger risk of errors.
- *More keystrokes during data entry*. Generally speaking, if you use text codes, you have to make a larger number of keystrokes than for numeric codes. Again, this means loss of time and increased likelihood of errors.

Due to these disadvantages of string variables, numeric variables are used where possible. The disadvantage of numeric codes is that it is not intuitively clear what codes like 1, 2, etc. mean. This ambiguity can be avoided by assigning labels to the values of a variable. In SPSS parlance, these descriptions are called *value labels* (see Section 5.4).

3.3   Entering the data

The last step in the transformation from data source to data file is entering the data into the data file, by using either the spreadsheet of the Data View (see Section 4.5) or the module Data Entry (see Chapter 7). Keying in the data may not be a terribly interesting activity, but it certainly is one on which the quality of all subsequent analyses depends. For that reason it is of paramount importance, not just to get it done as quickly as possible, but to keep the number of errors to an absolute minimum.

When you use the completed questionnaires as your starting material, make sure you first write the codes on all forms before entering the data. Simultaneously determining the codes and entering the data is a good recipe for making errors.

You should also allow ample time for checking the data file for any errors. Remember that a single incorrect entry may lead to flawed values for a whole series of variables: inadvertently skipping one variable leads to incorrect values for all subsequent variables.

Let us end with an obvious remark that cannot be overemphasised: whenever you have completed the data file, immediately make a back-up on another, separately and securely stored medium. There is nothing as tiresome as having to repeat a chore like this...

3.4   **The tennis survey**

To illustrate how SPSS works, we will use a survey among tennis players. Respondents are asked to answer the ten questions shown in Table 3.6. The

Table 3.6   The questionnaire used in the tennis survey

1 How many times a month, on average, do you play tennis?	... times

2 Which type of play do you practice?
    1 Singles only
    2 Doubles only
    3 Both singles and doubles	

3 How much did you spend on court rental last year?	... dollars
4 How much did you spend on tennis wear last year?	... dollars
5 Did you buy new tennis shoes last year?	Yes/No

6 If so, how much did these shoes cost?
    1 Less than 50 dollars
    2 Between 50 and 100 dollars
    3 More than 100 dollars	

7 How often do you go to see a tennis tournament?
    1 Rarely
    2 Occasionally
    3 Often	

8 What is your gender?	Male/Female
9 What is your age?	... years
10 What is your net monthly income?	... dollars

questionnaire is simple in design: each respondent can provide only one answer to each question, which implies that each question translates into a single variable.

Table 3.7 contains the corresponding code book. As you can see, the first variable in the code book refers to the respondents' number. Furthermore, questions 5 and 8 have been translated into string variables. The reason is that this survey will be used in the following chapters, where we also want to illustrate how to deal with string variables. As stated above, in real-life surveys numeric coding is usually preferred.

Table 3.7   The code book for the questionnaire used in the tennis survey

Question no.	Variable name	Variable description (variable label)	Coding (value labels)
–	RespNum	Respondent number	Number: 1…n
1	TimesTennis	Average number of times played (per month)	Number of times
2	SingleDouble	Play singles only, doubles only, both	1 = Singles only 2 = Doubles only 3 = Singles and doubles
3	CourtRental	Sum spent on court rental (last year)	Amount in dollars
4	TennisWear	Sum spent on tennis wear (last year)	Amount in dollars
5	NewShoe	Bought new tennis shoes last year?	Y = Yes N = No
6	ShoePrice	Shoe price category	1 = Less than 50 dollars 2 = Between 50 and 100 dollars 3 = More than 100 dollars
7	TournamentVisit	Frequency of going to see tennis tournaments	1 = Rarely 2 = Occasionally 3 = Often
8	Gender		F = Female M = Male
9	Age		Number of years
10	Income	Net monthly income	Amount in dollars

4 Session 1: The first steps

This chapter is the first in a series of three sessions aiming to illustrate:

1 **The structure of SPSS.** What windows are available in SPSS? Where do I find the command that I want SPSS to execute? How do I enter data, view the output or request help?

2 **How SPSS is used.** What steps do I have to follow in order to benefit from SPSS in my research? What comes first, what comes later? What do I have to do myself, what can SPSS do for me?

3 **What you can do with SPSS.** With SPSS you can make frequency tables, perform regression analysis, compute variables, select cases, create three-dimensional bar charts and perform t-tests. The three sessions in Part I of this book offer a global overview. Part II contains detailed discussions of all these commands.

4 **How best to use SPSS.** What is particularly useful, which procedures are less practical? What frequently made errors should I be aware of? How can I speed up the more time-consuming steps? Knowing such matters facilitates the use of SPSS.

Sessions 1–3 are presented in such a way that you can follow them while seated at your computer desk. All mouse clicks and all keystrokes are explicitly noted, with additional explanations where necessary. You will be guided step by step through the SPSS software and perform precisely the same tasks that you will be doing later, when using SPSS for your own research.

The present session helps you familiarise yourself with SPSS. You will learn to understand the structure of SPSS, how to enter and analyse data, and how to view the results of the analyses. In this session a simple data file is created; this file is used in both this session and the two subsequent sessions to show the features of SPSS.

4.1 The start

SPSS can be started by:

- clicking 'Start' in the task bar, then selecting 'Programs' and finally 'SPSS for Windows' (see Figure 4.1); or
- double-clicking the SPSS icon in the desktop (see Figure 4.1).

*Figure 4.1   Starting SPSS from the Programs menu (left) or from the desktop
(right).*

After SPSS has been started, an information window appears that shows which
version is running, soon followed by the SPSS start window shown in Figure 4.2.
(There may be another window first, asking 'What would you like to do?'. In that
case, just click the button 'Cancel' to continue.)

The SPSS start window is called the *Data Editor*. With this window you can copy,
enter or change data. The Data Editor contains a spreadsheet consisting of columns
(the variables) and rows (the cases or respondents). Each answer will be stored in
a cell that uniquely corresponds to the combination respondent–variable.

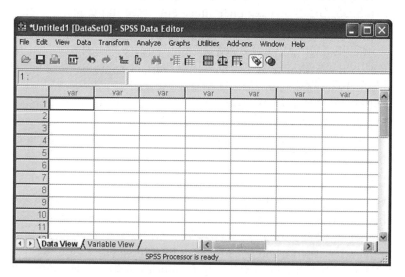

Figure 4.2   The SPSS start window with the Data Editor.

The Data Editor window consists of several components following the Windows
standard. The uppermost line is the *title bar* containing the name Data Editor,
followed by 'Untitled', meaning that the current data file does not have a name.
The next line contains the SPSS *menu*, followed by the *toolbar*, which is handy
for quickly executing frequently used commands. Then follows the spreadsheet
into which the variables and cases will be entered, at the bottom of which you
have two clickable tabs, referring to the Data View and the Variable View. At the
very bottom of the Data Editor window you see the *status bar*. Various messages
may appear in this line. The current message shows that SPSS is waiting for
instructions: 'SPSS processor is ready'.

At the far right in the title bar you find, from left to right, the Minimize button (dash), the Maximize button and the Close Window button (cross). The Maximize button toggles between full-size window and stacked windows, changing its appearance every time it is activated. Now click the Maximize button to ensure that the Data Editor occupies the full screen.

Before we proceed to enter our data, in the next section, let us now have a brief look at the menu first. SPSS is a package for analysing statistical data, so the most interesting option in the Data Editor menu is

Analyze

When you click this option a menu is displayed with a choice of several types of analysis. Because there are so many different analyses that you can perform with SPSS, the analytical techniques are listed in groups. As you can see, SPSS contains, for example, commands to compare the means of various groups or to perform correlation or regression analysis.

Various menu choices in their turn refer to other, subsequent menus. Where this is the case, an arrow indicates that a sub-menu is available. As you can see, all options in the Analyze menu refer to subsequent menus. Now click the second option in the Analyze menu, that is

Descriptive Statistics

This prompts another menu with various SPSS commands for summarising data (see Figure 4.3), such as commands to make frequency tables and crosstables. If you were to select one of these, you would get an error message because at this stage there are no data to analyse.

After this digression, we will show how to create a data file with SPSS. First, we leave the menu by clicking on one of the cells in the spreadsheet.

4.2   Creating a data file

In this and the next two sessions we illustrate the way SPSS works, using the tennis survey described in Chapter 3 as a simple example. To limit the amount of data typing we use only part of the questionnaire, as shown in Table 4.1.

As explained in the preceding chapter, the questions in the questionnaire are translated into variables. The code book shows how the answers to questions become values of variables in the data file. In this case each question has been translated into one variable. We have added a variable RespNum that takes the numbers identifying the respondents. Although SPSS automatically numbers

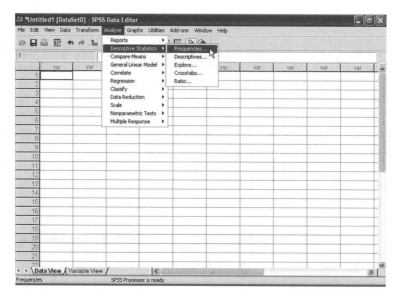

Figure 4.3   *The menu Analyze – Descriptive Statistics. Depending on the SPSS modules installed on your computer, your menu may contain more commands.*

Table 4.1   *Part of the questionnaire used in the tennis survey*

1	How many times a month, on average, do you play tennis?	... times
2	Did you buy new tennis shoes last year?	Yes/No
3	If so, how much did these shoes cost? 1 Less than 50 dollars 2 Between 50 and 100 dollars 3 More than 100 dollars	
4	What is your gender?	Male/Female
5	What is your age?	... years

cases, we recommend including this extra variable, because some SPSS commands (e.g. sorting and selecting) renumber the cases.

In the present example there are ten respondents. In this session, we will enter their answers into the Data Editor. The Data Editor looks like a spreadsheet, with variables in the columns and cases (the persons who answered the questions in our survey) in the rows. The cells accommodate the (coded) answers. The *cell pointer* indicates the cell that is ready to take your input.

We begin by entering the values of the first variable (RespNum). The top-left cell of the spreadsheet corresponds to the first variable (column) and the first case (row). If the cell pointer is not in this cell, then click the cell to place it there. Now type the number of the first respondent, i.e. the number

1

in this cell (note that you are actually typing in the line below the toolbar). Press Enter and the cell pointer will move down to the next row; at the same time SPSS generates the default name Var00001 for the new variable (first column heading). The digit 1 in the top left cell appears as 1.00, because the default SPSS notation for new variables has two decimals. Since this default notation can be changed it is possible that in your situation the default SPSS notation shows a different number of decimals.

Since we have ten respondents, you can continue by entering the numbers 2–10 in the successive cells in the column named Var00001. When this is completed your screen looks like that shown in Figure 4.4.

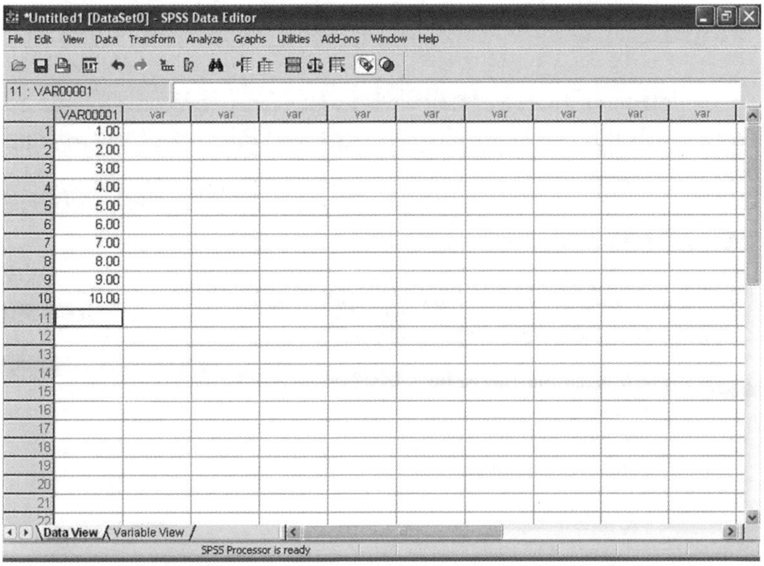

Figure 4.4   The Data Editor after entering the ten respondent numbers. (Depending on your default settings, the number of decimals may vary.)

The cell pointer is now ready and waiting at the position of the non-existent 11th case. One way of returning the pointer to the first case (row) is to repeatedly press the Arrow Up key a number of times. An easier and faster way is to key in

Ctrl+Home

by striking the Home key while pressing the Control key. The keystroke Ctrl+Home has the effect of returning the cell pointer to the top-left cell in the spreadsheet.

Likewise, the keystroke Ctrl+End directs the cell pointer to the last cell at the lower right, the one that corresponds to the last variable and the last case. This does not only apply to SPSS. In many other programs too, Ctrl+Home (Ctrl+End) can be used to instantly move the cursor position to the beginning (end) of a document.

4.3   Naming a variable

As we have seen, the variable containing the respondent numbers was automatically assigned the name Var00001. It would of course be more convenient to use another, intuitive name. The name can be changed with the other view of the Data Editor, which we access by clicking the tab

Variable View

at the bottom of the spreadsheet. Now the Variable View appears, as in Figure 4.5. As you will note, this window has the variables in the rows and their properties in the columns.

The current name Var00001 can be changed by typing, in the column 'Name', the preferred name

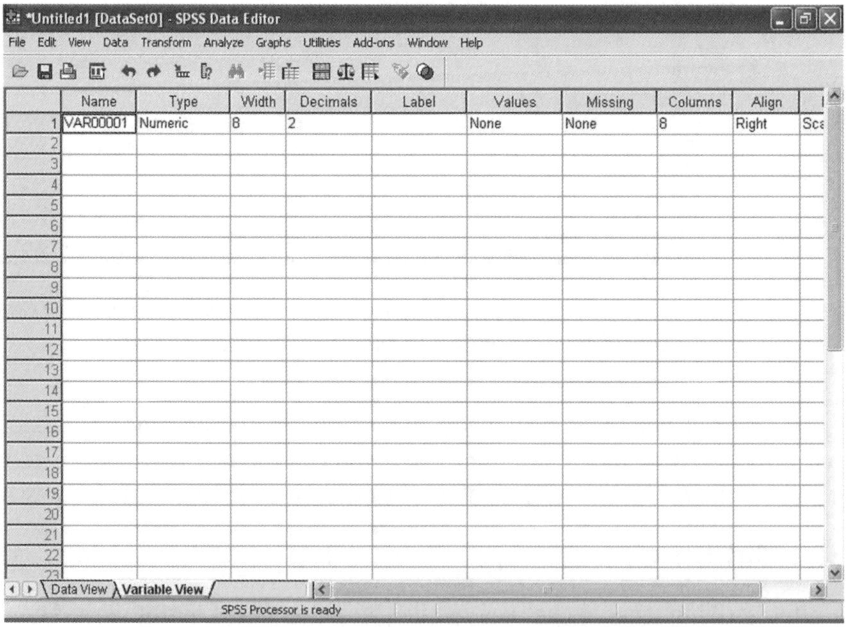

Figure 4.5   The Variable View of the Data Editor.

RespNum

Next, in the column 'Decimals' you can specify the number of decimals of a variable. The default value used by SPSS is 2, but the respondent number does not need to have decimals, so we specify zero decimals for RespNum by typing

0

under 'Decimals'. Now click the tab

Data View

to return to the previous screen and see the result. As Figure 4.6 shows, the variable name Var00001 has been changed into RespNum and the decimals have disappeared.

4.4 Defining the variables

As a next step, we could enter the data for the next variable, the answers to the first question ('How many times a month do you play?') into the second column. However, this is not what one normally does in practice. It is far more common to enter the data according to cases than according to variables (which was what we did for the respondent numbers, see Section 4.2). Naturally, this can only be done after all variables have been defined. That is what we will do in this section.

Variables are defined in the Variable View by using the code book (see Table 4.2). We return to this screen by clicking the tab

Variable View

According to the code book, the first question corresponds to the variable TimesTennis. Click the first cell in the second row and type the name

TimesTennis

Again, the number of times played does not have decimals; accordingly in the column 'Decimals' we type

0

In order to come up with short variable names, variable names often combine several words into one abbreviation. The name TimesTennis is an example of this. By assigning a description (*variable label*) to the variable name we can

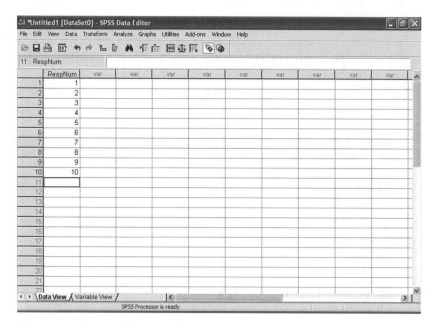

Figure 4.6   The Data View after changing the name and number of decimals of the first variable.

Table 4.2   The code book for the questionnaire used in the tennis survey

Question no.	Variable name	Variable description (variable label)	Coding (value label)
–	RespNum	Respondent number	Number: 1...n
1	TimesTennis	Average number of times played, per month	Number of times
2	NewShoe	Bought new tennis shoes?	Y = Yes N = No
3	ShoePrice	Shoe price category	1 = 50 dollars 2 = 50–100 dollars 3 = 100 dollars
4	Gender		F = female M = male
5	Age		Number of years

avoid having to use the code book each time we use a variable. In the column 'Label' you type the description from the code book

Average number of times played, per month

As you can see, SPSS automatically adjusts the column width (see Figure 4.7). In contrast to names of variables, labels are case sensitive. The SPSS output will show the labels exactly as they were specified in Variable View. When you now click the tab

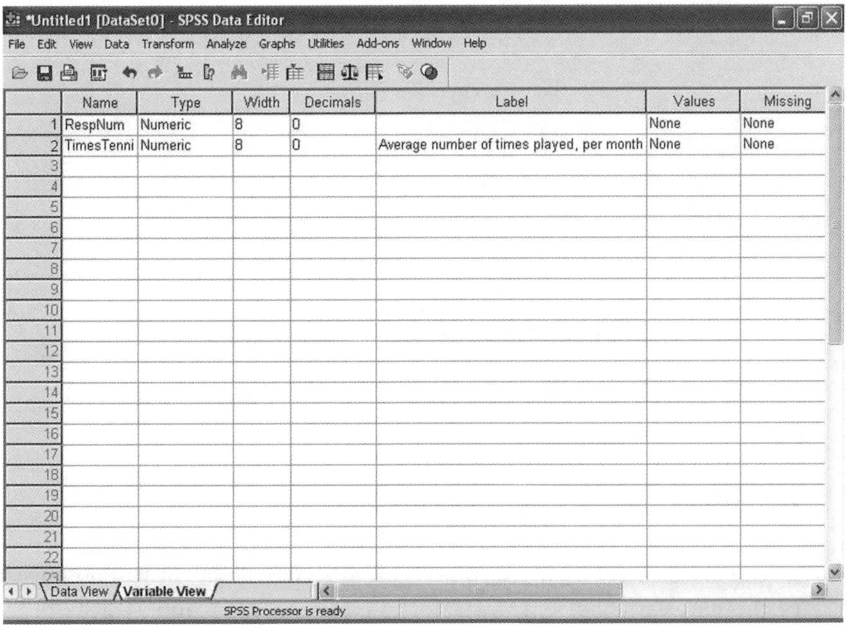

Figure 4.7   The Variable View after defining the variable TimesTennis.

Data View

at the bottom of the window, you will notice that SPSS has added the variable TimesTennis to the Data View (second column, Figure 4.8). All cells in this column contain a dot (or a comma depending on the settings on your PC). This is how SPSS shows missing values: as yet, no data have been entered for TimesTennis.

The next variable is NewShoe, which indicates whether or not the respondent bought new tennis shoes in the preceding year. To define this variable we do as before: first we click the tab

Variable View

then we type the name

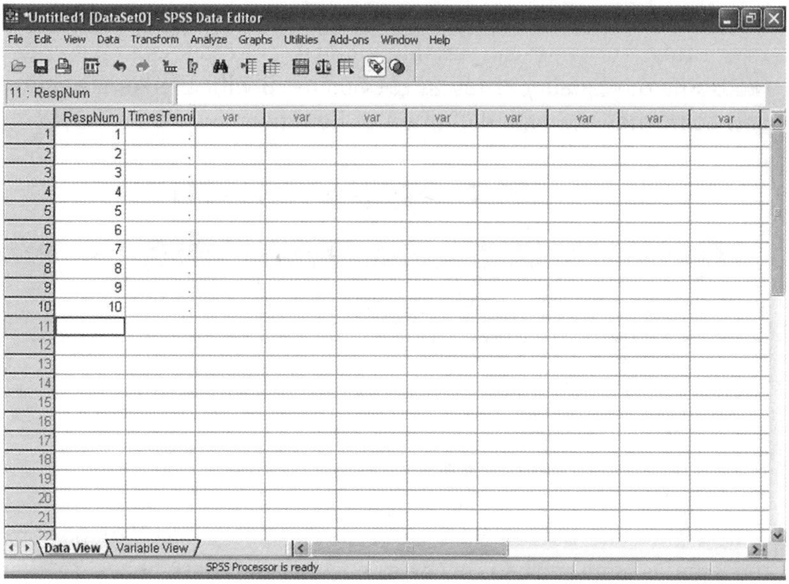

Figure 4.8   The Data View after defining the variable TimesTennis.

NewShoe

in the third row. When you press Enter, SPSS will fill in the default properties of the new variable. As shown in the columns 'Type' and 'Width', SPSS assumes that this is an eight-digit numeric variable. However, NewShoe has been defined as a one-position string variable, with the values Y (Yes) and N (No). This means that we have to change the variable type. The way to do this is as follows: click the icon with the row of dots following Numeric:

A dialogue box pops up, in which you can change the variable type. To specify a variable as a string variable, click the last option

String

Because the dialogue box shows a small circle in front of each type of variable (a radio button), you can select only one variable type.

In the right-hand part of the dialogue box you can specify the number of characters of a variable. The correct number of characters is specified by clicking the small box to the right of the word 'Characters' and typing

1

(and, where necessary, deleting the number 8 with the key Delete or Backspace). This completes the type definition of NewShoe (see Figure 4.9).

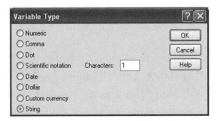

Figure 4.9   The dialogue box in which the type of the variable NewShoe is changed into a string variable with one character.

Now click the button OK to leave the dialogue box Variable Type. Note that the type as well as the number of characters (Width) have been adapted.

We also want to have a label for the variable NewShoe. In the column 'Label' we type

Bought new tennis shoes?

We now define the three remaining variables. The first is ShoePrice, indicating the price category for new tennis shoes bought. The name goes in the first cell in row 4:

ShoePrice

Because the survey does not ask for an exact price but just a price category (less than 50 dollars, between 50 and 100 dollars, more than 100 dollars) we may again set the number of decimals to zero. Under 'Decimals' we type

0

Finally, in the column 'Label' we specify the description:

Shoe price category

The next variable is Gender. In the fifth row you first type the variable name

Gender

Because this is a string variable we have to change the variable type. To do this, click the icon with the row of dots following Numeric (in the column

'Type'); again, the dialogue box appears in which you can change the variable type. Select the last option

String

and specify the number of characters in the right-hand part of the dialogue box:

1

Click the button OK to leave this dialogue box. The meaning of the variable name Gender being obvious, there is no need to specify a label here.

There is one more variable to define. In the first cell of row 6 type the name

Age

Since Age is a numeric variable, the default type is left unchanged and again there is no need for a label. The only thing we have to do is setting the number of decimals to zero. Under 'Decimals' we type

0

All six variables have now been defined (see Figure 4.10).

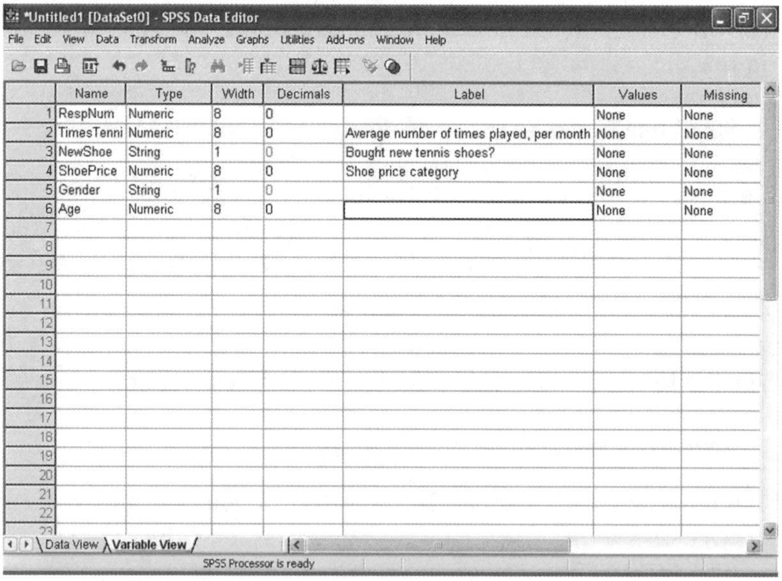
*Untitled1 [DataSet0] - SPSS Data Editor
File Edit View Data Transform Analyze Graphs Utilities Add-ons Window Help
Name Type Width Decimals Label Values Missing
1 RespNum Numeric 8 0 None None
2 TimesTenni Numeric 8 0 Average number of times played, per month None None
3 NewShoe String 1 0 Bought new tennis shoes? None None
4 ShoePrice Numeric 8 0 Shoe price category None None
5 Gender String 1 0 None None
6 Age Numeric 8 0 None None
Data View Variable View
SPSS Processor is ready

Figure 4.10 The Variable View with all defined variables.

4.5   Entering the data

To enter our data we use the Data View, so we leave the Variable View by clicking the tab

Data View

Note that SPSS has put dots (or commas) in the columns for the numeric variables to indicate that at this stage the values of these variables are missing. The cells below the string variables NewShoe and Gender are empty. Since a dot (or a comma) represents a valid value for these variables, SPSS leaves these cells empty.

In the headings of the columns we find the names of the relevant variables, not their labels. When you point the cursor at a name, SPSS shows the corresponding label.

The questionnaire used in this and the following sessions has been filled out by ten respondents. Their answers now have to be entered into Data View. We start with the answers of the first respondent. The first respondent plays tennis on average two times a month. Click the cell corresponding to the first case and the variable TimesTennis, then type

2

Now press the Arrow Right key to move on to the next variable (if you press Enter, the cell pointer jumps to the next line in the same column, which is not very practical because usually data is entered case by case). With the cell pointer now in the NewShoe column you can indicate that the first respondent did buy new tennis shoes last year, by typing

Y

Remember that the values of string variables are case sensitive. In other words, according to SPSS the answer Y is different from the answer y. It does not matter whether you use upper-case (capital) letters or lower-case letters, as long as use is consistent.

Now move right again to the variable ShoePrice. Because this respondent bought shoes in the lowest price category, enter

1

The first respondent being a woman, type

F

in the column Gender. The last variable is Age and her age is

33

years. After all data for the first respondent have been entered, the Data View appears as shown in Figure 4.11. Note that in the default setting, the values of the numeric variables are right-aligned and those of the string variables left-aligned. The *alignment* of the data is one of the properties of a variable we have not discussed yet (it can be changed in the Variable View).

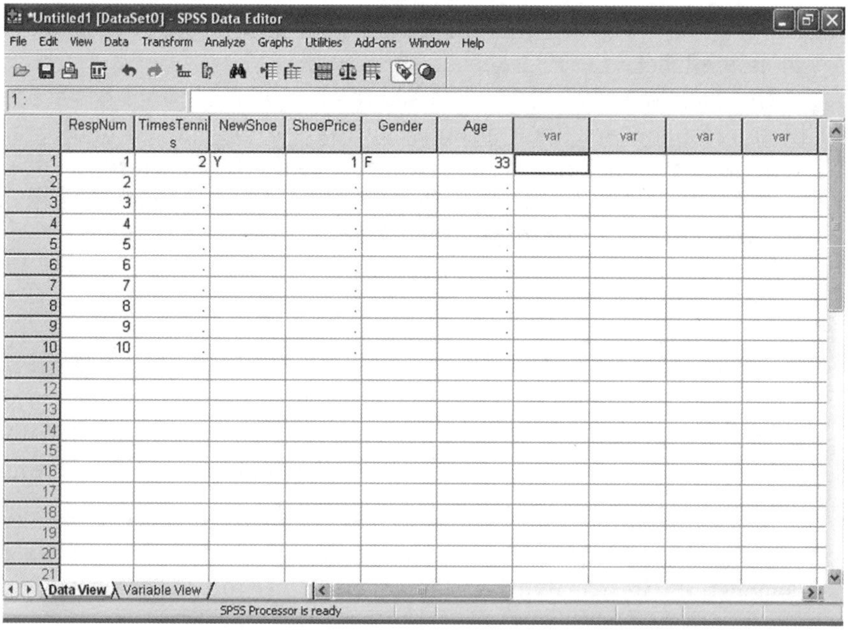

Figure 4.11   The Data View after entering the answers of the first respondent.

We will now enter the answers given by the other nine respondents. The answers of all ten respondents are shown in Figure 4.12. Before entering the answers of the second respondent you have to click the first cell in the second row. Because the second respondent did not buy new tennis shoes, you can skip the cell for ShoePrice (no entry is made).

Note that respondent 4 did not answer the question about his age and that the corresponding cell has the value 0 (zero). Alternatively, we could have skipped this cell. But because we will explain the concept of missing values in Chapter 6, we have given the variable Age of respondent 4 the value 0. When you have entered all data, the Data View should look as in Figure 4.12.

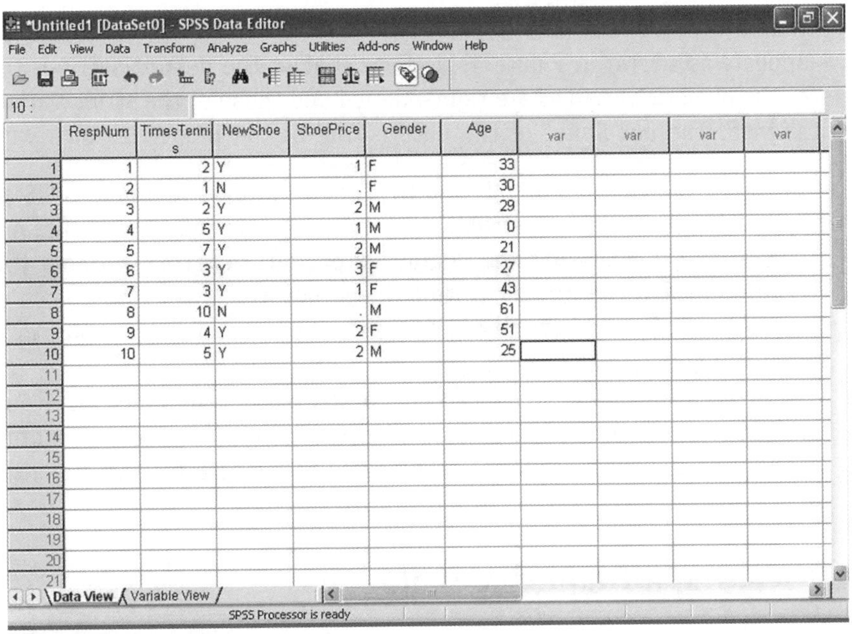

Figure 4.12   The Data View after entering the answers of all ten respondents.

Check the data for any mistakes. This is important because we will be using this file again in the following chapters to illustrate the way SPSS works and demonstrate its capabilities. Typing errors can be corrected by clicking the relevant cell and typing the correct entry.

4.6   Saving the data file

Before proceeding to the analysis of the data, we will first store the data file on a hard disk. It is certainly advisable, especially when you are dealing with large amounts of data, to save the file at regular intervals while still in the process of defining the variables and entering the data.

The contents of the Data Editor can be saved as follows. From the main menu, select

File

Then open the File menu and select

Save

In the next dialogue box, type the name of the data file in the box next to the item 'File name':

tennis

No extension (i.e. a dot followed by three letters) is required. SPSS automatically adds the proper extension, which depends on the type of file. As you can see, a data file receives the default extension '.save' (shown next to 'Save as type'). Clicking the arrow pointing down next to 'Save as type', you see a list of the other file formats that SPSS can create. For instance, you can also save files in Excel format.

Having selected the drive and folder according to your preference, you can save the file by clicking the button Save. The text 'Untitled' in the title bar of the Data Editor simultaneously changes to the name of the data file (i.e. 'tennis').

4.7   Making a frequency table

Until now we have only carried out various preparatory tasks that have to be completed before performing the actual analyses, such as defining variables, entering data and saving the data file. Our next step is the execution of a simple but very common type of analysis, i.e. making a frequency table. We will do that for the price categories of the tennis shoes bought.

Making a frequency table is a form of statistical analysis and so we choose from the main menu

Analyze

Since a frequency table is an example of a descriptive analysis, we select from the Analyze menu the option

Descriptive Statistics

The first option in the next menu is

Frequencies

When you click this option, a dialogue box appears in which you can make a frequency table (see Figure 4.13). The structure of the dialogue box for the Frequencies command is the same as that for many other types of analysis in SPSS. The left part shows all variables in the data file and under the heading 'Variable(s)', SPSS shows the variables to be analysed. SPSS uses various symbols to indicate different types of variable. A yardstick symbolises numeric variables, the symbol with the letter A (for alphanumeric) refers to string variables.

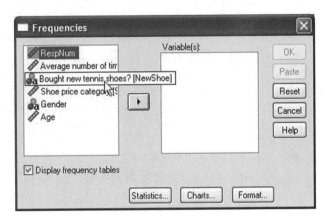

Figure 4.13   The dialogue box for making a frequency table.

In the list of variables, SPSS shows the variable labels, if these have been specified. When the cursor is pointed at a variable, such as NewShoe in Figure 4.13, SPSS will show a box with the full label, followed by the name of the variable in brackets. If, in your case, SPSS only shows the names of the variables but no labels, you can change this setting as follows: select Edit > Options from the menu and click the tab General, then under the item 'Variable Lists' make SPSS show variables including their descriptions (option 'Display Labels') and in the order in which they were entered (option 'File'). Now click OK to confirm and leave this dialogue box.

In the centre of the dialogue box Frequencies, between the two boxes, you see a button with an arrow, by which the variables are moved from one box to the other. The buttons at the bottom of the dialogue box usually refer to additional options of an SPSS command. In the case of Frequencies these are the buttons: Statistics, to request descriptive and summary statistics, Charts, to create bar charts and histograms, and Format, for changing the layout of the table. Finally, on the right we see the five buttons you will find in most SPSS dialogue boxes, namely:

- *OK* to execute the command;
- *Paste* to copy the command to the Syntax Editor;

- *Reset* to clear all settings and all variables entered;
- *Cancel* to cancel the command;
- *Help* for an explanation on the command being specified.

We will make a frequency table for the price categories of tennis shoes. So, first click the variable ShoePrice in the list of variables on the left in the dialogue box, then the button with the arrow right. This will move the variable ShoePrice to the list of variables to be analysed. Note that clicking the button with the arrow right does not only move ShoePrice from the left to the right, it also changes the arrow right into an arrow left. The system is such that when you click a variable in the list on the left, the button will show an arrow right, whereas clicking a variable in the list on the right will produce a button with an arrow left.

If you click the button with the arrow left, ShoePrice is moved back to its original location in the list of all variables and the arrow left is changed back into an arrow right. In this way you can select variables for analysis and place them back again. If you are skilled in using the mouse, there is a quicker way of selecting a variable, namely by double-clicking it.

Make sure that ShoePrice is selected and placed under the heading 'Variable(s)'. We will not use any of the more advanced options of Frequencies; therefore the command is ready to be executed. Execute it by clicking OK.

4.8   Browsing the output in the Viewer

The Frequencies command produces output and therefore SPSS activates a new window *Viewer* in which you can browse the results of the analyses (see Figure 4.14). If the Viewer occupies only part of the screen, maximise the window by clicking the Maximize button, that is, the middle one of the three buttons at the far right in the title bar.

The structure of the Viewer window is similar to that of the Data Editor. In the title bar we see the name SPSS Viewer and the name of the output file. Because the latter has not yet been defined, SPSS uses the default name 'Output1'. The next line contains the menu, with many options being identical to those in the Data Editor. In addition to general options like File, Edit and View, you will find Analyze and Graphs in each SPSS window. Below the menu is the toolbar (two lines). Finally, at the very bottom of the window we have the status bar, now displaying the message 'SPSS Processor is ready', because the frequency table is complete.

The specific part of the Viewer is the central part, where the results of the analyses are shown. A vertical bar divides this portion of the window into two parts. The part on the left contains the *outline* pane, an overview of the full

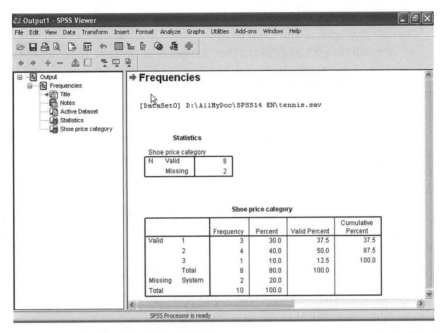

Figure 4.14   The SPSS Viewer for browsing the output with the frequency table of the variable ShoePrice.

output contained in the Viewer. SPSS presents the output in the form of objects, that is, separate elements allowing further processing (more on this below). We see that the output generated by Frequencies is organised in the form of five objects: Title, Notes, Active Dataset, Statistics and 'Shoe price category' (the last of these refers to the frequency table that has been made). Actually, the outline is nothing more than a list of names of all objects present in Viewer. The part to the right of the bar is the *content pane* containing the actual output, such as tables, charts and text output.

The quickest way of finding tables and charts in the Viewer is by clicking them in the outline pane; SPSS will then show them in the content pane. In both panes, a red arrow indicates which output object is currently selected. In this example, we see that SPSS points to the object 'Title' in the outline pane and that this refers to the title 'Frequencies' in the content pane. In the outline pane, now click the object

Shoe price category

As you will have noted, the red arrow in the outline pane has moved to this object, while in the content pane the frequency table has been selected. If, under different circumstances, the frequency table had not been visible, SPSS would now have retrieved and displayed it.

The icon for 'Shoe price category' in the outline pane symbolises an open book showing a data table. By double-clicking this icon

you close the book:

In the content pane, the frequency table now disappears. A double-click on the closed book will reopen it; the Viewer will then show the frequency table again.

Upon careful inspection of the outline pane, you will notice that by default one element of the output of Frequencies is not shown. This is the element 'Notes', indicated by the closed book. Double-click the closed book to show the contents of Notes (see Figure 4.15).

The frequency table is now no longer on the screen. Clicking (not double-clicking!) the object 'Shoe price category' in the outline pane brings it back

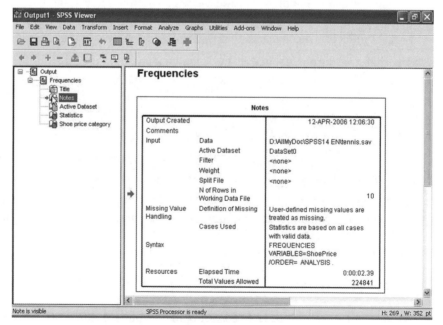

Figure 4.15   The Viewer after opening the object 'Notes'.

into view. This way you can easily find your way around in the SPSS output and show or hide parts of it. In Sections 6.7 and 6.8 we go into more detail, by showing how to change, save and print output in the Viewer.

4.9   The output of Frequencies

As we have seen in the previous section, the output of Frequencies consists of five objects: Title, Notes, Active Dataset, Statistics and the frequency table 'Shoe price category'. In this section we briefly discuss these objects. 'Title' only refers to the title Frequencies, and 'Active Dataset' to the name of the data file used; the other objects are more interesting.

'Notes' provides a summary of the data SPSS has used for the analysis. This object forms part of the output of every SPSS analysis. The most important information in the Notes table (see Figure 4.15) concerns:

- the name of the data file, in this example tennis.sav;
- any selections ('Filter'), weightings ('Weight') and file split-ups applied ('Split File'); none of these having been made in this example, the corresponding entries read '<none>';
- the number of cases in the data file (10);
- how SPSS has handled missing values ('Missing Value Handling'; also refer to Section 6.4);
- the syntax of the command, that is, the analysis written in the special SPSS command language; we briefly discuss the use of the SPSS syntax in Section 6.11.

The fourth object is called 'Statistics' (Table 4.3), a table with the number of cases with valid and missing values. The table shows that for eight respondents the variable ShoePrice has a valid value, while in two cases the value is missing (because two persons did not buy tennis shoes, see Figure 4.12).

The last object is the frequency table that Frequencies was all about (Table 4.4). The heading 'Shoe price category' at the top of this table is identical to the label

Table 4.3   The output object 'Statistics' with an overview of the number of valid and missing cases

Statistics

Shoe price category

N	Valid	8
	Missing	2

Table 4.4   The frequency table of the price category of the tennis shoes bought

Shoe price category

		Frequency	Percent	Valid Percent	Cumulative Percent
Valid	1	3	30.0	37.5	37.5
	2	4	40.0	50.0	87.5
	3	1	10.0	12.5	100.0
	Total	8	80.0	100.0	
Missing	System	2	20.0		
Total		10	100.0		

of the variable ShoePrice. If we had not specified a label for the variable, the heading would have shown the name of the variable.

The first column contains the values of ShoePrice. Note that SPSS has divided them into two categories: valid values and missing values. SPSS has found three valid values, namely the numbers 1, 2 and 3. The meaning of the codes may be looked up in the code book (Table 4.2).

The second column, with the heading 'Frequency', shows the number of times that each of these values occurs in the data file; in other words, the absolute frequency. We see that three respondents bought tennis shoes at a price less than 50 dollars (category 1). The largest number of respondents (four) is found in the second category, with tennis shoes of between 50 and 100 dollars. Two respondents have a missing value.

SPSS computes two totals, 8 and 10, respectively. The first is the number of respondents for whom a valid value was measured. The second total, in the last line, corresponds to the total number of respondents in the data file and includes the two persons who did not answer the question because they had not bought tennis shoes.

The third column, with the heading 'Percent', gives the percentages (relative frequencies) computed as absolute frequencies divided by the total number of cases. For the first price category this amounts to 30.0% (3 cases out of 10).

In the column 'Valid Percent' we find the relative frequencies for each of the price categories expressed as percentages of the total number of valid responses. For the first price category this amounts to 37.5% (3 cases out of 8).

Finally, the last column contains the cumulative percentages. For each the price category this is the sum of the valid percentages corresponding to this category and all lower categories.

4.10   Exiting SPSS

We have reached the end of the first session. In this first session you have learned the basics of SPSS for Windows. The most important objective was to make you become familiar with the structure of the program. As we have seen, SPSS has separate windows for your data (the Data Editor) and your output (the Viewer). The Data Editor contains two views, the Data View and the Variable View, for entering and changing data and variables. The Viewer is used to browse the results of the analyses, and contains an outline pane and a contents pane. In the Data Editor and the Viewer you find very similar menus. For example, from both windows you can start a statistical analysis.

In addition to exploring these basic SPSS features, you have performed a number of elementary but important tasks, namely defining variables and entering data based on the code book, saving the data file and performing a simple analysis (i.e. making a frequency table). In the following session we go on from here and demonstrate how to create a bar chart and compute a new variable.

We end this session by exiting SPSS. From the main menu, select

File

and in the File menu select the last option

Exit

Whenever you close a window whose content has been changed, SPSS asks whether you wish to save the new content. In this example we have already saved the data, and therefore we are now asked only if we wish to save the content of the Viewer. If you want to save the frequency table, click the button Yes; otherwise, click No to leave SPSS.

5   Session 2: Charts and computations

The previous session was a first step in learning how SPSS works. We now continue our journey by performing some further basic tasks such as opening a file, getting help information, creating a bar chart and computing a new variable. Additionally, we discuss some commands of a more advanced nature that illustrate the many options to specify preferred settings instead of using default ones. In these exercises we use the data file that we created in the first session.

Like the other two sessions, this chapter has been designed such that you can follow all procedures while seated at your computer desk. All required keystrokes and mouse clicks are noted and where necessary explained.

5.1   Opening the data file

After starting up the program (see Section 4.1) the first thing you see is an information window, followed by a dialogue box with the question: 'What would you like to do?' (Figure 5.1). The options offered in this dialogue box are: start the SPSS tutorial, type in new data, get data from a database (via a query) or open a data file (the default selection). Below this last option you see a box in which SPSS displays recently used data files. It often occurs that you wish to continue work with a file used in a previous session, so this list is a very practical tool for making a quick start with SPSS.

The dialogue box contains the name of the data file that we created in the previous session:

tennis.sav

First click the file name, then confirm by clicking OK to have the Data Editor loaded with the data from the first session (see Figure 5.2). It is possible that your SPSS version has been installed in such a way that the initial dialogue box does not appear. In that case, open the data file from the Data Editor menu by clicking File > Open. Select the desired drive and folder and open the file named tennis.

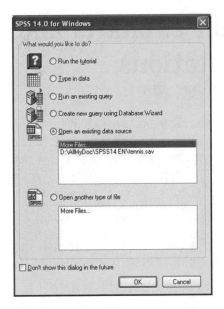

Figure 5.1   The start dialogue box to instruct SPSS what you intend to do.

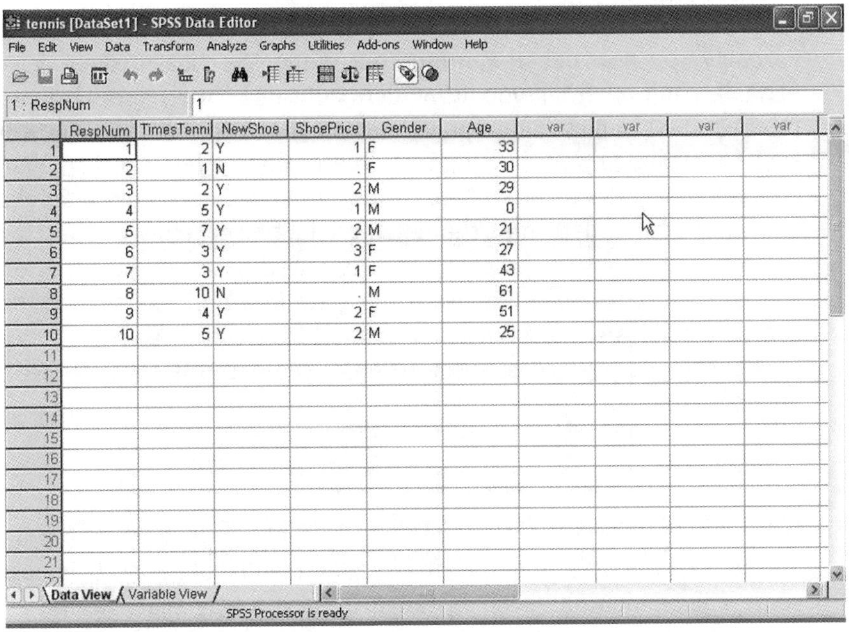

	RespNum	TimesTenni	NewShoe	ShoePrice	Gender	Age	var	var	var	var
1	1	2	Y	1	F	33				
2	2	1	N	.	F	30				
3	3	2	Y	2	M	29				
4	4	5	Y	1	M	0				
5	5	7	Y	2	M	21				
6	6	3	Y	3	F	27				
7	7	3	Y	1	F	43				
8	8	10	N	.	M	61				
9	9	4	Y	2	F	51				
10	10	5	Y	2	M	25				

Figure 5.2   The Data Editor with the data from the first session.

If the Data Editor occupies less than the full screen, maximise this window with the Maximize button as described in the previous chapter (Section 4.1).

5.2   Creating a bar chart

In this section we will create a bar chart for the price category of tennis shoes. SPSS contains multiple options for doing this; the Graphs menu contains three different commands to create bar charts. The reason for this rather confusing situation is the long history of the software package. What used to be easy can now be accomplished in an even simpler manner, but for the sake of users of the older SPSS versions the software designers kept the old options in the program.

We will create a bar chart in this section in the easiest way possible, by using the Chart Builder. Select in the menu of the Data Editor the option

Graphs

and then in the Graphs menu the command

Chart Builder

Probably you now get a warning concerning the measurement level of your variables and whether you have defined value labels (see Figure 5.3). We skipped these topics in the previous session: in this chapter we will see why it is important to provide complete definitions to your variables.

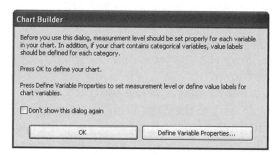

Figure 5.3   A warning of the Chart Builder related to defining the correct measurement level of variables and assigning value labels.

However, we will now ignore this warning. To prevent SPSS from repeating this warning, click on 'Don't show this dialog again'. After you click the OK button, the Chart Builder appears (see Figure 5.4).

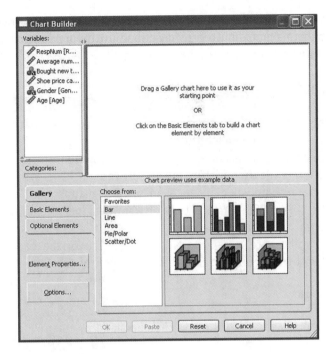

Figure 5.4   The start window of the Chart Builder.

In the upper left corner of the Chart Builder SPSS displays the variables, the large rectangle to the right will show a preview of the chart to be created and the bottom half of the window contains tabs and buttons for the design of the chart.

Currently the tab Gallery is shown. This tab contains the most often used charts, namely bar charts, line charts, area charts, pie charts and scatterplots. In most cases, SPSS can create multiple variants. For example, six variants of a bar chart are shown.

In this case we will create a simple bar chart So, drag the picture of the first bar chart (Simple Bar) to the chart preview. The preview now shows a bar chart in which the horizontal and vertical axes are still empty (see Figure 5.5). We do not need the dialogue box of Element Properties that (probably) has also popped up. Close this box by clicking the button with the cross in the title bar.

In the next step, you determine the variables that have to be shown in the bar chart. Drag the variable 'Shoe price category' to the horizontal axis (X-axis).

SPSS displays a preview of the bar chart (see Figure 5.6). As you can see, the various categories are shown as vertical lines instead of bars. The reason for this is that we defined ShoePrice as a continuous variable. SPSS uses the term 'scale variable'; see also the message in the box below the variables list. To solve this problem we first have to adjust the measurement level of ShoePrice. This is what we do in the next section.

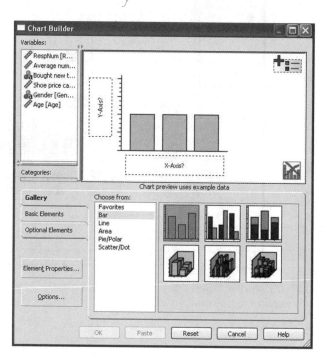

Figure 5.5   The Chart Builder after making the first step in creating a bar chart.

5.3   Changing the measurement level of a variable

Changing the measurement level of a variable takes place in the Variable View of the Data Editor. This is the tab with the variable properties. So, close the Chart Builder window (by clicking the button with the cross in the title bar). Now you are back in the Data Editor, probably in the Data View. Click the tab

Variable View

at the bottom of the spreadsheet to switch views. The Variable View contains the measurement level in the last column, called Measure. The row of ShoePrice shows that the current measurement level is 'Scale'. This refers to interval or ratio variables. ShoePrice, however, is an ordinal variable (see Section 2.5.1).

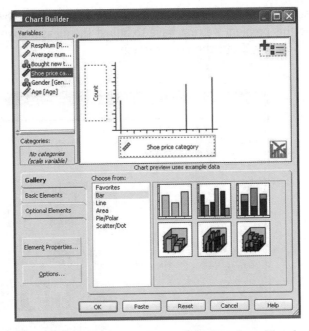

Figure 5.6   The Chart Builder shows a preview of the bar chart. The chart contains vertical lines instead of bars because ShoePrice is a continuous (scale) variable.

To change the measurement level click the cell containing the current measurement level of ShoePrice. Then an arrow appears in this cell. Click the arrow and select Ordinal.

With the correct measurement level we can create the bar chart with the Chart Builder. Select in the menu of the Data Editor again the option

Graphs

and in the Graphs menu

Chart Builder

Drag in the Chart Builder the picture of a simple bar chart to the preview area and close the dialogue box of Element Properties.

The next step is dragging the variable 'Shoe price category' to the horizontal axis (X-axis). Because ShoePrice has been changed into an ordinal variable, SPSS now displays a bar chart with bars (see Figure 5.7). Now click the button OK to execute the command.

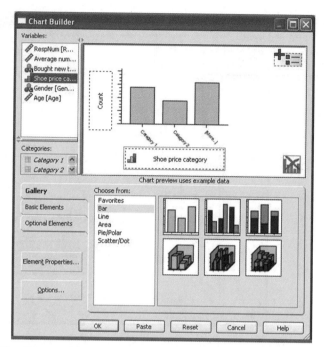

Figure 5.7   The Chart Builder with the correct preview of a bar chart.

To show the output, SPSS opens the Viewer in a new window. If the Viewer opens in a reduced window, maximise the window so that you can see the bar chart in full (see Figure 5.8).

The vertical axis of the bar chart displays the number of cases (Count) and the horizontal axis the various categories of ShoePrice. The tallest bar (4 cases) belongs to value 2, that is, the middle category of 50–100 dollars (see the code book, Table 4.2). Category 3 has the lowest number of cases.

In the outline pane of the Viewer you can see that the output consists of four objects. The first of these, the title, is marked by an arrow. The second one, 'Notes', is represented by a closed book. When you double-click this icon, an overview of the data used in creating the bar chart is displayed. This table is very similar to the one discussed in the previous session (see Figure 4.15).

5.4   The description of the coding

You will have noted how cumbersome it is having to refer to the code book each time you want to know the meaning of a code. What price category corresponds to the value 1 of the variable ShoePrice? How much do shoes from

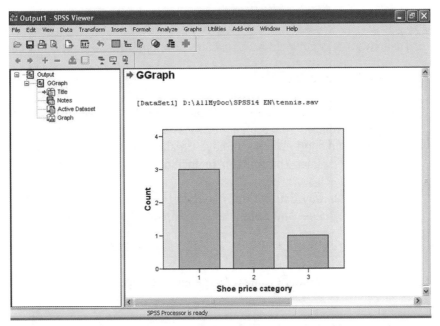

Figure 5.8   The bar chart of the price category of tennis shoes shown in the Viewer.

the third group cost? It would be much easier if SPSS displayed the meaning of these codes in the bar chart. This can be done by defining value labels. In the same way that a variable label explains the name of a variable, a *value label* is a description assigned to a value of a variable.

For stating the value labels, we have to return to the Data Editor. Click the button 'Tennis – SPSS Data Editor' in the task bar at the bottom of the screen, shown as

*tennis [DataSet1] - SPSS Data Editor

(Alternatively, from the Viewer menu you can select the option Window and then click the Data Editor in the next menu.) Now you return to the Variable View.

The value labels have to be specified in the column 'Values'. In this column, click the cell corresponding to ShoePrice (in the fourth row). As we saw before, when defining the variable type, an icon with a row of dots appears in the cell. Click this icon:

None

and the dialogue box Value Labels will pop up. You can now define the labels as follows: click the input field next to 'Value', and key in the first code, that is

1

Then click the input field next to 'Label' and type the description of code 1:

Less than 50 dollar

Like variable labels, value labels need to be concise since tables and charts often allow limited space for labels. Make sure, therefore, that the labels are both clear and short. When you have finished typing the label, the button Add is highlighted. Click this button to include it as the first item in the list of value labels.

In a similar way you can now specify the other two labels: click the input field next to 'Value' and enter the second code:

2

Then click the input field next to 'Label' and type the label corresponding to code 2:

Between 50 and 100 dollar

Finally, click the button Add to include this description in the list of value labels. Now you can define the third value label. Click the input field next to 'Value' and type:

3

Then click the input field next to 'Label', enter the description:

More than 100 dollar

and click Add. After you have defined the three labels, the dialogue box Value Labels looks as shown in Figure 5.9. The three labels are separate elements in the list of value labels. This becomes clear when you click the labels one by one. By selecting a value label, you can change or remove it (with the corresponding buttons). Many SPSS dialogue boxes in which you have to specify a number of elements feature these buttons Add, Change and Remove.

Save the labels in the dialogue box Value Labels by clicking OK. You then return to the Variable View, where the first part of the list of labels is displayed.

In the Data View you can have displayed either the codes or the value labels. Click the tab

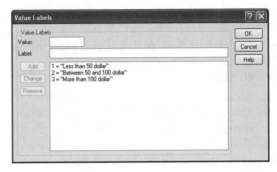

Figure 5.9   The dialogue box after entering the three value labels for the variable ShoePrice.

Data View

at the bottom of the Variable View. Depending on the way SPSS is installed on your computer, you will see either codes or labels in the column of ShoePrice. If codes are shown, you can change the setting to display value labels, by first selecting from the menu

View

and then the option Value Labels. Clicking this option will result in replacing the ShoePrice codes by the corresponding labels (see Figure 5.10). Showing value labels is particularly useful when analysing individual cases. Because the default column width is 8, the spreadsheet only shows the first part of the value label.

5.5   Using the toolbar

Most commands so far were given via the menu, but in many cases there is a quicker alternative available, namely by using the toolbar. The buttons enable you to execute commands by a single click that would otherwise require several menu selections.

Each button shows an icon symbolising the action that is summarised by the button. The meaning of a button is shown when you aim the mouse pointer at it. From your experience with other programs you will already be familiar with the first three buttons:

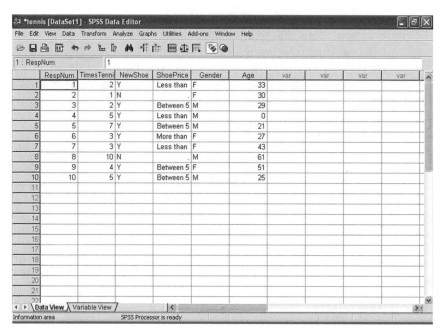

Figure 5.10   The Data View in which the codes of ShoePrice have been replaced by value labels.

These are the well-known buttons used for opening, saving and printing files or parts of file

Because we have added value labels to the variable ShoePrice in the preceding section, it is a good idea to save the data file on a disk. If you click the button Save File, the button with the diskette symbol, SPSS will save the data file under the existing name (tennis.sav).

The toolbar is a very handy tool, enabling you to speed up SPSS work. For that reason we describe a few other buttons as well in the remainder of this session and the next one. If you use SPSS a lot, we recommend that you customise the toolbar, to include the commands that you frequently use (see Section 20.2).

Towards the end of the previous section we demonstrated how to make SPSS show value labels. An alternative way of doing this makes use of the toolbar. When you place the mouse pointer on the button

the description 'Value Labels' will be displayed. If you click this button, SPSS will show the codes instead of the labels in the Data Editor. Upon clicking once more, the labels reappear. This is a fast and easy way of switching between these options. Now make sure labels are shown.

In the previous section we specified value labels in order to make the bar chart easier to interpret. We can now create the bar chart again by selecting the option Graphs in the menu, followed by choosing Chart Builder, as we did before. However, SPSS has a button for recalling a command executed before. This is the button Dialog Recall

(when you look closely, this button appears as a stylised dialogue box). SPSS now shows a list of commands you have used before, leaving out general commands such as saving and opening of files. The list now probably contains two commands, namely:

Chart Builder

Frequencies

The box contains these two commands because these are the only two analyses that we have carried out during this session and the previous one. It is also possible that your window contains only the first of the above commands – or, instead, more than these two – depending on the way SPSS is installed on your computer.

Because we now again want to create a bar chart, click the command

Chart Builder

This opens the dialogue box with the settings of the previous bar chart. Note that the button Dialog Recall saves you a couple of keystrokes: working from the menu you would have had to select Graphs, followed by Chart Builder.

The Chart Builder still contains all settings of the bar chart created before. You will now also understand the usefulness of the Reset button that you find in the dialogue box of each statistical technique. The Reset button removes all specific settings and selected variables; you will use it to repeat an analysis with different variables and settings.

Click OK to create the same bar chart again. The Viewer now shows the bar chart with the value labels instead of the codes 1, 2 and 3 (Figure 5.11).

Because the Viewer now contains more than one chart, the outline pane is useful for viewing the previous bar chart again. At the topmost GGraph command in the outline pane, click

Graph

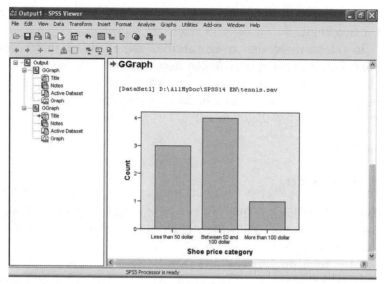

Figure 5.11   The bar chart of ShoePrice in the Viewer where the categories are identified by value labels.

(single click, or the book icon will close), and the first bar chart reappears, the one without value labels. Clicking the bar chart icon at the second command will get you back again to the one you just created.

By clicking the elements in the outline pane you can easily recall and view interesting parts of the output. You can also do this in the content pane, the right-hand part of the Viewer, with the scroll bar at the far right of the window. The outline pane is particularly useful when you know which part of the output you want to see, and when you have a lot of output. If you do not have much output, scrolling the content pane will often be more practical.

5.6   Improving the appearance of the bar chart

In this section we further improve the appearance of the bar chart of price categories of tennis shoes. You can do this in two ways, namely by providing a more detailed specification of the bar chart when defining one, or by changing an existing chart. Many changes are possible by either method, so you can take the route of your own preference. To illustrate both methods, we give some examples of each method.

We discuss four examples, in which we turn the vertical bars into horizontal bars, add a title to the chart, change the order of the bars and add shading to the bars. For the first two examples we adapt the design specifications of the chart; for the other two changes we use the Chart Editor to modify an existing chart.

To extend the design specification of the chart, we first have to recall the Chart Builder. Click on the Dialog Recall button

and select

Chart Builder

You find additional features in the various tabs. First we turn the vertical bars into horizontal bars and then add a title to the chart.

5.6.1 Turning vertical bars into horizontal bars

By rotating the bars, the vertical bars become horizontal bars. The Chart Builder currently displays the tab Gallery; for rotating the bars you need the tab Basic Elements, so click on this tab.

To rotate the bars you have to click the button Transpose. SPSS then shows a bar chart with horizontal bars in the preview (see Figure 5.12).

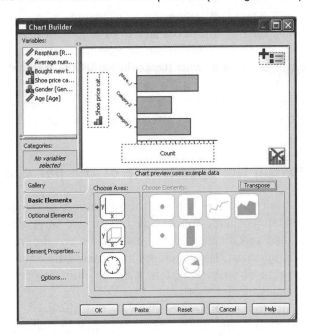

Figure 5.12   The bar chart in the Chart Editor with horizontal bars.

5.6.2 Adding a title

To add various descriptions to the chart, such as titles and footnotes, you click the tab Optional Elements. As you see, you can specify two titles, a subtitle and two footnotes.

You add a title by dragging the button 'Title 1' to the chart preview. It does not matter where you drop the button, since each title and footnote has its own position in the chart.

Next, the dialogue box Element Properties appears. In the upper part the element 'Title 1' is highlighted. Below you find an input field in which you can specify a title, for example:

How expensive are tennis shoes?

(see Figure 5.13). To confirm you have to click the button Apply.

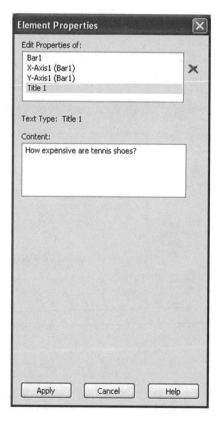

Figure 5.13   The dialogue box Element Properties after specifying a title.

The upper part of the dialogue box Element Properties contains a list of the various chart elements. Bar1 refers to the information represented by a bar; in our example this is the number of cases (count). You can change this into the percentage of cases or some other statistic. The element X-axis1 refers to the variable ShoePrice.

To create the bar chart with the new specifications, click in the Chart Builder on the OK button. Now the new bar chart is shown in the Viewer (see Figure 5.14).

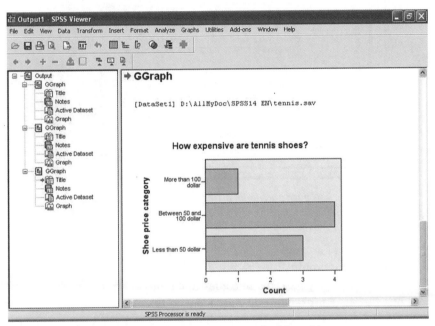

Figure 5.14   The bar chart with transposed bars and with a title.

5.6.3   Changing an existing chart

The second method of improving the appearance of a chart is by changing an existing chart. This is done in the Chart Editor. This window appears when you double-click an existing graph in the Viewer. Double-click the bar chart just now created. To improve its appearance we change the order of the bars, and add shading to the bars.

After you have double-clicked the chart, SPSS opens a new window, the Chart Editor. The 'big' bar chart in the Viewer becomes hatched to indicate that it is being edited (see Figure 5.15).

Besides the Data Editor and the Viewer, the Chart Editor is the third main window of SPSS. Like the other two windows, the Chart Editor has its own menu and buttons. The menu contains various commands for changing charts.

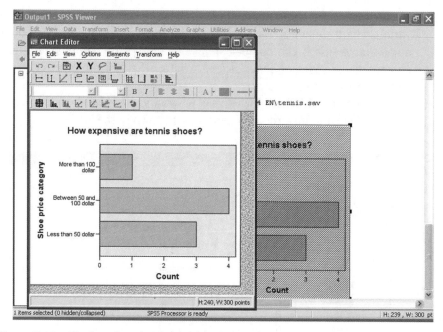

Figure 5.15   The bar chart loaded in the Chart Editor with the Viewer containing the hatched bar chart in the background.

The starting point for changing a chart is that each chart is composed of a number of elements. This becomes apparent when you click the chart in various places. For example, if you click the text 'Count' on the horizontal axis, a box will appear around the text. Similarly, when you click one of the numbers on the horizontal axis, these are also placed in a box. When you click a bar, the bar will be surrounded by bold lines. Each chart consists of separate elements that have their own properties such as location, colour and size. Each of these can be changed.

Changing the properties of a chart is very simple. To illustrate the procedure we discuss two examples, in which we change the order of the bars, and add shading to the bars.

5.6.4   Changing the order of the bars

In Figure 5.15 the highest category (more than 100 dollar) is at the top. If you prefer to have the bars in descending order, this bar will become the bottom one. This can be arranged as follows. Double-click one of the bars. The Properties dialogue box then appears, in which you have to click the tab Categories (see Figure 5.16).

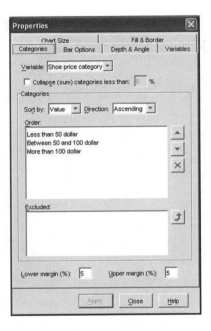

Figure 5.16   With the tab Categories (in the Properties dialogue box) you can change the way the various categories are displayed.

Behind 'Sort', in the middle of the dialogue box, you find the specification of how SPSS shows the various categories: based on the value sorted in ascending order. This is why under 'Order' the category 'Less than 50 dollar' is listed first. It seems surprising that the order of the three categories under 'Order' is the exact opposite from the order in which they are shown in the bar chart. The reason is that SPSS starts the listing from the horizontal axis, and therefore the category 'Less than 50 dollar' comes first.

To reverse the order of the bars, we need to change the sort direction. Click on the arrow behind Ascending and select Descending. Click the button Apply to change the bar chart (see Figure 5.17).

5.6.5   Bars with shadow
The final change involves the presentation of the bars. We show how you can add shadow to the bars. For this we again need the Properties window that you probably still have on your screen (if not, double-click one of the bars). In the dialogue box Properties click the tab Depth & Angle (see Figure 5.18).

Under Effect, select 'Shadow' (the current setting is 'Flat'). You can also specify how much shadow you want. You get a preview of this under Angle (top right) by shifting the (horizontal and vertical) slide controls. When you are

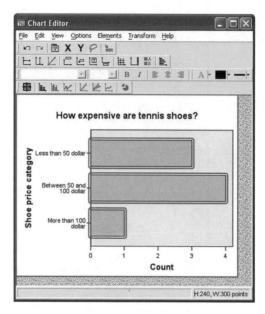

Figure 5.17   The bar chart in which the order of the bars is reversed.

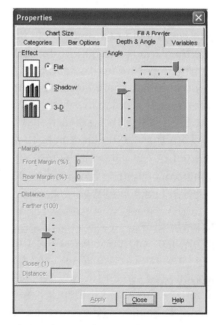

*Figure 5.18   With the tab Depth & Angle (in the dialogue box Properties)
you can change the way the bars are shown.*

satisfied with the effect, click the button Apply to implement the settings in the bar chart (Figure 5.19).

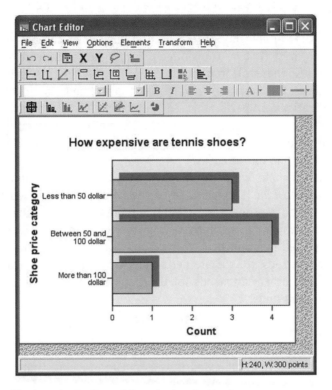

Figure 5.19   The bar chart after adding shadow to the bars.

To summarise, in this section we have seen that you can easily change existing charts. All you have to do is to select (double-click) the element you wish to change. There also is a Properties dialogue box for the horizontal and vertical axes, in which many properties can be specified. Finally, you can use the menu, in particular the option Chart, and the toolbar to change the chart properties.

We now return to the Viewer, so close the Chart Editor by clicking the button with the cross in the title bar of the Chart Editor. The Viewer reappears, now showing the changed bar chart.

5.7   Computing variables

When you start using SPSS in a research project, the first step is to create the data file, after which you can proceed to the analyses. Some situations, however, require another step in between, namely that of *transforming the data*.

Sometimes you want to analyse only women, or only persons who play tennis at least five times a month. Another example is if you need a crosstable with the ages of the respondents and the price paid for the tennis shoes. To avoid getting a very large crosstable, you first have to group the many different values of the variable Age into a limited number of categories. In all situations the data must first be transformed. Sometimes this involves transforming the cases (respondents), for example when you need to select or sort cases. Sometimes the variables have to be transformed, for instance when making classifications or performing computations. Part II of this book contains a detailed discussion of the various transformation commands in SPSS. The transformation of variables is the subject of Chapter 9 while Chapter 10 discusses the transformation of cases.

As an example, we perform a computation in this section. Suppose that you want to know what percentage of the persons interviewed play less than 25 times a year. We then need a variable representing the number of times played per year, which can be derived from the variable TimesTennis, the number of times played per month.

Computations in SPSS are performed with the Compute command. This command, and other commands for the transformation of variables, can be found in the menu under

Transform

Now click the first command in the Transform menu, that is

Compute

A dialogue box pops up in which you can specify the computation (see Figure 5.20). The upper part of this dialogue box represents the actual computation:

Target Variable = Numeric Expression

First you specify a name for the variable to be computed (the target variable). Type below 'Target Variable'

YearTennis

as the name for the variable corresponding to the number of times per year a respondent plays. Next, you specify the computation ('Numeric Expression'). A computation may have three components: variables from the list of variables; numbers and arithmetic operators (like +, − or /) from the keypad; and functions, e.g. for extracting a root, rounding or drawing random numbers from a probability distribution.

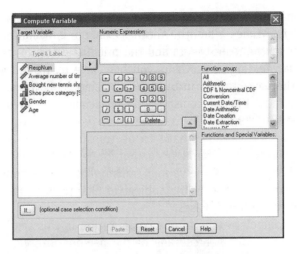

Figure 5.20   The dialogue box of the Compute command.

For the sake of convenience we assume that to compute YearTennis we may multiply the monthly average TimesTennis by 12. The way to specify this computation is as follows: double-click in the list of variables TimesTennis, the number of times played per month, to place this variable into the formula (you can also click TimesTennis and then the button with the arrow right).

The second part of the computation is:

*12

You can either type this on your keyboard, or click the three symbols in the keypad of the dialogue box. This completes the specification of the computation (Figure 5.21).

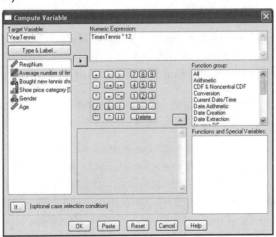

Figure 5.21   Calculating the variable YearTennis in the dialogue box of the Compute command.

Before executing the computation, we specify a label for YearTennis with the button Type&Label. When you click this button, a dialogue box will be displayed, in which you can specify a variable label and the type of variable. You could type a label for YearTennis (such as 'Number of times played, per year'), as we did before. However, we now use the other option, so click

Use expression as label

This means that the computation specified above will become the label assigned to YearTennis (see Figure 5.22). Although this is not a very elegant label for use in a report, it is a very practical function, as it reduces the amount of typing and avoids any ambiguity in the label.

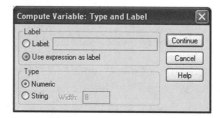

Figure 5.22   The dialogue box in which the computation is assigned as variable label of the new variable (the button Type&Label of the Compute command).

In the lower half of the dialogue box you can specify the type of the new variable YearTennis. As you can see, the default type is numeric, so there is no need to change it.

To execute the computation, click the button Continue in the dialogue box 'Type and Label', followed by OK in the dialogue box Compute.

The Viewer only shows the results of analyses. To see the computed variable you have to switch to the Data Editor. This time, we use an alternative way of doing this, namely by clicking the button Goto Data, the button with the matrix

In the Data View the new variable YearTennis appears in a new column next to Age, the last variable in the spreadsheet. As you can see, SPSS assigns the computed variable two decimals (by default). If desired, you can change this in the Variable View. Compare YearTennis and TimesTennis to verify that the computation is correct. When you direct the mouse pointer to the variable name YearTennis at the top of the column, a box with the label will appear, showing the computation (see Figure 5.23).

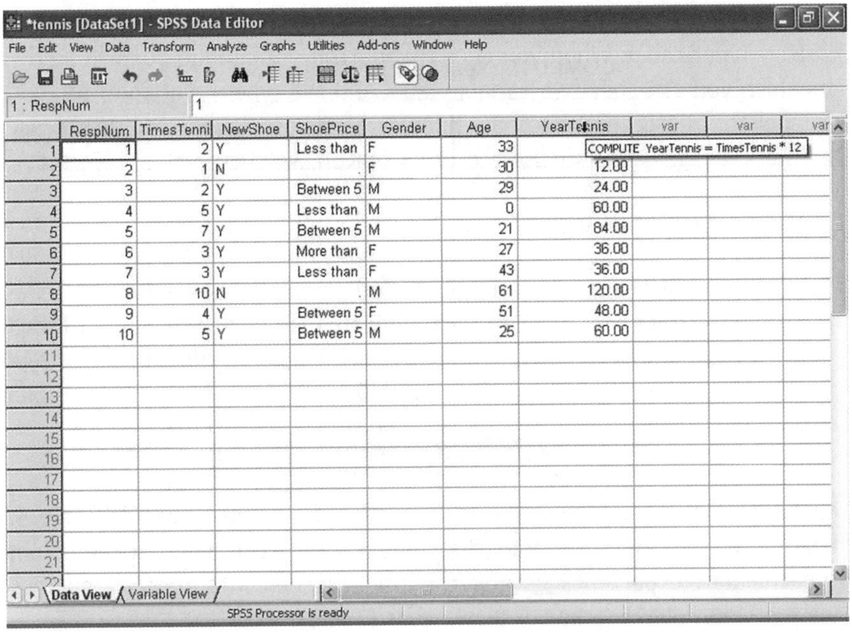

	RespNum	TimesTenni	NewShoe	ShoePrice	Gender	Age	YearTennis	var	var	var
1	1	2	Y	Less than	F	33				
2	2	1	N	.	F	30	12.00			
3	3	2	Y	Between 5	M	29	24.00			
4	4	5	Y	Less than	M	0	60.00			
5	5	7	Y	Between 5	M	21	84.00			
6	6	3	Y	More than	F	27	36.00			
7	7	3	Y	Less than	F	43	36.00			
8	8	10	N	.	M	61	120.00			
9	9	4	Y	Between 5	F	51	48.00			
10	10	5	Y	Between 5	M	25	60.00			

Figure 5.23 The Data View after computing the new variable YearTennis.

We have computed YearTennis because we wanted to know what percentage of the respondents play 25 times or less on an annual basis. The easiest way to find out is to make a frequency table for YearTennis. As explained in the preceding session, this can be done from the menu, by first selecting

Analyze

then

Descriptive Statistics

and finally

Frequencies

Now, a dialogue box appears in which a frequency table can be specified. In the list of variables, double-click the new variable

YearTennis

to place YearTennis in the list of variables to be analysed (or single-click the variable and then the button with the arrow right). Next, click OK to execute the

Table 5.1   The frequency table of the new variable YearTennis

COMPUTE   YearTennis = TimesTennis * 12

		Frequency	Percent	Valid Percent	Cumulative Percent
Valid	12.00	1	10.0	10.0	10.0
	24.00	2	20.0	20.0	30.0
	36.00	2	20.0	20.0	50.0
	48.00	1	10.0	10.0	60.0
	60.00	2	20.0	20.0	80.0
	84.00	1	10.0	10.0	90.0
	120.00	1	10.0	10.0	100.0
	Total	10	100.0	100.0	

command. The Viewer now shows the frequency table shown in Table 5.1. The heading of the table describes the computation performed. In the column with the cumulative percentages you can find the percentage of all persons interviewed who play 25 times or less a year (30%).

5.8   Exiting SPSS

Here we reach the end of the second session, in which we have extended and deepened our knowledge of SPSS, building on what we learned in the first session. We have not only discussed several basic commands but also illustrated the wide range of features of the program. The basic commands include opening a data file, creating a bar chart, entering value labels and computing a new variable. When changing the properties of a chart, we saw that SPSS has many possibilities of choosing settings other than the default ones. Furthermore, the use of the toolbar showed that many frequently used commands can be executed by a single keystroke. This can speed up work considerably. In the third and final session we take the introduction further, showing how to select cases, how to deal with the important concept of missing values and how to include SPSS tables and charts in a report written with a word processor.

To end this session, we exit SPSS. Refer to the menu

File

and click

Exit

Upon exiting SPSS you will be asked whether you want to save the contents of the Viewer and of the Data Editor. Saving is not strictly necessary for the next session. If you wish to save the contents, click Yes. Otherwise, click the button No twice to exit SPSS without saving anything.

6 Session 3: Performing statistical analyses

In this third and final session we introduce further basic tasks, as we did in the preceding sessions. We will make a selection of cases, create a scatterplot and specify a code for missing values. Of course your research is not finished after completing the analyses: we will therefore show how to improve the format of the SPSS output, and how the output can be saved, printed and copied to a word processor to be included in your research report. Again, we use the data file that you created in the first session.

   Like the other two sessions, this chapter has been designed such that you can follow all procedures while seated at your computer desk. All required keystrokes and mouse clicks are noted and explained where necessary.

6.1 Selecting cases

Not every analysis requires all cases; some of them may not be relevant. Suppose you are trying to answer questions like: How often do young people play on a monthly basis? What is the average age of the respondents who bought tennis shoes from the lowest price category? What percentage of male respondents bought new tennis shoes last year? To answer such questions we have to analyse only part of the cases; in other words, we must first select a group of cases. In this section we show how to answer the question of what percentage of male players bought new tennis shoes last year.

   After SPSS has been started (see Section 4.1) SPSS asks you: 'What would you like to do?' Again, we use the data file that you created in the first session. Accordingly, click

tennis.sav

at the bottom of the dialogue box; then click OK. If the dialogue box does not appear, open the data file by selecting File > Open in the Data Editor menu. If necessary, select the desired drive and folder, then open the file tennis. The Data View displays the data entered in the first session, with the value labels for ShoePrice specified in the second session. If necessary, maximise the window.

To answer the question of what percentage of the men bought new tennis shoes, we must first select all male respondents. To do so, choose from the menu

Data

Almost at the bottom of the Data menu you find the command

Select Cases

When you click this command, a dialogue box appears in which you can specify the type of selection you want. As the box shows, the present selection means that all cases are used in analyses. Other options include selecting cases based on a condition or at random. You can also select a range of cases ('Based on time or case range'). To select only male respondents, click the second option:

If condition is satisfied

Now, the button If is highlighted (see Figure 6.1). By clicking this button you can express the conditions that the cases have to meet. The dialogue box

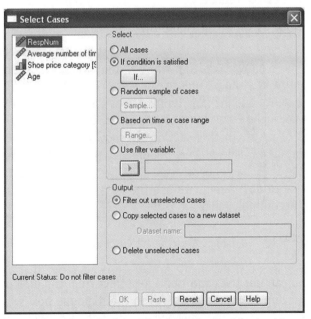

Figure 6.1   The dialogue box for specifying the desired selection; in this example the selection of cases that meet a condition.

'Select Cases If' contains the same three components that we encountered in the previous session when specifying a computation with the Compute command, namely the list of variables, the keypad and the list of functions.

In this example, we have to select those cases where the variable Gender has the value M. First include the variable, by double-clicking

Gender

in the list of variables. Next, click the 'equals' sign

=

in the keypad (or type in from your keyboard), and finally type the desired value of the variable

'M'

Make sure that the letter M is in single quotation marks. If these are omitted, SPSS will assume that the letter M is a name of a variable. Since there is no variable M, SPSS will return an error message indicating that you have entered a nonexistent variable. Furthermore, the use of upper-case M or lower-case m makes a difference. If you used capitals when entering the data, you must also use them here (or use lower case if that is what you did before). The complete condition is shown in Figure 6.2.

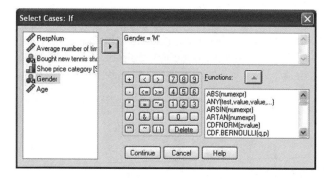

Figure 6.2   The dialogue box 'Select Cases If' with the condition to select men.

You can put the condition into effect from the dialogue box 'Select Cases If' by clicking Continue, and then in the dialogue box Select Cases, clicking OK.

SPSS indicates the selection in the Data View with a slash through the row number for the filtered cases (women) (see Figure 6.3). This means that these cases

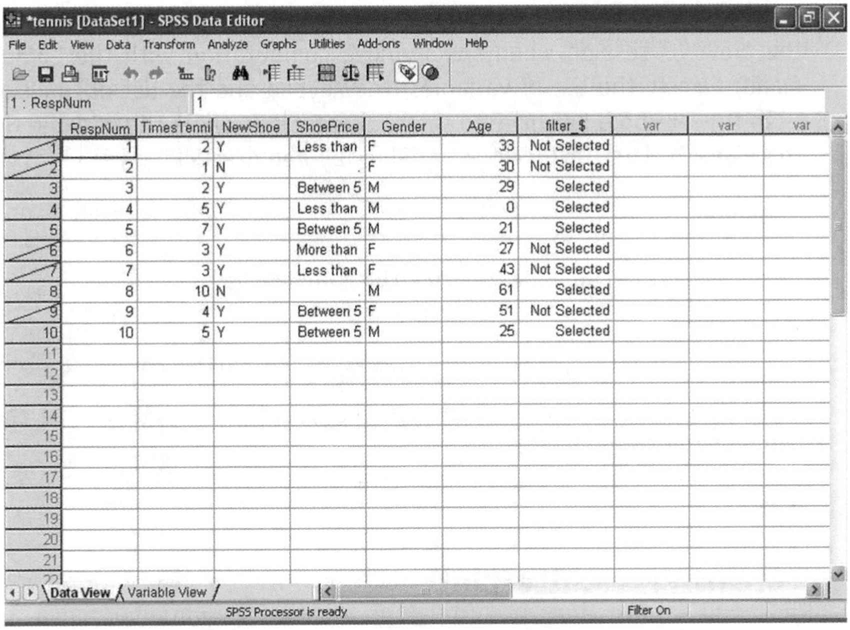

	RespNum	TimesTenni	NewShoe	ShoePrice	Gender	Age	filter_$	var	var	var
1	1	2	Y	Less than	F	33	Not Selected			
2	2	1	N	.	F	30	Not Selected			
3	3	2	Y	Between 5	M	29	Selected			
4	4	5	Y	Less than	M	0	Selected			
5	5	7	Y	Between 5	M	21	Selected			
6	6	3	Y	More than	F	27	Not Selected			
7	7	3	Y	Less than	F	43	Not Selected			
8	8	10	N	.	M	61	Selected			
9	9	4	Y	Between 5	F	51	Not Selected			
10	10	5	Y	Between 5	M	25	Selected			

Figure 6.3 The Data View shows which cases are selected.

are not used, but not deleted. Furthermore, SPSS shows the new filter status in the status bar at the bottom of the window: 'Filter On'. Finally, SPSS has automatically added a new variable Filter_$, that you can find in the last column, next to Age. For the cases selected (Men), the variable Filter_$ has the value 1 (with the value label 'Selected'), while for the women Filter_$ equals 0 (zero, labelled 'Not Selected').

We are interested in the percentage of the male players who bought new tennis shoes. So we need a frequency table of the variable NewShoe. From the menu we select

Analyze

next

Descriptive Statistics

and then

Frequencies

Now select from the list of variables the variable that indicates whether a respondent bought new shoes

NewShoe

by double-clicking it. Next, click OK to execute the command. The frequency table will now appear in the Viewer (see Table 6.1). It turns out that the data file contains five men: four of them bought new tennis shoes last year (80%).

Table 6.1   The frequency table of NewShoe containing only the male respondents

Bought new tennis shoes?

		Frequency	Percent	Valid Percent	Cumulative Percent
Valid	N	1	20.0	20.0	20.0
	Y	4	80.0	80.0	100.0
	Total	5	100.0	100.0	

6.2   Creating a scatterplot

All analyses so far performed in this and the preceding sessions were descriptive analyses that tell us something about the distribution of a single variable. In research projects we are often also interested in the relation between variables. Is there a relation between age and how often people play tennis? Do older people play more often than young people because they have more time available? Or do younger people play more often because they exercise more? Either situation seems plausible, and a scatterplot can provide an insight into the actual relation between the two variables. In a scatterplot one variable is shown on the vertical axis and the other one on the horizontal axis, and the cases are presented as a cluster of points. The form and the direction of the cluster indicate the relationship between the variables.

A scatterplot can be made as follows. From the menu, select

Graphs

and from the Graphs menu select

Chart Builder

The bottom half of the Chart Builder contains the tab Gallery. Select in this tab the bottom option

Scatter/Dot

As was the case with bar charts, SPSS can create multiple kinds of scatterplots. In this example we want a simple scatterplot with two variables. So, drag the first icon of a scatterplot to the chart preview. If the dialogue box Element Properties appears, close it because we do not need it.

In a scatterplot you need to specify a variable for both the horizontal and the vertical axes. The common way is to specify the dependent variable on the vertical axis: in this example how often one plays tennis. Drag this variable to the vertical axis (Y-axis).

The independent variable, the cause, is Age. Drag this variable to the horizontal axis (X-axis). The command is now complete (see Figure 6.4). Click OK to execute the command.

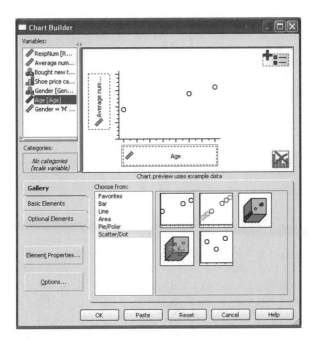

Figure 6.4   The use of Chart Builder to create a scatterplot with TimesTennis on the vertical axis and Age on the horizontal axis.

The resulting scatterplot now appears in the Viewer (see Figure 6.5). Each case is shown as a point in the chart. The form and the direction of the cluster of points provide information on the strength and the direction of the relationship between age and playing frequency. However, before drawing any conclusion from the chart, we note two things: first, the chart contains only five points; and second, one person is included who has an age of zero years. The cause of the first problem is that the selection of male respondents is still

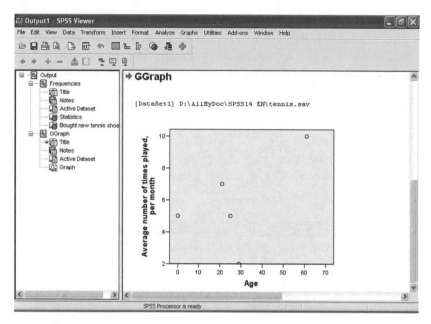

Figure 6.5   The scatterplot with TimesTennis and Age in the Viewer.

active; the second problem arises because we used a valid code for a missing value. In the next two short sections we will solve both problems.

6.3   Deactivating a selection

The scatterplot contains only five cases because the selection of men is still active. This is a common and dangerous mistake when using SPSS: for a certain analysis you have selected a subset of cases and for subsequent analyses you forget to tell SPSS to use all observations again. There are two ways to note this mistake, both of which, however, are easily overlooked. The first of these is the message in the status bar of the Data Editor, signalling that you have selected a subset of the cases Filter On'; see Figure 6.3). However, the output of an analysis is shown in the Viewer and the status bar of the Viewer does not contain this message. Secondly, for every analysis SPSS reports the number of cases used in the table 'Notes'. The problem here is that, by default, this table is closed. If you double-click the icon of a closed book next to 'Notes' (under GGraph) in the outline pane of the Viewer, Table 6.2 is displayed. As you can see, SPSS has used only five cases ('N of Rows in Working Data File'). Precisely because both ways of noticing this problem are easily overlooked, the mistake of accidentally leaving the selection on is so common. Moreover, many statistics, for example a mean or a standard deviation, do not signal whether the correct number of cases was used.

Table 6.2   The output object Notes belonging to the scatterplot. SPSS has used only five cases

Notes

Output Created		02-MAY-2006 10:40:44
Comments		
Input	Data	D:\AllMyDoc\SPSS14 EN\tennis.sav
	Active Dataset	DataSet1
	Filter	Gender = 'M' (FILTER)
	Weight	<none>
	Split File	<none>
	N of Rows in Working Data File	5
Syntax		GGRAPH /GRAPHDATASET NAME="graphdataset" VARIABLES=Age TimesTennis MISSING= LISTWISE REPORTMISSING=NO /GRAPHSPEC SOURCE=INLINE.
Resources	Elapsed Time	0:00:02.44

So we now have to 'switch off' the selection. This can be done with the same command Select Cases that we used to specify the selection. Accordingly, from the Data Editor menu select

Data

and then, from the Data menu, the command

Select Cases

The dialogue box Select Cases shows the currently active condition (If Gender = 'M'). You regain access to all cases by clicking the first option

All cases

Note that the condition Gender = 'M' remains available next to the button If. The condition is no longer active, however, as indicated by the grey colour. If on some later occasion you need to perform another analysis for male respondents only, you do not have to specify the entire selection criterion again. All you have to do then is to click the option 'If condition is satisfied'.

You actually regain access to all cases by clicking OK. If you now switch to the Data Editor by clicking 'Tennis – SPSS Data Editor' in the task bar at the bottom of the screen, you will note that the slashes in the row numbers of the spreadsheet have disappeared. Also, the message 'Filter On' in the status bar at the bottom of the window has been removed.

6.4   Specifying missing values

It is not uncommon that a variable does not have valid values for all cases. This situation is referred to as missing values and missing cases. There can be various reasons for this. A respondent may have refused or been unable to answer a question, or was never even asked a certain question. The question concerning the price of tennis shoes would not, of course, be asked to players who did not buy any. In such cases the variable ShoePrice is skipped when entering the data. SPSS then automatically assigns a missing value to the variable ShoePrice, indicated by a comma or a dot in the Data View. Such missing values are called I missing value; *system missing values*, that is, missing values recognised by the SPSS system itself.

Sometimes questionnaires are returned with categories of answers that one cannot use. Well-known examples include 'Undecided', 'Don't know' and 'Not applicable'. In most analyses one prefers to leave out such cases. A comparable situation occurs when a special code is entered where no answer was received, like the code 0 for Age. In that case you have to ensure that SPSS treats the value 0 as a missing value. If you were to compute the average age straight away, SPSS would use all cases with the value 0, because 0 is a valid value for a numeric variable. You therefore have to instruct SPSS that 0 is, in this case, the coding for missing values. This code for missing values that is specified by the SPSS user is referred to as a *user missing value*.

The code for missing values is a property of a variable and is specified in the Variable View. Click the tab

Variable View

at the bottom of the spreadsheet to switch over to this window.

The code for missing values must be specified in the column 'Missing'. So, click the cell in the column 'Missing' and the row Age (the 6th row). As we saw before, an icon with a row of dots now appears in the cell. Click this icon. In the resulting dialogue box, SPSS offers three options for the specification of codes for missing values. At this stage, no codes have been specified ('No missing values'). You may enter one or more separate values ('Discrete missing values'), or a range of values ('Range plus one optional missing value').

In this exercise we specify only one code; therefore, click the option

Discrete missing values

In the first input field you then type the number zero

0

The specification is ready (see Figure 6.6); leave the dialogue box Missing Values by clicking OK.

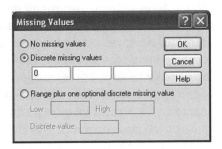

Figure 6.6   The dialogue box for assigning the code that has been used for missing values.

The scatterplot that we created at the beginning of this session was flawed on two accounts: the selection (Men) had been left active, and the variable Age had the (valid) value 0. In this and the preceding section we have corrected both mistakes, so we can now create a correct scatterplot. The quickest way to do this is by clicking 'Dialog Recall'

SPSS then shows a list of the most recently executed commands. At the top we see the Select Cases command that we used in the preceding section to regain access to all variables. In this example you have to click the second item in the list:

Chart Builder

Next, the dialogue box used for the previous scatterplot reappears. In this dialogue box the number of times respondents play is plotted on the vertical axis and age on the horizontal axis. Because we do not want to change this, click OK straight away. The Viewer now presents the scatterplot with nine points, the case with Age = 0 has been left out (see Figure 6.7).

When creating the first scatterplot, we had two seemingly opposite hypotheses: older people play more often because they have more time available, and young people play more often because they generally spend more time exercising. The scatterplot, in fact, seems to confirm both hypotheses. It is the middle group, of players between 30 and 50 years, who play least often.

6.5 Interpreting the scatterplot

Scatterplots give information on the strength and the direction of the relationship between two variables. The closer the points in the cluster resemble a straight (or curved) line, the stronger the relationship between the two variables. The scatterplot also gives information on the direction of the relation: do older players play more often, or is the opposite true? To test for such (linear) relationships, techniques like correlation analysis and regression analysis are used. Scatterplots are often used by way of preliminary analysis, to assess whether applying such techniques is worthwhile.

It frequently happens that most points fit the cluster reasonably well but a few of them do not. It is worthwhile to take a closer look at these outliers, to see whether an explanation can be found for the deviations from the general pattern. The first step in such an analysis is to determine which cases are the outliers. These cases can be examined in the Data View to look for possible explanations. Identifying the outliers and finding them in the Data View can be a lot of work, but SPSS offers a powerful tool for this, called point identification.

Note that in the scatterplot in Figure 6.7 there is one senior respondent who plays very often. We might be interested to know the exact age of this respondent (the plot suggests it is slightly over 60) and whether this player is a man or a woman. This is a type of question for which point identification is a useful feature.

In order to use point identification we first have to transfer the scatterplot to the Chart Editor (point identification is not possible in the Viewer), by double-clicking the chart.

In the toolbar of the Chart Editor you have to click the button Data Label Mode

Moving the mouse pointer across the chart you will note that the mouse pointer changes from an arrow into a square. Use this square to click the case that we want to analyse. This is the case on the top right in the scatterplot (see Figure 6.8).

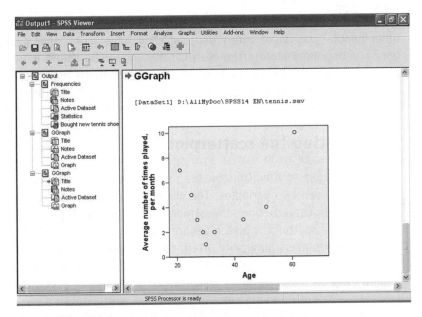

Figure 6.7   The correct scatterplot with the variables TimesTennis and Age (containing all cases and without the missing value of Age).

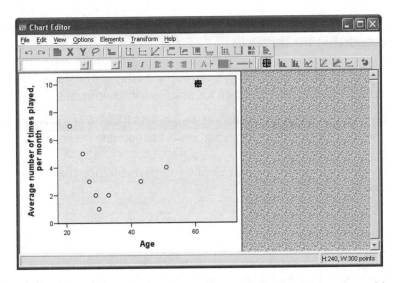

Figure 6.8   Selecting a case in the scatterplot that you want to analyse with point identification (data label mode).

When you click this case, the number of the case is shown respondent 8. It is turns out that the senior player who plays frequently is respondent 8. The number 8 can be removed from the plot by clicking this case once more. Thus, by clicking points of special interest, you can alternately view and suppress the corresponding case numbers.

Now make sure that the case number (8) is visible in the chart and switch off point identification by clicking the corresponding button once more. To find the exact age of this respondent and determine if it is a man or a woman, we have to search for this case in the Data Editor. The easiest way to do this is by clicking the button 'Go to Case'

In the Data Editor, you have to recall the Data View, so click the tab

Data View

at the bottom of the Variable View. SPSS has already highlighted the case we are interested in, which makes it easier to view its details (see Figure 6.9).

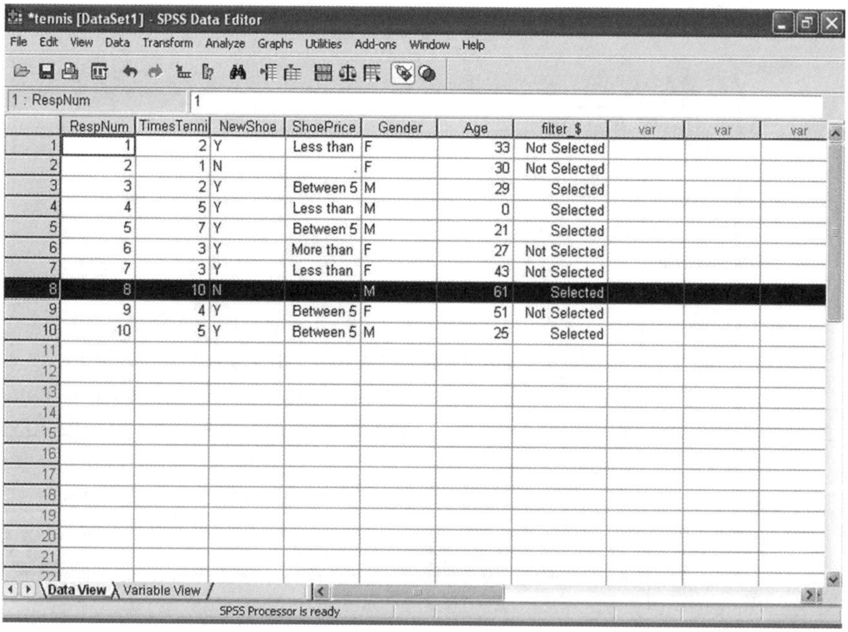

	RespNum	TimesTenni	NewShoe	ShoePrice	Gender	Age	filter_$	var	var	var
1	1	2	Y	Less than	F	33	Not Selected			
2	2	1	N	.	F	30	Not Selected			
3	3	2	Y	Between 5	M	29	Selected			
4	4	5	Y	Less than	M	0	Selected			
5	5	7	Y	Between 5	M	21	Selected			
6	6	3	Y	More than	F	27	Not Selected			
7	7	3	Y	Less than	F	43	Not Selected			
8	8	10	N	.	M	61	Selected			
9	9	4	Y	Between 5	F	51	Not Selected			
10	10	5	Y	Between 5	M	25	Selected			

Figure 6.9   The Data View with the highlighted case.

From the Data View you see that the respondent is a 61-year-old man. Although he plays very often, he did not buy new tennis shoes last year.

Point identification in combination with the button 'Go to Case' is a convenient way of analysing extreme cases and looking for explanations why a given case deviates from the overall pattern.

6.6   Making a crosstable

Scatterplots are useful to explore the relationship between two continuous variables. Is there a relation between age and how often people play tennis? This is a question for which we created a scatterplot in the previous sections. When we are dealing with variables grouped into categories, we use a crosstable to study the relation between two variables. Do women and men buy new shoes equally often? Do women and men buy shoes that are about equally expensive? A crosstable can provide insight into the answer to such questions.

In this section we make a crosstable to answer the question whether men and women buy new tennis shoes equally often. The Crosstabs command can be found as follows. First select:

Analyze

next

Descriptive Statistics

and then

Crosstabs

In the resulting dialogue box you can specify the variables in the crosstable. You have to specify a variable for the rows in the crosstable and a variable for the columns. One usually places the *independent variable* (the 'cause') in the *rows* and the *dependent_variable* (the 'effect') in the *columns*. The reason is that humans can more easily compare numbers when they are shown in the same column than when presented in the same row. In our case Gender is the independent variable (the cause) while the dependent variable (the effect) refers to whether or not a person bought new tennis shoes.

Accordingly, you have to first click the variable

Gender

then the arrow in front of 'Row(s)'. When you have done this, Gender will be placed in the list of variables under 'Row(s)'. Next, click the variable that indicates whether a person bought new shoes:

NewShoe

and then click the arrow in front of the list of variables for 'Column(s)'. Basically, this completes the command (see Figure 6.10). In a standard crosstable each cell

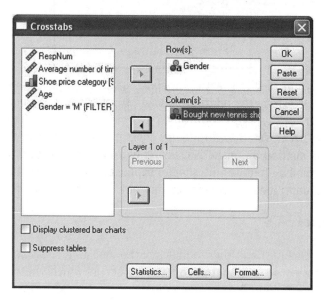

Figure 6.10   The dialogue box for making a crosstable.

will show the number of cases belonging to that cell, for instance the number of men who bought new tennis shoes, or the number of women who did not. In this example we want SPSS also to show percentages in the table.

Because we want to change the cell content, you have to use the button Cells. When you click this button, the dialogue box Cell Display appears. This dialogue box contains the statistics that SPSS can place in a cell. The default selection is a single statistic, namely the observed number of cases for a cell ('Observed' under Counts).

We now want each cell to show row percentages as well. Since the rows contain the independent variable Gender, we will get a table showing, for either gender, the percentages of respondents who did, or did not, buy new shoes. Accordingly, refer to 'Percentages' and click the option 'Row' (see Figure 6.11).

Do not leave the dialogue box yet. You can ask for help at many places within SPSS by clicking the right mouse button. In a dialogue box, for example, you can

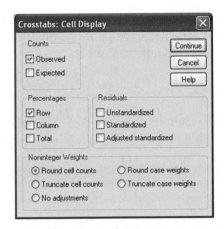

Figure 6.11   The dialogue box for specifying which information SPSS should display in the cells of the crosstable (recalled with the button Cells of the Crosstab command).

direct the mouse pointer to the subject you want information on and then right-click the mouse. To give an example: suppose you are wondering what 'Expected' (under Counts) means. In order to find out, move the pointer to

Expected

(without clicking) and then right-click the mouse. A small box will now pop up that contains an explanation on the object at which the mouse is currently pointed (see Figure 6.12). As you can see, 'Expected' refers to the number of

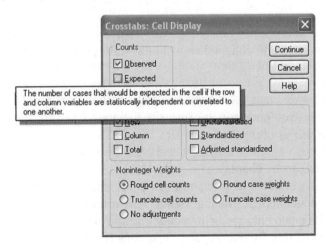

Figure 6.12   Requesting help about a subject in a dialogue box with the right mouse button.

cases in a cell if the row variable and the column variable were statistically independent (this is the expected or theoretical frequency used for the chi-square test).

Let us now return to the crosstable. By clicking Continue you exit the dialogue box Cell Display. Next, click OK in the dialogue box Crosstabs and the crosstable will appear in the Viewer (see Table 6.3). As the table shows, five men and five women were interviewed, and in both groups there was one person who indicated that he or she had not bought new shoes. Both 80% of the men and 80% of the women bought new tennis shoes.

Table 6.3   The crosstable with gender by buying new tennis shoes

Gender * Bought new tennis shoes? Crosstabulation

			Bought new tennis shoes?		Total
			N	Y	
Gender	F	Count	1	4	5
		% within Gender	20.0%	80.0%	100.0%
	M	Count	1	4	5
		% within Gender	20.0%	80.0%	100.0%
Total		Count	2	8	10
		% within Gender	20.0%	80.0%	100.0%

6.7   Changing a table in the output

In the previous chapter we showed how a bar chart can be changed (Section 5.6). Tables, too, can be changed in a similar way. In this section we discuss three examples in which we:

1.   change the structure of the table;
2.   change the format of the table;
3.   change the content of the cells.

The table to be changed is the crosstable from the previous section, showing the relation between gender and buying new shoes. To change a table, you first have to double-click it in the Viewer. This produces several effects (see Figure 6.13). The menu changes, with a new option Pivot, and a window Pivoting Trays and a Formatting Toolbar appear. These new features are all tools to change the various elements of a table. Depending on the way SPSS has been installed on your computer, your screen may look differently. As we will not be using the

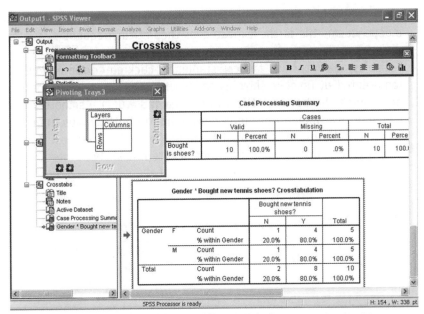

Case Processing Summary

	Cases					
	Valid		Missing		Total	
	N	Percent	N	Percent	N	Perce
Bought is shoes?	10	100.0%	0	.0%	10	100.(

Gender * Bought new tennis shoes? Crosstabulation

			Bought new tennis shoes?		
			N	Y	Total
Gender	F	Count	1	4	5
		% within Gender	20.0%	80.0%	100.0%
	M	Count	1	4	5
		% within Gender	20.0%	80.0%	100.0%
Total		Count	2	8	10
		% within Gender	20.0%	80.0%	100.0%

Figure 6.13   The Viewer with additional tools to change tables (recalled by double-clicking a table).

Formatting Toolbar initially, we close it for now, by clicking the cross on the far right in the title bar.

6.7.1   Changing the structure of the table

In SPSS parlance, tables are often referred to as 'Pivot Tables'. Pivoting a table means interchanging various elements in the table, for example rows and columns. This works as follows. Click the title bar of the window 'Pivoting Trays' (see Figure 6.14). If this window is not displayed, you can open it from the menu by selecting Pivot Pivoting Trays.

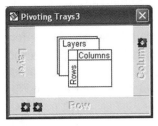

Figure 6.14   The Pivoting Trays window to change the structure of a table.

The window contains a symbolic representation of the contents of the crosstable and the order in which these are displayed. SPSS distinguishes three dimensions: layers, rows and columns. Because our crosstable contains two variables, we only have rows and columns. Each element in a row or column is represented by an icon showing four arrows that bend around the corner. The grey bar at the bottom of the window shows which elements are in the rows (there are two). The grey bar on the right contains the column elements (only one in this case).

To find out the meaning of an icon, aim the mouse pointer at it. Now point at the icon on the left in the bottom bar of the window (corresponding to rows)

A box will appear below the mouse pointer, showing the word Gender. Likewise, the second icon refers to Statistics. Thus the rows contain two elements: the variable Gender, and the requested statistics (the number of cases and the row percentage; see Table 6.3). Because Gender precedes Statistics, the values of the variable Gender (in other words, men and women) determine the basic breakdown of the rows. For each value of Gender, the statistics that we have computed define the next split of rows. As a result the table contains for either gender two rows, one for each statistic.

To explain the concept of the division and subdivisions of rows, we interchange the two elements. Click the icon on the left in the Row bar (corresponding to Gender)

Keep the left mouse button down and drag the icon across to a position in the Row bar to the right of the second icon (Statistics). As you can see, the basic division of the rows in the table is now defined by the statistics. The first row contains the number of cases ('Count'), while the second row shows the percentages. On the next level, these rows are each subdivided into two, according to the two different values of Gender (see Table 6.4). In this way you can interchange main divisions and subdivisions within rows or columns.

Besides changing the order of the elements in a row or column, it is also possible to move elements from rows to columns, and vice versa. We show this by dragging the statistics to the Column bar. Move the mouse pointer to the icon that is now on the left in the Row bar (Statistics)

Table 6.4   *The crosstable of gender by buying new tennis shoes in which the*
statistics determine the main division in rows, and the values of Gender the
subdivision

Gender * Bought new tennis shoes? Crosstabulation

| | | | Bought new tennis shoes? | | Total |
			N	Y	
Count	Gender	F	1	4	5
		M	1	4	5
	Total		2	8	10
% within Gender	Gender	F	20.0%	80.0%	100.0%
		M	20.0%	80.0%	100.0%
	Total		20.0%	80.0%	100.0%

and drag this icon to the Column bar, placing it below the icon already there
(NewShoe). In the new situation the Row bar contains only one icon, corresponding to Gender. Consequently, we get a new crosstable with just two rows,
corresponding to men and women, respectively (plus a third row for totals, of
course). In the Column bar we see two icons. The upper one represents the
variable NewShoe and the lower one Statistics. Consequently, the main division
of the table is determined by having, or not having, bought shoes, while each
column is broken down further (the subdivision) into a column for Count and
one for the percentages (see Table 6.5).

Table 6.5   *The crosstable of gender by buying new tennis shoes in which the NewShoe*
determines the main division in columns, and the statistics the subdivision

Gender * Bought new tennis shoes? Crosstabulation

| | | Bought new tennis shoes? | | | | Total | |
| | | N | | Y | | | |
		Count	% within Gender	Count	% within Gender	Count	% within Gender
Gender	F	1	20.0%	4	80.0%	5	100.0%
	M	1	20.0%	4	80.0%	5	100.0%
Total		2	20.0%	8	80.0%	10	100.0%

In order to end with a table in a more manageable form, we change the table structure once more. Drag the lower icon (Statistics) from the Column bar back to the Row bar, placing it to the right of the icon that refers to gender. Thus we now have the table as we had it at the start (see Table 6.3). The basic division in the rows is determined by gender, while the rows for men and for women are broken down into separate rows for the two statistics.

Thus, the table structure can be changed by dragging the elements in the rows and the columns in the window 'Pivoting Trays'. We now move on to changing the content of a table, so close the window 'Pivoting Trays'.

6.7.2   Changing the appearance of the table
By default, crosstables in SPSS contain vertical lines separating the columns, and some horizontal lines separating the rows. The appearance of the table, in terms of the lines it contains, is determined by the 'TableLooks' settings. To change these from the Viewer menu, select

Format

followed by

TableLooks

A dialogue box is then displayed that shows a large number of TableLooks (Figure 6.15). The list on the left contains the names of the various standard TableLooks, while the right-hand part of the dialogue box shows what a TableLook looks like. You will note the many possibilities for changing the appearance of a table by moving from one item in the list to another, either by clicking the mouse or by using the arrow keys.

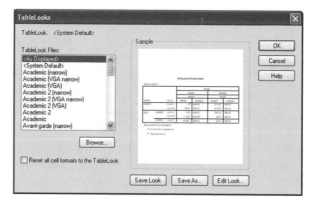

Figure 6.15   The dialogue box TableLooks for determining the appearance of the table.

How your table should look is partly a matter of taste, partly one of helping the reader to digest the information the table contains. When it comes to personal taste, you can choose a very vivid look (such as the TableLooks 'Hotdog' or 'Contrast') or an austere format like 'Report'. The second aspect to consider is the ease of information transfer to the reader. Research into the way people take in tabled information confirms the popular wisdom that one can have too much of a good thing. In particular, one should limit the use of vertical lines, colours and shadings. A plain table, like the TableLook 'Academic' for example, may not look all that smart, but in many cases your reader will prefer it. By way of illustration, Table 6.6 shows the crosstable in the TableLook 'Contrast', while Table 6.7 shows the same table in the style 'Academic'.

Table 6.6   The crosstable in the TableLook 'Contrast'

Gender * Bought new tennis shoes? Crosstabulation					
			Bought new tennis shoes?		Total
			N	Y	
Gender	F	Count	1	4	5
		% within Gender	20.0%	80.0%	100.0%
	M	Count	1	4	5
		% within Gender	20.0%	80.0%	100.0%
Total		Count	2	8	10
		% within Gender	20.0%	80.0%	100.0%

Table 6.7   The crosstable in the TableLook 'Academic'

Gender * Bought new tennis shoes? Crosstabulation					
			Bought new tennis shoes?		Total
			N	Y	
Gender	F	Count	1	4	5
		% within Gender	20.0%	80.0%	100.0%
	M	Count	1	4	5
		% within Gender	20.0%	80.0%	100.0%
Total		Count	2	8	10
		% within Gender	20.0%	80.0%	100.0%

6.7.3   Changing the cell content

There are three ways to change the content of a cell:

- by changing the text or numbers; or
- by changing the presentation style of text or numbers; or
- by changing the appearance of the cell.

We briefly discuss each of these.

The text in a cell can be changed by double-clicking the cell. We illustrate this by giving the table a new heading. Double-click the cell with the rather awkward heading

Gender * Bought new shoes? Crosstabulation

To indicate that the text has been selected, SPSS highlights it by showing it in a different colour (by single-clicking you select the cell itself rather than its content). You may now type a new heading, for instance:

Purchases of new shoes: breakdown by gender

When you now click another cell, the new heading is shown centred.

One of the good features of SPSS is that the software is intelligent enough to note that it has used the same term multiple times in a table. This enables you, for example, to replace all instances of 'Count' by the term 'Number of cases', by a single action. This is accomplished as follows. Double-click any one of the three cells containing the label

Count

SPSS shows the text in this cell in a different colour, while the other two cells containing 'Count' are highlighted. Now type:

Number of cases

and click any other cell in the table. SPSS then automatically changes the text in all three cells (see Table 6.8).

The text style in a cell can be changed with the Formatting Toolbar; this is the toolbar that we initially disabled. You can retrieve this toolbar by selecting from the menu

Table 6.8   The crosstable in which the label Count has been changed into 'Number of cases' and with a new heading (new text and increasedfont size)

Purchases of new shoes: breakdown by gender

			Bought new tennis shoes?		
			N	Y	Total
Gender	F	Number of cases	1	4	5
		% within Gender	20.0%	80.0%	100.0%
	M	Number of cases	1	4	5
		% within Gender	20.0%	80.0%	100.0%
Total		Number of cases	2	8	10
		% within Gender	20.0%	80.0%	100.0%

View

and

Toolbar

The Formatting Toolbar now reappears (Figure 6.16). The first button (with the bent arrow) is used to undo changes and the next one (four arrows bending around a corner) retrieves the 'Pivoting Trays' window discussed above.

As an example we change the font size of the heading. Click the cell with the heading. SPSS then shows the font ('Arial') and font size (9 points) of the heading in the empty fields in the toolbar (see Figure 6.16).

To change the font size, click the arrow next to the number of points (9). A pull-down menu appears with a list of numbers of points. Select a higher number, for example 14, and click it. The table heading is now shown enlarged (Table 6.8).

With the next four buttons you can specify the text properties bold (B), italics (I), underline (U) and colour (icon A and palette). The following four buttons are used to specify the justification within the cell.

Figure 6.16   The Formatting toolbar to change the text style in a cell (recalled with View Toolbar).

Now close the toolbar by clicking the cross on the far right in the title bar of the Formatting Toolbar.

The appearance of the cell can be changed by changing the properties of the cell. If, for instance, one of the cells contains a remarkable result, you can draw readers' attention to it by giving the cell a different colour or shading. Suppose we had assumed that only a small percentage of men had bought new tennis shoes. In that case the finding that 80% of the men have bought new shoes would be a striking result. We therefore change the appearance of this cell.

The dialogue box for changing the appearance of cells may be retrieved via the menu (Format > Cell Properties). But there is another way of doing this. Within SPSS you can often get access to a relevant menu with the right mouse button. So, aim the mouse pointer at the cell with 80% men and then right-click the mouse. Now, the context-dependent menu of Figure 6.17 pops up.

As you can see, this menu also contains commands for retrieving TableLooks, Pivoting Trays and the Formatting Toolbar (this is the option 'Toolbar' below Pivoting Trays). In this case, click

Cell Properties

Figure 6.17   The context-dependent menu, recalled by clicking the right mouse button in a cell.

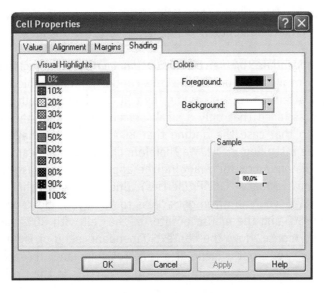

Figure 6.18 *The dialogue box for determining visual highlights and cell colours (recalled with Cell Properties and Shading)*

Now a dialogue box containing four tabs appears; from these, select

Shading

In this box you can specify the degree of shading and the cell colour (Figure 6.18). Shading cells ('Visual Highlights') is not recommended because it diminishes the readability of the cell contents. It is better to select a different background colour to attract the reader's attention. Below 'Sample' SPSS shows the current settings (that is, no visual highlight and black characters on a white background).

In order to change the background colour, click the arrow next to 'Background' to retrieve an overview of available colours. Click the box with the lightest shade of grey (to make a cell stand out, even pale grey is enough). Below 'Sample' you see an example of the selected combination of colours.

With the other tabs you can change various cell properties. Examples are the number of decimals (with the tab 'Value'), horizontal and vertical alignment within a cell (with 'Alignment') and the cell margins (with 'Margins'). To see how the table looks with one highlighted cell, click OK to exit the dialogue box (see Table 6.9).

Table 6.9 The table in which a cell is marked by changing its background colour into grey (with Format > Cell Properties)

Purchases of new shoes: breakdown by gender

			Bought new tennis shoes?		
			N	Y	Total
Gender	F	Number of cases	1	4	5
		% within Gender	20.0%	80.0%	100.0%
	M	Number of cases	1	4	5
		% within Gender	20.0%	80.0%	100.0%
Total		Number of cases	2	8	10
		% within Gender	20.0%	80.0%	100,0%

6.8 Saving and printing output

Having completed a number of analyses, you will probably wish to save some of the results to include them in a report or to print them. The Viewer enables you to save, delete, print and copy the SPSS output or part of it. In this section we discuss the first three of these options. How to include output in a report produced in a word processor will be the subject of the next section.

SPSS presents the output objects in the outline pane of the Viewer in hierarchical form. This means that some elements are connected at a higher level. In the present example there are three levels of hierarchy:

- *All output:* this is the highest level and refers to all objects in the Viewer. In the outline pane, click 'Output' and you will notice that all objects are selected.
- *All results of an analysis:* the second level refers to all output belonging to a single analysis. For example, click the icon 'Frequencies' and the five corresponding objects will be highlighted ('Title', 'Notes', 'Active Dataset', 'Statistics' and the frequency table 'Bought new tennis shoes?').
- *Separate objects:* under 'Crosstabs', click 'Case Processing Summary' and only this object will be selected.

The hierarchy implies that when you click an element at a certain level, all objects at lower levels will automatically be selected as well. Now suppose that we wish to save our output. In that case we first have to decide whether we want to keep all output or only parts of it. For example, there is no need to save the first scatterplot, because there were mistakes in it. In the output of the first 'GGraph' command, click

Graph

The first scatterplot with only five data points and a zero as a valid value for Age then appears in the content pane. The second scatterplot is the correct one, so the first one may be deleted. In fact, this applies to all output belonging to the first scatterplot. Therefore, click the first command

GGraph

in the outline pane. All four objects belonging to it have now been selected ('Title', 'Notes', 'Active Dataset' and 'Graph'). These objects can now be removed from the Viewer, by pressing Delete.

The Viewer now only contains the output from the commands Frequencies, GGraph and Crosstabs. You can save this output either by clicking the button with the floppy disk

or via the menu, with the command Save File As. In the dialogue box Save As you then have to key in a filename and a storage location (drive and folder).

Printing the output of an analysis is very simple. First you select the results that you want to print. If you want to print multiple objects, use the 'Shift' or 'Ctrl' key to select the objects. Using these keys in combination with the left button on the mouse is a convenient way of selecting a group of elements (this works in many other programs as well).

Suppose we want to select four elements from Crosstabs, namely Notes, Active Dataset, Case Processing Summary and the crosstable itself. What you have to do is the following. First click

Notes

(with the left mouse button). Now press the Shift key and keep it down. Then move the mouse pointer to the object that refers to the crosstable

Gender * Bought new tennis shoes? Crosstabulation

Then release the Shift key. As you will note, not only this object, but also the objects in between, i.e. Active Dataset and Case Processing Summary, have been selected. Thus the Shift key can be used to select a group of consecutive objects.

You only have to click the first and the last ones, and all objects in between are also selected.

In a similar manner, several separate objects can be selected with the Ctrl key. We will now select the frequency table, the scatterplot and the crosstable. In all three cases this is the last object of the analysis. Begin by clicking the last object of the Frequencies command

Bought new tennis shoes?

Now keep the Ctrl key down all the time and click the scatterplot

Graph

followed by the crosstable

Gender * Bought tennis new shoes? Crosstabulation

Finally, release the Ctrl key. You will note that only the three objects that you clicked have been selected.

The selected objects can be printed either with the button Print or the Print command in the File menu. You can also request a preview of the printed output by clicking the button Print Preview.

6.9   Transferring output to a report

The usual procedure in a research project is that SPSS is used to perform the statistical analyses while the research report is written with a word processor. The report needs to contain the relevant parts of the SPSS output, for example some interesting tables and charts. In this section we show how SPSS output can be transferred to a word processor. In this example we use Microsoft Word as the word processor. If you use another word processor, similar commands can be executed.

Start your word processor and then return to the Viewer. As a first exercise we will insert the last scatterplot we created into a text in the word processor. The procedure is as follows. Click this object in the outline pane of the Viewer:

Graph

You will probably find that the scatterplot is still shown shaded. The reason is that it is still present the Chart Editor. You may exit that window, but there is no real need.

In the menu, click

Edit

and from the Edit menu select the command

Copy objects

Now switch to your word processor by clicking its button in the task bar, in this case

Microsoft Word

In the word processor you can type the text of your report. In this case you could type a paragraph explaining the scatterplot (see the text in Figure 6.19).

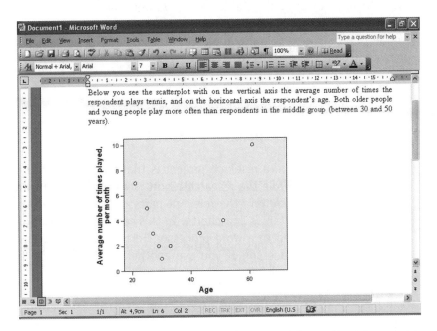

Figure 6.19   The Word window with the sample text and the scatterplot created in SPSS.

When ready, retrieve the scatterplot as you always do in Windows, by selecting from the menu

Edit

followed by

Paste

The chart is now displayed as an object in your text (see Figure 6.19).

In a similar way you can transfer tables from the Viewer to a word processor. To do this, return to the Viewer by clicking the button 'Output1 – SPSS Viewer' in the task bar.

We now want to select the frequency table of NewShoe that we created in the beginning of this session, the one including only men. In the output of Frequencies, click the object

Bought new tennis shoes?

We now have to copy this table in the Viewer. There are two methods, with Copy Objects or with Copy. To show the differences between the two methods, we first follow the same route as we did for the scatterplot. Refer to the Viewer menu and select

Edit

and then, in the Edit menu,

Copy objects

Switch to the word processor, by clicking the relevant button in the task bar

Microsoft Word

Now insert a few blank lines below the scatterplot and then retrieve the table by going to the menu and selecting

Edit

followed by

Paste

The frequency table appears in the word processor in SPSS format (see Figure 6.20).

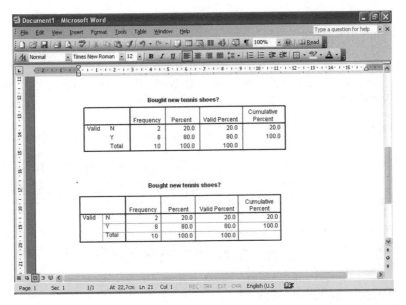

Figure 6.20   *The frequency table inserted in Word as a picture in the SPSS layout (above, with Copy Objects), and as a Word table (below, with Copy).*

You cannot edit this table in Word, because Word regards the table as a picture. If you want to be able to edit the table in Word, you have to follow the other route.

Begin by returning to the Viewer by moving to the task bar and clicking the button 'Output1 – SPSS Viewer'. Check whether the frequency table is still selected in the Viewer and select from the menu

Edit

and then

Copy

Return to the word processor by clicking the relevant button in the task bar

Microsoft Word

Insert a couple of blank lines below the frequency table and recall the table by choosing from the menu

Edit

and then

Paste

The frequency table is now pasted as a Word table (see Figure 6.20). When you click on the table you will notice that now you are able to change the table contents.

Whether to use Copy or Copy Objects in the Viewer thus depends on whether you want to be able to edit the table in the word processor. If you are pleased with the SPSS format, the best way is to use Copy Objects. If you want to change the table in the word processor, e.g. remove or add rows and columns, you have to copy the table in the Viewer by using Copy.

6.10   Some useful Data Editor options

As we are nearing the end of the final session we take one more look at the Data Editor. Its basic functions were explained in the first session, where we showed how this window is used to define variables and enter data. The Data Editor features a number of handy options that make performing these tasks much easier. In this section we discuss the following options:

- opening multiple data files;
- changing the column width with the mouse;
- deleting variables and cases; and
- undoing changes.

First of all we have to switch from the word processor to the Data Editor. Move to the task bar and click the button 'Tennis – SPSS Data Editor'.

6.10.1 Opening multiple data files
SPSS version 14 is the first SPSS version that enables users to open multiple data files simultaneously. You can also copy variables and data in the usual way from one data file to the other. By using the task bar or with the option Window in the SPSS menu you switch between the various files. The latest data file that you have viewed is called the Active Dataset. SPSS uses the data from this window to perform the next analyses. In the output of each analysis SPSS reports with Active Dataset has been used.

6.10.2 Changing the column width
At the start of this session we attached value labels to the various price categories of tennis shoes. As you will note in the Data View under ShoePrice, only

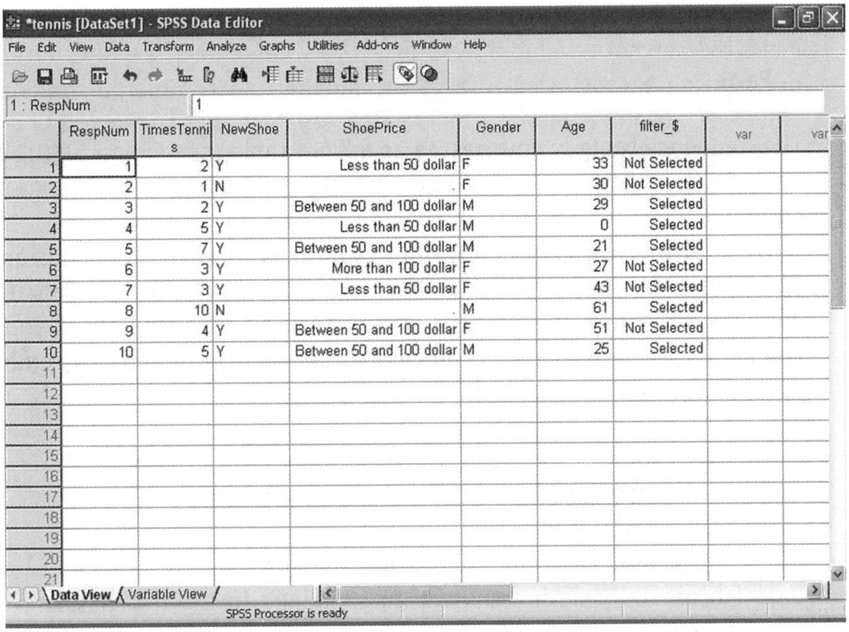

*tennis [DataSet1] - SPSS Data Editor

File Edit View Data Transform Analyze Graphs Utilities Add-ons Window Help

1 : RespNum   1

	RespNum	TimesTennis	NewShoe	ShoePrice	Gender	Age	filter_$	var	var
1	1	2	Y	Less than 50 dollar	F	33	Not Selected		
2	2	1	N		F	30	Not Selected		
3	3	2	Y	Between 50 and 100 dollar	M	29	Selected		
4	4	5	Y	Less than 50 dollar	M	0	Selected		
5	5	7	Y	Between 50 and 100 dollar	M	21	Selected		
6	6	3	Y	More than 100 dollar	F	27	Not Selected		
7	7	3	Y	Less than 50 dollar	F	43	Not Selected		
8	8	10	N		M	61	Selected		
9	9	4	Y	Between 50 and 100 dollar	F	51	Not Selected		
10	10	5	Y	Between 50 and 100 dollar	M	25	Selected		

Data View / Variable View /

SPSS Processor is ready

Figure 6.21   The Data View after changing the column width of ShoePrice.

the first part of the value labels is visible. To see the entire label, you have to increase the width of the column.

This can be done as follows. Aim the mouse pointer at the dividing line in the margin between the columns ShoePrice and Gender. The mouse pointer changes to a double-headed arrow.

When the mouse pointer has changed its shape, click the left button on the mouse and keep it down. Move the mouse pointer to the right until the value labels of ShoePrice are completely visible and then release the left button (see Figure 6.21).

6.10.3 Deleting variables and cases

Variables as well as cases can easily be removed from the Data Editor. The last column of the spreadsheet contains the variable Filter_$. This variable was automatically generated when we selected the male respondents at the beginning of this session. You can remove this variable as follows. Click the name of Filter_$ in the margin of the spreadsheet and then press Delete. SPSS then removes the variable Filter_$. (Alternatively, in the Variable View you can click the row number of a variable and then press Delete.)

Cases can be deleted in a similar way. Suppose you want to delete case 8. Click row number 8 and SPSS will highlight this row. Then press Delete and

SPSS removes the case. This example also demonstrates why it was useful to make the separate variable RespNum. SPSS renumbers the rows after deleting or inserting a case. This affects the numbers in the margin, but leaves the values of RespNum intact. This variable enables you to trace any given case to the corresponding respondent, even after removing cases from the Data Editor.

6.10.4   Undoing changes

It may happen that you make some undesired change in the Data Editor, for example by inadvertently deleting a variable or a case or by overwriting an existing value with a new number. In such situations you can use the function 'Undo'. From the menu, select

Edit

and then click the first command

Undo

As you can see, case 8 is reinserted in the Data View.

6.11   Epilogue: learning to work with SPSS

We have now come to the end of the third, and final, session. Although the exercises in the three sessions (Chapters 4, 5 and 6) have not turned you into an advanced SPSS user, they should definitely enable you to start using the software yourself. At the beginning of Chapter 4 we mentioned four goals to be achieved; each of these will be briefly discussed below.

1. **Getting to understand the structure of SPSS.** SPSS has different windows for different tasks. The two most important are the Data Editor and the Viewer. The Data Editor contains two tabs, the Data View and the Variable View. The Data View is used for entering, viewing and changing data, while the Variable View is used for defining variables. In the Viewer you can review the output of the analyses and also change, print and copy it to a word processor. Furthermore, SPSS includes the Chart Editor, for changing charts, and the Syntax Editor (which we did not discuss), for using the SPSS command language. All SPSS windows have the same basic structure, but each window contains specific content and (partly) a specific menu.

2. **Understanding the way SPSS is used in a research project.** The first step in each SPSS project is to create a data file. You have to define the variables (in the Variable View) and enter the data (in the Data View). The next step is the analysis of the data. Sometimes there is an intermediate stage in which the data are transformed (like computing new variables or selecting cases). When all analyses have been done, the charts and tables can be transferred to a word processor to be included in a research report.

3. **Exploring the possibilities offered by SPSS.** In these three sessions we discussed only a small fraction of the many SPSS features. Part II of this book contains a detailed description of many SPSS applications. The menu Analyze gives access to the various groups of statistical analyses, each of which in turn leads to submenus containing several techniques. Each group is discussed in detail in Part II (see Chapters 12 and 14–19). Furthermore, SPSS enables you to create a great variety of charts. We have already discussed bar charts and scatterplots; in Chapter 13 other kinds of charts, such as line graphs and pie charts, are discussed. Finally, SPSS has commands for transforming variables (like computing and categorising into groups; see Chapter 9), transforming cases (like selecting and sorting; see Chapter 10) and transforming data files (like merging and aggregating; see Chapter 11).

4. **Optimising SPSS procedures.** In these three sessions we have not only explained how to use SPSS, but also given practical advice. It is recommended always to provide your variables with variable labels and value labels. This takes some extra effort initially, but it really pays off. Furthermore, using the buttons instead of the menu can save you a lot of time. Another useful feature is that often you can change the properties of an element (a variable name or a cell in a table) by double-clicking that element. In addition, we have discussed how some common mistakes are made with SPSS, such as leaving a selection active during a subsequent analysis that should involve all cases (see Section 6.2).

The number of options of SPSS is so large that, after these three sessions, you may well feel that you can no longer see the forest for the trees. In various ways this book therefore helps you find your own way about SPSS:

* *The table of contents*. The contents of the three sessions have been rigorously organised into sections to treat only one topic per section. With the table of contents you can therefore easily find a specific subject.
* *A general discussion of the many options of SPSS*, with references to the sections where these are discussed in detail is presented in Chapter 2.

- *A table with statistical techniques and a table with types of charts* can be found on the inside back cover. These tables will help you select the appropriate technique and chart, given your research questions and the available data, and also contain references to the relevant sections that describe the corresponding SPSS commands and output.
- *The extensive index* at the back.

Best wishes for your successful research projects with SPSS!

Part II

Working with SPSS and Data Entry

Part I introduced you to SPSS. In three sessions we showed how to make and analyse a simple data file. In Part II we take a detailed look at the many options and features of both the SPSS Base Module and the module Data Entry. This part consists of three groups of chapters. In the first group, Chapters 7–11, we discuss a number of topics preceding statistical analyses. Next, Chapters 12–19 discuss the most important statistical techniques in the SPSS Base Module. Finally, in Chapter 20 we show how you can customise SPSS.

The first few chapters of Part II deal with subjects that precede the actual analyses. Chapter 7 discusses the features of Data Entry. This module facilitates data entry and helps to increase your data quality by performing automatic checks. It also has useful features for designing and conducting questionnaires.

The following chapters discuss data management features of the SPSS base module. Creating a data file and importing data from other software is the subject of Chapter 8. Next we discuss how to transform data. The transformation may involve the variables (Chapter 9), cases (Chapter 10) or the entire data file (Chapter 11).

Starting with Chapter 12 we discuss various statistical techniques: descriptive analyses (Chapter 12), charts (Chapter 13), crosstables and the chi-square test (Chapter 14), analysing multiple response data (Chapter 15), describing groups and testing for group differences with the t-test (Chapter 16), analysis of variance (Chapter 17), correlation and regression analysis (Chapter 18) and non-parametric tests (Chapter 19).

All chapters (and sections) are structured in the same way. First, a technique is introduced by discussing some examples. Then we focus on the hypotheses (the null hypothesis and the alternative hypothesis), the assumptions and related techniques. This discussion helps you to decide whether in your specific situation a certain technique is the most appropriate one. Next, a practical example shows how to specify the SPSS command. The SPSS output is then presented, discussed and interpreted. Finally, we discuss possible extensions of the analysis.

Part II closes with a chapter on how to customise SPSS to your personal preferences by changing the default settings.

7 Designing and conducting questionnaires with Data Entry

The SPSS module Data Entry makes it easy to design professional-looking questionnaires that can be used for mail, telephone and internet surveys. While you are designing the questionnaire, the software automatically defines variables and labels. That is why, even for mail surveys, it is better to use Data Entry rather than a word processor (such as MS Word). Moreover, you will save time by using Data Entry and the resulting questionnaires are more attractive. You can also use Data Entry to create online forms. In that case you have to save the questionnaire in HTML code (this can be done in the Builder with the command File > Export > To).

Data Entry is particularly well suited for designing questionnaires – not only because you can use it to make questionnaires that look good. With Data Entry you can include rules that specify the acceptable answers, the logical relationships between questions (the combination of 8 years old and high school education is improbable, for example), as well as rules for skipping questions or automatically assigning values.

The structure of this chapter is as follows. Section 7.1 discusses the basics of designing a questionnaire, emphasising the various types of question and how to add questions and change the properties of variables. Section 7.2 focuses on the questionnaire layout. We discuss aspects like colours, italics and special effects as well as the use of supporting elements, such as pictures, arrows and boxes. Checking and skip and fill rules to ensure error-free and efficient data entry are discussed in Section 7.3, while entering the data is the subject of Section 7.4.

Finally, a brief general introduction into Data Entry: after you have started the Data Entry Builder, the screen shown in Figure 7.1 will be displayed. At first sight this composition of three windows may not seem easy to understand, but it will become less daunting when you are familiar with the functions of the various components. The upper window, called the 'Form', shows the questionnaire. The lower window contains the 'Builder', which shows the variables you have defined. The features of both the Form and the Builder are extensively discussed in this chapter.

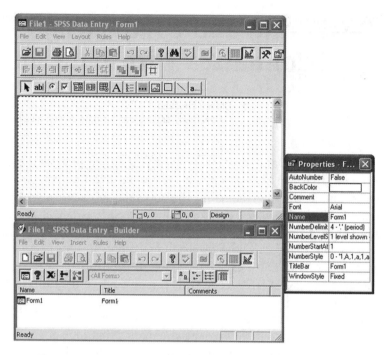

Figure 7.1   The start screen of SPSS Data Entry with the Form (the upper window) and the Builder (the bottom window).

7.1   Designing the questionnaire

Designing a questionnaire involves determining how the questions and answers should be organised in the form and, if needed, changing the properties of the variables that are automatically created by Data Entry. The present section discusses the following three subjects:

1. the various types of question distinguished in Data Entry;
2. placing questions in the question form;
3. changing the properties of a variable.

In this section we assume that initially all questions and variables are yet to be specified. When you open an existing data file in the Builder, Data Entry offers to create a questionnaire for it. You obtain the best-looking questionnaire by selecting the option 'Create Questions based on Default Types'. Data Entry then creates a questionnaire, based on the available variables and labels. If needed, you can then modify the form's appearance (see Section 7.2).

Table 7.1   An overview of the six types of question Data Entry distinguishes

Question types

Open question: *1. Text box question*

Closed question:
How many anwers can a single person give?

One answer per person:
Are the response categories related?

Independent response categories (nominal):

2. *Option button question*

3. *Drop-down list question*

4. *Single-selection list box question*

Response categories form a scale (ordinal):
5. *Scale button matrix*

Multiple answers per person:
6. Multiple response question: *Check box question*

7.1.1 Question types

Designing a questionnaire takes place in the design view of the 'Form', that you can open via the command View > Design. The first step in entering a question is to specify its type. Data Entry distinguishes between six types of question (see Table 7.1 for an overview). The question types are inserted with the buttons in the 'Toolbox'. These are the buttons in the third row of buttons in Figure 7.1; in case the Toolbox is not shown on your screen, you can open it via View > Toolbox. Table 7.1 also tells you which button in the Toolbox corresponds to which type of question (the name of the button pops up when you aim the mouse pointer at the button). The following subsection describes how to actually insert questions. We now first discuss the various types of questions.

The first subdivision in Table 7.1 is between open and closed questions. An *open question* is created with the button 'Text box question'. As the name suggests, the default variable type is a string variable. In case you require a numeric variable, you have to change the variable type to numeric after

A. Open question (string variable)

Who is your favourite tennis player?   _____

B. Open question (numerical variable)

What is your age?   _____

Figure 7.2   Two open questions. The first question is connected with a string variable (the answer is text), the second question with a numerical variable (the answer is a number).

adding the question (see Section 7.1.3). Figure 7.2 shows two examples of open questions.

The second main category in the scheme is that of *closed questions*. Data Entry distinguishes between two classes of closed questions, depending on the number of answers a respondent can give. If each respondent can give only one answer, you have a *closed single-answer question*. An example is the question 'What is your gender? Female/Male'.

Depending upon the relationship between the various answers, Data Entry distinguishes between two different forms of closed single-answer questions. The answers are either unique but arbitrary values (e.g. male versus female) or form a ranking scale (e.g. from 'Disagree entirely' to 'Agree entirely'). If the range of answers does not form a scale, the variable is nominal; otherwise the variable is ordinal (see Section 2.5.1).

For nominal questions, Data Entry distinguishes between three variants, depending on how the answers are to be displayed in the questionnaire. Figure 7.3 summarises these variants; the following is a brief description:

1. **Option button questions:** all possible answers are shown on the screen, preceded by an option button.
2. *Drop-down list questions:* the various answers are shown in a drop-down list. This has the advantage that the question uses only one line in the question form, but the disadvantage is that the answers only become visible after one has clicked the arrow on the far right in the response box. This type cannot be used in a mail survey.
3. **Single-selection list box questions:** all possible answers are shown in a box. With the arrow keys you can select an answer. If the answers do not all fit

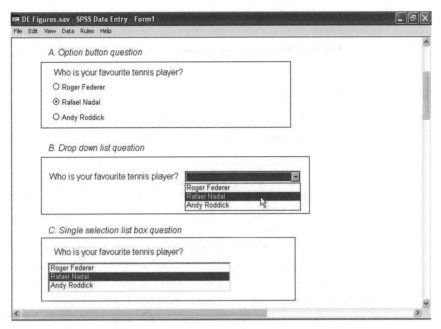

Figure 7.3   Three variants of a closed single-answer question in which the various response categories are independent (they are nominal and do not form an ordinal scale).

into the box, Data Entry automatically adds a scroll bar to the box. This type cannot be used in a mail survey.

The other variant of a closed single-answer question is an *ordinal question*, when the answers form a scale, either ascending or descending. Questions of this type can be added with the button 'Scale button matrix'. Such questions are often used when asking people about the extent of their agreement with a statement (see Figure 7.4 for an example).

When each respondent can give more than one answer to a closed question, this is a *multiple response question*, for which you have to use the button 'Check box question' in the Toolbox. In this case the respondent can select all applicable answers from a list of all possible answers. An example from the tennis survey concerns the type of play: singles or doubles. It is of course also possible that a respondent plays both (see Figure 7.5). Data Entry defines a separate variable for each response category (with the values 1 if checked off and 0 if not checked off), plus a set for the entire group (see Chapter 15 for the use of sets).

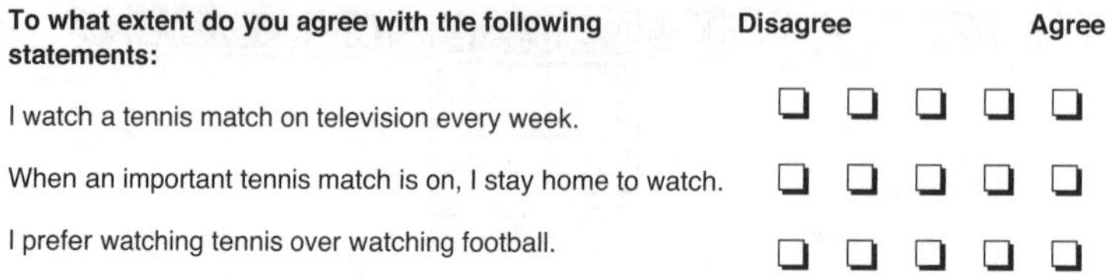

To what extent do you agree with the following statements:	Disagree				Agree
I watch a tennis match on television every week.	❏	❏	❏	❏	❏
When an important tennis match is on, I stay home to watch.	❏	❏	❏	❏	❏
I prefer watching tennis over watching football.	❏	❏	❏	❏	❏

Figure 7.4   An example of a question where the response categories form an ordinal scale ('scale button matrix').

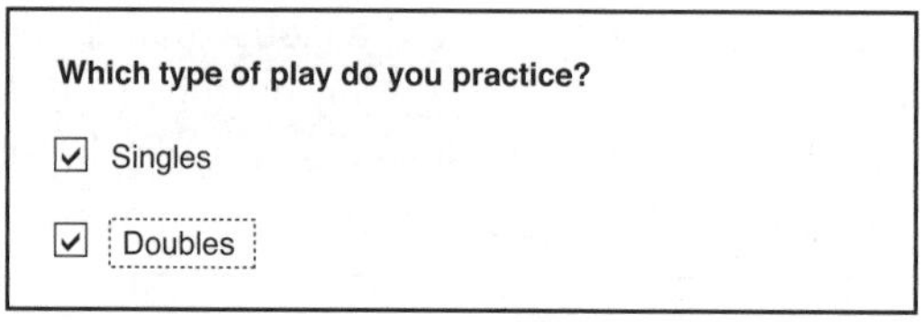

Which type of play do you practice?

☑ Singles

☑ Doubles

Figure 7.5   An example of a closed question with multiple responses.

7.1.2 Inserting questions

Inserting a question in the Form is done as follows:

1. Click the desired question type in the Toolbox and keep the left mouse button down.
2. Move the mouse pointer to define the position and the number of sub-questions or response categories.
3. Click the desired position of the question in the Form and create a rectangle in which the question is to be placed.

By way of example we show how to add a closed single-answer question. The question is 'What is your gender?' with the response categories Female and Male. Proceed as follows.

Step 1: While in the Toolbox (the third line of buttons in Figure 7.1), click the button called 'Option button question' (see also Table 7.1) and keep the left mouse button down.

Step 2: A design matrix is now displayed in which only the top-left cell contains an option button. You have to indicate the number and the arrangement of the answers. Each option button in the design matrix represents one response category. By filling a row, a column or a rectangle with option buttons you can determine the arrangement of the answers in the Form.

The most convenient arrangement is to have the various response categories one below the other. Only when considerations of space dictate otherwise should you consider placing them next to each other (in extensive mail surveys, for example). Rectangles are used only when the number of response categories is very large.

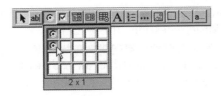

Figure 7.6   Creating a closed single-answer question with two response categories that will be shown as two option buttons below each other.

In our example you have to move the mouse pointer one row down to fill the top two cells in the first column with option buttons (see Figure 7.6). Thus you have prepared a question with two possible answers, displayed one below the other.

Step 3: Release the left mouse button and move to the position in the form where you want to place the question. The mouse pointer has changed its appearance to a plus sign with an option button. The question can now be placed in the Form as an object (a rectangle), as follows:

- Click the position in the Form where you want to have the upper left corner of the question and keep the left mouse button down.
- Now move the mouse pointer to the desired position of the lower right corner. Data Entry shows the rectangle into which the question will be placed. Release the button when you have made a rectangle of the desired dimensions.

The rectangle contains all elements of a closed single-answer question, namely (see Figure 7.7):

- *a question*, at this stage reading 'Question Text' (default);
- *a variable*, with the default name 'Var00001';
- *option buttons* for both response categories, indicating that for this question a respondent can select only one answer; and
- *the response categories*, each having the default description 'ResponseItem'.

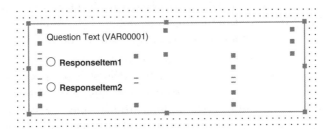

Figure 7.7   Part of the form after adding a closed single-answer question with two response categories.

The black squares form the corners of the various components of the question. The entire question (the rectangle) is an object, but the text of the question and the response categories also are objects that may be enlarged, reduced, moved or deleted just like any other object.

Step 4: Now we have to enter the actual question and the response categories. Obviously, you have to double-click these objects. Double-click 'Question Text' and the text will be highlighted and can be changed. Type the question:

What is your gender?

Then double-click 'ResponseItem1' and type

Female

Finally, double-click 'ResponseItem2' and type

Male

This completes the question (see Figure 7.8).

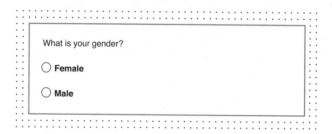

Figure 7.8   The gender question after specifying the question text and the response categories.

The design matrix for different question types

After clicking a question type button in the Toolbox, you have to specify, in the design matrix, the number of sub-questions or response categories. Use the mouse pointer to select the numbers of rows and columns in the design matrix (Figure 7.6). The meaning of the design matrix varies according to the type of question (see Table 7.2).

There are cases in which it is not possible to type the description of a response category by double-clicking a default term offered by Data Entry (as above, for the list of option buttons). In such cases you have to click the part where you want to have the answers, after which you call up the properties of the variable with the right mouse button (Variable Properties). The tab Values can then be used to specify response categories (see Section 7.1.3).

Table 7.2   The meaning of the cells (rows and columns) in the design matrix for each question type

Question type	Meaning of the design matrix
1. Text box question (open question)	Each cell is a separate question (variable)
2. Option button question	The entire matrix is one question (variable). Each cell is a response category
3. Drop-down list question	Each cell is a separate question (variable)
4. Single-selection list box question	Each cell is a separate question (variable)
5. Scale button matrix	Each row is a separate question (variable). Each column is a response category
6. Check box question (multiple response question)	The entire matrix is one question. Each cell is a response category. Each response category is a separate (0/1) variable

7.1.3 Modifying the properties of a variable

The Builder window shows a list of variables when you insert questions in the Form (if this list does not appear, then call it up with View Variables). The properties of a variable can be changed as follows:

- *in the Builder*: by double-clicking the variable; or
- *in the Form*: by clicking the question with the right mouse button and then selecting 'Variable Properties' from the menu that pops up.

In both cases the dialogue box of Figure 7.9 is displayed. In the little box next to Variable Name the default name of the variable (Var00001) has already been changed into Gender. Below that you find the variable label and the text of the question. Because the option 'Link with variable label' is active, Data Entry automatically uses the text of the question as the variable label. If you do not wish to use the question itself as the variable label, you can disable this option and change the variable label.

A useful feature is that during data entry you can automatically assign default values to variables (see Figure 7.9). This is the value of the variable when a new case is added. The usual default value is 'System missing', but with the drop-down list you can also select 'Same as previous case' and 'Increment previous by 1'.

The other tabs in the dialogue window Variable Properties are used to change various other properties. Some examples are the variable type (via the tab Format) and the codes used for missing values (via the tab Missing Values). With the tab Values you can change the following value properties (see Figure 7.10):

- *Specify value labels*. And, depending on whether or not you check off the option 'Link', change the description of the response categories (response items).

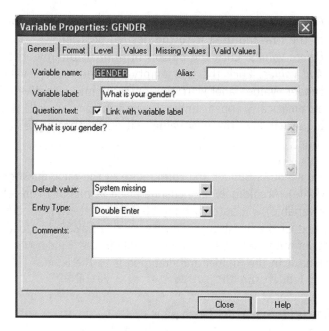

Figure 7.9   The dialogue box for defining variables.

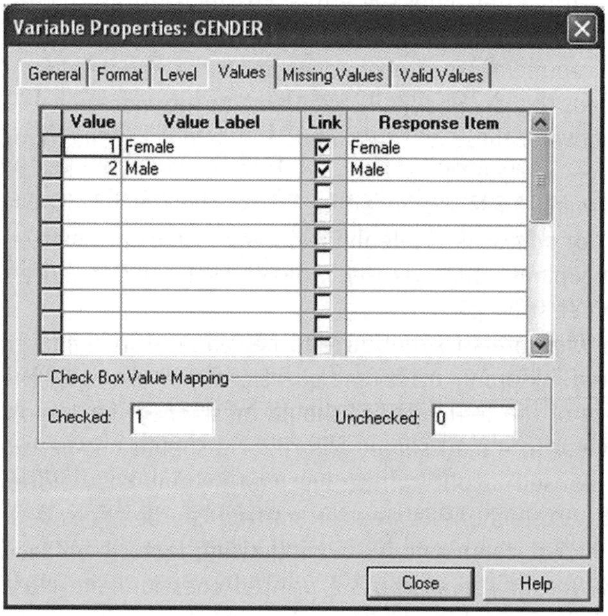

Figure 7.10   The tab Values for editing the response categories.

- *Change the order of the values*. Select a row by clicking the button in front of the row and drag it to the desired position.
- *Delete values*. Click the button in front of the row, then press Delete.
- *Add values*. Click the first empty row and enter a value and a description (under 'Value label'). If the option 'Link' is active, the value label will automatically appear under 'Response Item' as well. When you exit the dialogue window, the new value will automatically be added to the question form.

The windows Builder and Form relate to the same questionnaire (and the same SPSS file). Accordingly, any change made in one of them (e.g. a new description of a variable) will automatically be implemented in the other (e.g. by changing the text of the question). Likewise, you can also add a question to the Form by first defining the corresponding variable in the Builder (via Insert Variable), then clicking it in the Builder and dragging it to the Form.

7.2   Questionnaire layout

When you have entered all questions, the layout of the questionnaire has to be considered. The aim is to present the questions such that they can be answered efficiently with minimum risk of errors. Possible errors include skipping questions inadvertently, and ambiguity on how or where a question has to be answered. The layout requirements strongly depend on the way in which the questionnaire is to be used, that is, in a mail, telephone or internet survey. Some relevant differences between these methods affecting layout are the following:

- *Page format*: A4 or letter format versus the size of a screen.
- *Number of pages*: in a telephone survey it does not matter if each question is on a separate page (screen), but it makes a difference in case of a mail or internet survey.
- *The routing*: refers to the route to be followed in completing the questionnaire, e.g. skipping irrelevant questions. For example, the question about the price of the tennis shoes should be skipped if a respondent did not buy new shoes. In a mail survey the routing should not be too complex, and a well-organised layout can do much in helping to avoid errors. When dealing with a telephone survey the routing can be controlled by the software, meaning that complexity is not a limiting factor (see Section 7.3).
- *The position of the answers*: a printed questionnaire must clearly indicate where the answers have to be written; in a telephone questionnaire or a webpage the cursor will automatically advance to the position of the next answer.

Questionnaire layout is specified by deciding on the following elements:

1. **The position of the questions**: the amount of interspace, use of indentation and position of the response categories. You move objects (questions or answers) by clicking an object and dragging them to the desired position.
2. **The style of the elements composing the questionnaire.** Some properties that you can modify are colour, use of frames, font and font size, print style (italics or bold) and the background (see Section 7.2.1).
3. **The use of supporting elements:** title, comments or explanations, pictures, boxes, lines and arrows (see Section 7.2.2).

It is also possible for different elements (objects) to overlap. You can use the Layout > Layer command to indicate which object should be in the foreground and which one in the background.

Improving the layout of the questionnaire is a step-by-step process. You make some change (drag a question, use bold print, increase font size, etc.), inspect the result and then consider further improvements. In the case of a telephone survey you can use View > Form Entry to see what the screens would look like during a telephone interview (return to the design view with View > Design). In the case of a mail survey you can see the questionnaire by selecting File> Print Preview (or by clicking the corresponding button); when done, return to the design view by clicking the button Close.

Let us end with a warning: while improving the appearance of the questionnaire, always bear in mind that the true aim is to enhance both the speed and the accuracy of answering the questions. The exercise is not about creating a work of art!

7.2.1 The style of questionnaire elements

The style of each element in the questionnaire can be modified by changing its properties. All properties of an element are accessible via the Properties window. After you select View > Properties, this window will automatically appear when you click an element (object). The Properties window shows the current values of all properties. If you click one of these properties and then press the function key F1, help information on that property will be displayed. The value of a property can be changed by clicking the property. In some cases you can then type a value; in other cases a button with dots will lead you to a dialogue box containing all values that that property can take. For instance, if you click the property 'Font' and then the button with the dots, a dialogue box will be shown that contains the various fonts (such as Arial, Courier, and Times New Roman), the available styles (like italics and bold) and the font size (number of points). You can use the Properties window to change the properties of the question form, entire questions, question text and individual answers.

Question form
The properties of the question form include the colour of the background ('BackColor'), the name in the title bar ('TitleBar', the default title is Form1) and the window style ('WindowStyle').

Entire question
The most important properties of the entire question (i.e. the question text and all response categories) are:

- *background colour*: 'BackColor';
- *border* ('BorderStyle') with the values 'None', 'Box' and 'Underline';
- *colour of the border*;
- *width of the border*;
- *presentation style*: 'SpecialEffect', with the values 'Flat' (i.e. level), raised above the form ('Raised') and sunken below the form ('Sunken'). A requirement for the last two effects is that the question has a border.

Question text
The important properties of the question text are:

- *automatic adaptation to the size of the object*: 'AutoSizeToFit';
- *background colour*: 'BackColor';
- *border*: ('BorderStyle') with the values 'None', 'Box' and 'Underline';
- *font*: for specifying font, style (italics and bold), font size and special effects (strike out and underline);
- *text colour*: 'FontColor';
- *alignment of the text*: 'HorizontalAlignment' (centre, left, right);
- *presentation style*: 'SpecialEffect', with the values 'Flat' (i.e. level), raised above the form ('Raised') and sunken below the form ('Sunken'). A requirement for the last two effects is that the question text has a border.
- *position within the question*: the distance from the top-left corner of the entire question is determined by the properties 'Left' and 'Top'.

Response
The important properties of a response category in an option button list are (the answers for other types of question have similar properties):

- *automatic adaptation to the size of the object*: 'AutoSizeToFit';
- *background colour*: 'BackColor';
- *description*: 'Caption';
- *position of the text relative to the option button*: 'CaptionPosition' (values: left and right);
- *font*: for specifying font, style (italics and bold), font size and special effects (strike out and underline);
- *text colour*: 'FontColor';

- *alignment of the text*: 'HorizontalAlignment' (centre, left, right) and VerticalAlignment (centre, top, bottom);
- *presentation style*: 'SpecialEffect', with the values 'Flat' (i.e. level), raised above the form ('Raised') and sunken below the form ('Sunken'). A requirement for the last two effects is that the answer has a border;
- *position within the question*: the distance from the top-left corner of the entire question is determined by the properties 'Left' and 'Top'.

7.2.2 Use of supporting elements

The clarity of the questionnaire can be further enhanced by adding supporting elements. Headers and footers can be added via View > Headers/Footers (use your own text or page numbers, date and time). Use the buttons in the Toolbox (accessible via View > Toolbox) to insert the following elements: text, pictures, frames, lines and arrows (see also Figure 7.11). Below we briefly discuss each of these elements.

Figure 7.11   Buttons from the Toolbox for adding supporting elements, namely (1) text, (2) pictures, (3) rectangles and (4) lines and arrows.

Text

Besides questions and answers, a questionnaire may also contain a title, an introduction, headings, comments, explanations and descriptions. All such text elements can be inserted via the button Text (the capital A) in the Toolbox. The properties of a text object are very similar to those of the question text (see Section 7.2.1).

Pictures

With the button Picture in the Toolbox you can insert pictures. Click the property 'Picture' in the Properties window to paste the picture.

Rectangles

Frames can be added with the button Rectangle. The properties of a rectangle are very similar to those of a border for an entire question (see Section 7.2.1). You can also fill the rectangle with a colour.

Lines and arrows

Especially for mail surveys, lines and arrows can be of great help in finding the next question. Lines and arrows can be inserted with the button Line. The default option is an arrow at the end, but you can change this into a line by assigning the property 'ArrowStyle' the value 'None'. Arrows can be included at the start, end or both ends of a line. You can also change the colour, style and width of lines and arrows. A line or arrow is always straight; Data Entry has no bent or hooked lines. To create a hooked arrow you have to construct it in parts, for example by first inserting a vertical line (without arrowhead) and then adding a horizontal arrow.

7.3   Defining checking and routing rules

Data Entry has three options to ensure quality input and to achieve maximum efficiency of data entry. You can make arrangements for:

1. **Defining valid answers:** you specify all acceptable answers to a given question, typing other answers leads to an error message.
2. **Checking rules to define logical relationships between answers:** some combinations of answers may form a contradiction. For instance, you may require that the sum of three variables equals 100. If this condition is not met, an error message will be displayed.
3. **Skip & Fill rules:** Skip rules are used to skip questions, depending on the answers to previous questions. Fill rules can be used to change the answer to a question already asked, or a question that was skipped.

All these rules can be defined with the 'Rule Wizard' that you can activate via Rule Wizard (see Figure 7.12).

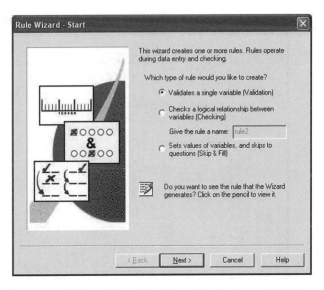

Figure 7.12   The start window of the Rule Wizard (activated with Rules and Rule Wizard).

Changing rules

The Rule Wizard can be used for specifying rules, not for changing them. The rules are saved in a special programming language (JScript, the Microsoft version of JavaScript). Unless you are able to write programs in this language, there is but one option for changing a rule: delete the rule and specify a new one. Rules can be deleted in the design view of the Form (View > Design), with the Rules > Rule Scripts command. Select the rule to be deleted from the drop-down list, and delete it with Scripts > Delete Script.

7.3.1 Valid answers

Rules that specify the valid answers to a given question are called validation rules. Validation rules can be defined by selecting the option 'Validation' in the start window of the Rule Wizard, then pressing the button Next.

The next dialogue box shows all variables for which no validation rule is available. Begin by checking off those variables that have the same set of valid answers. Next, you can indicate how you want the user to be alerted to the error: by a sound, a standard message or a custom-made message (click 'Custom alert message' and type the message).

Click Next once again to open a dialogue box in which you can specify which values are valid (see Figure 7.13).

Valid values can be specified in three different ways. The first is to select the categories of valid values, namely the answers specified in the questions, user missing values and system missing values.

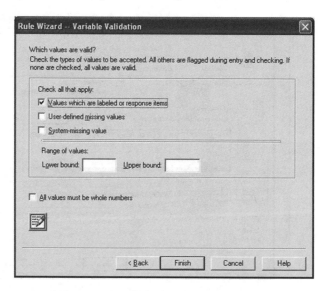

Figure 7.13   The dialogue box for specifying validation rules, to specify which responses are valid answers.

The second possibility applies to numeric variables and consists of stating the range in which the value should fall (i.e. between 'Lower bound' and 'Upper bound').

Finally, and again for numeric variables only, you may require the answer to be an integer (i.e. no decimals, 'All values must be whole numbers'). Click the button Finish to end specifying the validation rule.

A dialogue window similar to Figure 7.13 can also be opened via the dialogue window for defining variables (Variable Properties) and the tab Valid Values. For two reasons it is usually preferable to work with the Rule Wizard: it enables you to specify the same validation rule for several variables instead of just one, and to create your own error message.

7.3.2 Logical relationships between answers

Logical relationships between questions may exist in many ways. It is improbable that a business with fewer than ten employees has a turnover exceeding 100 million dollars. It is unlikely that someone younger than 18 years has an income of more than 100,000 dollars. A person living within 10 kilometres from work is unlikely to need more than one hour to get there. In all such cases you can specify a 'checking rule' to detect unlikely combinations of answers.

To specify a checking rule click 'Checking' in the start window of the Rule Wizard. Because a checking rule is not linked to a variable, you have to give the rule a name. After that, click Next to continue.

In the next dialogue box you can specify the checking rule (see Figure 7.14) in the form of an 'if–then' relation. First you have to state the condition under 'If':

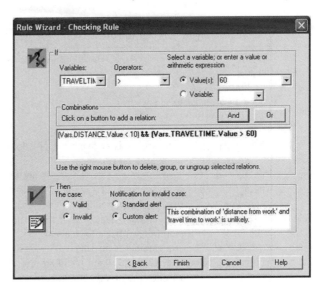

Figure 7.14   The dialogue box for specifying checking rules, to identify unlikely combinations of answers.

- select a variable from the drop-down list;
- select an operator from the drop-down list (e.g. equals, smaller than, larger than);
- state a value, or specify a variable from the drop-down list.

In the example of Figure 7.14 the rule specified is that if a person lives within 10 kilometres from work, it is unlikely that the travel time exceeds 60 minutes. Accordingly, the variable selected was Distance, the operator '<' (smaller than) and the value '10' was entered next to 'Value(s)'.

The condition in the checking rule may consist of multiple conditions. Thus, after the first condition (If Distance < 10), the button And was clicked to indicate that the respondent has to meet both conditions. The second condition was specified by selecting the variable TravelTime, the operator '>' (larger than) and typing the value '60'. The complete condition then reads: If Distance < 10 and TravelTime > 60.

A checking rule is an if–then rule, and therefore the condition (if) must be followed by an action (then). The action can be specified under 'Then'. You can indicate whether the case is 'Valid' or 'Invalid' if the condition(s) is (are) met. Finally, you can define the message to be given: in the form of a standard alert or a custom alert (click 'Custom alert' and type the message; see Figure 7.14). Then click the button Finish.

Besides 'smaller than' and 'larger than' there are a number of other operators to choose from (see Table 7.3).

Table 7.3 The operators you can use in conditions

==	Equal
!=	Unequal
<	Less than
<=	Less than or equal to
>	Greater than
>=	Greater than or equal to
Any	Whether the value of a variable is among a list of values (after Values you specify the list as numbers separated by commas)
NotAny	The opposite of Any, so the value of a variable is not among a list of values
Range	Whether the value of a variable is in a range of numbers that you specify (after Values you specify the range as minimum comma maximum)
IsLabeled	Whether the value of a variable equals one of the value labels (you select the value label from the drop-down list after Values)
IsMissing	Whether the value of a variable is missing
IsValid	Whether the value of a variable is valid (valid are those values that are specified as valid in the Valid Values tab of Variable Properties)
IsNotValid	The opposite of IsValid

7.3.3 Skip and fill rules

Respondents do not always have to answer every question. If someone did not buy new tennis shoes, we do not have to ask about the price of the shoes. Depending on the answer to a question, other questions are asked or skipped. *'Skip rules'* are used to define which question comes next, following a certain response.

Normally, the questions (variables) that are skipped are assigned the value system missing value. Sometimes this is not the right solution. Suppose that you are interested in the total amount of money a player spends on tennis. You then have to fill in 0 rather than a system missing value for the amount spent on tennis shoes if someone did not buy new shoes. For such situations you can define a *'fill rule'* to assign a value to the skipped question. Another useful application of fill rules concerns string variables. A common problem with string variables is that SPSS distinguishes between upper-case and lower-case characters. For Yes/No questions, the answer Y is not the same as the answer y, as far as SPSS is concerned. This means that you yourself have to ensure that only upper case is used, or only lower case. After answering a Yes/No question, you can use a fill rule to change lower-case y or n into upper-case Y or N (or vice versa). Thus you can ensure that the data file contains upper-case values only (or lower-case only).

To specify skip and fill rules, you have to click the third option, 'Skip & Fill', in the start window of the Rule Wizard. After pressing Next, a dialogue box shows all questions for which no skip and fill rules have been defined. In this dialogue box you have to check off all questions for which you want to specify the same skip and fill rule. When done, click Next.

In the next dialogue box you can specify the skip and fill rule (see Figure 7.15). Like checking rules, skip and fill rules are examples of if–then relations. Therefore, the upper half of the dialogue box is identical to that of the checking rule (see Section 7.3.2 for a description of this part of the dialogue box).

In the example of Figure 7.15 the condition has been defined as:

If NewShoe = 'Y'

Obviously, there are two possibilities: either the condition is satisfied, or it is not. If the condition is satisfied, the actions specified below 'Then' will be executed. If the condition is not met, the 'Else' actions will be carried out. For both Then and Else you can specify:

- which question is to be presented next, with the button 'Skip to a Question'; and
- which variables will automatically be assigned a value, with the button 'Fill Values'.

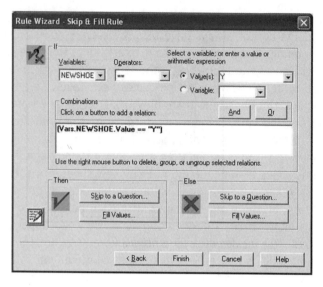

Figure 7.15   The dialogue box for specifying skip and fill rules, to skip questions and to assign values to variables.

The dialogue box for 'Skip to a Question' offers three options (see Figure 7.16):

- go to the next question in the questionnaire; or
- go to a specific question (you can select the desired question in the drop-down list); or
- go to the following case ('Go to next case'); in other words, terminate this interview.

The dialogue box for a fill rule consists of a table with all defined variables (see Figure 7.17). In the empty column you can specify the value that is to be

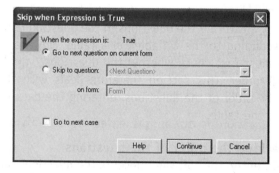

Figure 7.16   The dialogue box for a skip rule.

Figure 7.17   The dialogue box for a fill rule.

assigned to a variable. The example of Figure 7.17 shows the fill rule for Else (if the respondent did not buy new tennis shoes). Two variables get a new value in this case:

- NewShoe gets the value 'N', to ensure that if lower-case letters have been typed, these are automatically replaced by upper case (note that in this case the condition NewShoe = 'Y' ought to be extended by a second condition OR NewShoe = 'y');
- ShoePrice is assigned the value 0 (zero), instead of the default value system missing value.

7.4   Entering data

Data Entry enables you to enter the data (answers) in either of two possible ways, i.e. by answering the questions in the questionnaire or by typing the values corresponding to the variables in a table. However, before you enter any data, you must first check whether the questions (variables) are presented in the correct order. This section therefore deals with the following subjects: checking the order of the questions, entering the data in the form and typing the data in the table.

7.4.1 Checking the order of the questions
During data entry, the software presents the questions one by one in the order in which they were formulated (unless, of course, skip rules dictate otherwise).

It can happen that you have inserted questions or changed their order by dragging questions in the Form. In such situations the order in which Data Entry presents the questions may no longer be right. You can view the order in which Data Entry handles the questions by selecting from the menu Layout > Tab Order and Numbering.

In this overview you can see the sequence in which Data Entry will move through the questions (see Figure 7.18). If this sequence is not correct, questions can be moved around by clicking and dragging them to their correct positions (or with the arrow buttons).

Figure 7.18   The overview of the sequence in which Data Entry will move
through the questions (recalled with Layout and Tab Order).

7.4.2 Entering data in the form

Data can be entered in the question form by selecting from the menu View > Form Entry. Data Entry automatically shows the first question of the first case (respondent). Answers may be typed, clicked or checked off. When you press the Enter (or the Tab) key, the program moves on to the next question. After the last question has been answered, the first question for the next respondent is automatically displayed.

The toolbar contains a number of buttons that make it easier to navigate through the cases (the buttons with the black arrows). If this toolbar is not on your screen, you can call it up from the menu via View > Toolbars, and checking off Case Navigation. These buttons enable you to go to the next (previous) case, to the first (last) case, to the next case containing an error, to insert a new case and to overrule an error message.

7.4.3 Entering data in the table

It is also possible to enter the data in a table. In the menu, select View > Table Entry. For variables with a limited number of response categories, Data Entry shows a drop-down list of possible answers. If in the Data menu the option 'Display Response Items' has been selected, this list will show the value labels; if not, numbers are displayed.

The important advantage of the Data Entry table over the Data Editor of SPSS is that it allows you to check the data during data entry. However, it is also possible to check an existing file, via Rules > Check File.

8 Creating a data file

When creating a data file, one of two possible situations applies: either the data have yet to be entered, or the data are available in another software package. Both situations are discussed in this chapter.

In the first session (Chapter 4) we explained how to define variables in SPSS. Section 8.1 deals with this subject in greater detail. All properties of a variable are discussed, as well as several time-saving commands, for instance to assign the same properties (e.g. value labels) to several variables, or to use a selection of variables.

The next two sections deal with the features of the SPSS Data Editor, that is, the Data View and the Variable View. Here, too, the basic functions have already been discussed in the sessions. This chapter discusses other useful options. Section 8.2 deals with entering and moving variables and cases. Section 8.3 shows how to find specific information in the Data Editor, such as a specific case, variable or value of a variable.

In the final three sections we discuss how to access data files created by other software. Section 8.4 describes how to import non-SPSS data files such as Excel files. Complex selections from databases (e.g. Access) or spreadsheets can be made with the SPSS Database Wizard (see Section 8.5). The third possibility of importing external files concerns ASCII files and is discussed in Section 8.6.

8.1 Defining variables

The first step in creating a data file is to define the variables. For this one uses the Variable View of the Data Editor. The basics of defining the variables are discussed in Section 4.4. The present section gives a comprehensive overview of all properties that can be specified: name, type, number of positions and decimals, variable labels and value labels, missing values, alignment and measurement level. Except for the number of decimals, we briefly discuss each of these properties. In the remainder of this section we pay attention to three functions that are useful in defining and handling variables: assigning the same properties to multiple variables, obtaining an overview of variables and working with a selection of variables.

8.1.1 Variable names

Each new variable in SPSS is automatically assigned the default name 'Var' followed by five digits starting from 00001 (Var00001 and so on). You can use names according to your own preference, bearing in mind the following restrictions:

- the maximum length is 64 characters;
- the name must begin with a letter;
- the name may contain letters and digits, plus the following symbols: dot, underscore (_), dollar sign ($), hash (#) and at sign (@); spaces or commas are not allowed.

Within these limitations, you may choose any name, with the exception of reserved words (words pertaining to the SPSS command language), which may not be used as variable names.

8.1.2 Type of variable

The two main variable types are numeric variables and string variables. The default assumption is that a variable is numeric. In addition, SPSS distinguishes between many other variable types, i.e. variants of the numeric type like dates and currencies. SPSS accepts several standard date formats; in case you are using a different format, you can define it via Data > Define Dates.

8.1.3 Length and decimals

SPSS has two properties related to the length of variables. The first of these is Width, which refers to the maximum length of a variable. A string variable with a Width of 8 can contain text of up to eight characters. This restriction does not apply in the same way to numeric variables: for numeric variables of Width 1, SPSS accepts 10 as a valid value. For numeric variables one can also specify the number of decimals. The default number values of width and decimals can be changed with Edit > Options and the tab Data (see Section 20.1).

The second property is Columns and refers to the number of positions shown in the Data View, that is, the width of the column. As we have seen in Section 6.10, it is also possible to use the mouse for changing the column width in the Data View. This is usually more convenient than using the Variable View.

8.1.4 Labels

SPSS distinguishes between a description of the name of a variable, the *variable label* (in the Variable View, property Label), and descriptions of the values of a variable, the value labels (in the Variable View, property Values). Although the maximum label lengths are fairly generous, 256 and 60 characters, respectively, the actual number of characters shown in the output is often smaller, so try to keep the descriptions as short as possible (see Section 5.4 for defining value labels).

8.1.5 Coding of missing values

The property Missing in the Variable View refers to the values (codes) that SPSS has to interpret as *user missing values* (see also Section 6.4). There are three ways in which you can specify these values:

- *as separate values*, with a maximum of three ('Discrete missing values');
- *as a range of values*, by specifying lowest and highest value ('Range of missing values');
- *as a range of values, plus one separate value* ('Range plus one discrete missing value').

8.1.6 Alignment

The default alignments are right alignment for numeric variables and left alignment for string variables. With the property Align you specify the desired arrangement (left, centre and right).

8.1.7 Measurement level

The measurement level of a variable determines which statistical techniques can be performed (see Section 2.5). The property Measure distinguishes between three measurement levels, namely 'scale' (interval or ratio), ordinal and nominal.

8.1.8 Copying properties

When the survey contains a number of Yes/No questions, almost all properties of the corresponding variables are the same. Only the names and variable labels will be different. Instead of having to enter all the common properties for each variable, you can copy them. You can do this both in the Variable View and with the Copy Data Properties Wizard. The second option offers the most extensive features, but takes more keystrokes. We discuss both methods briefly (in both instances only the properties of a variable are copied, so the definition of a variable and not the values in the Data View).

Copying properties in the Variable View is possible in two ways, depending upon whether you want to copy all properties of a variable or just a single property. In the first case you click the row number of the variable whose properties you want to copy. Next you copy this row with Edit > Copy (or the keystroke Ctrl-C). Click the number of the first empty row in the Variable View and specify with Edit > Paste Variables how many new variables you want (and their names). If you want to copy a single property: first click the cell with the property you want to copy and copy it with Edit Copy (or the keystroke Ctrl-C). Click the cell to which this property has to be copied and paste the property with Edit > Paste (or the keystroke Ctrl-V). In both cases you can switch to another dataset between copying and pasting, enabling you to copy variable properties from one data file to the other.

Copying properties with the Copy Data Properties Wizard requires more steps but offers more features. You start the wizard with Data > Copy Data Properties. In step 1 you specify the data file containing the properties you want to copy; this is the current data file (the Active Dataset) or another data file (in that case the variable names have to identical). In step 2 you select both the variables with the properties you want to copy (the source variables) and the variables that should be assigned these properties (the target variables). In step 3 you specify which properties have to be copied. You can also select properties of the data file to be copied, such as Multiple Response Sets or Variable Sets. Finally, the execution of the copy data properties command takes place in step 5.

8.1.9 Overview of all variables defined
With the command Display Data File Information in the File menu you get an overview of all defined variables and their properties.

8.1.10 Working with multiple data files
SPSS enables you to open multiple data files simultaneously. However, in each analysis you can only use data from a single data file. With the Window command you can switch between data files (or windows).

You make a *copy of the current dataset* with the command Data > Copy Dataset. If needed you can save this dataset under a different name.

During a research project often multiple versions are made of the same data file. This happens when you save the data file under a different name, for example after you have computed new variables or deleted part of the cases. To ease keeping track of the differences between the various files, you can *add comments to a data file* with the command Utilities – Data File Comments. SPSS adds a date to each comment.

8.1.11 Protecting the data file
To protect you from unintentionally overwriting a data file you can mark the file as 'Read Only' (with File > Mark File Read Only). You can still change such a file, but you can only save these changes under a different name. The protection is cancelled with File > Mark File Read Write.

8.1.12 Working with a selection of variables
Normally, SPSS dialogue boxes show all variables in the data file. If you need only a limited group of variables for several analyses, you can save time by selecting this group of variables. To do this, you first have to define a *set of*

variables with Utilities > Define Sets. In the dialogue box you specify a set name and the relevant variables. The next step is to select this new set with the Utilities > use sets command and leave out the other available sets used (these include the default sets All Variables and New Variables). The variables that have not been selected remain available in the Data Editor, but no longer appear in dialogue boxes.

8.2   Operations in the Data Editor

In Section 4.5 we discussed the subject of data entry. This section deals with inserting and moving variables and cases in the Data Editor.

8.2.1 Inserting variables or cases

A *new variable* can be inserted in the Data View as follows:

1. Click the column before which you want to place the new variable.
2. Click the button Insert Variable. A new column will appear, with the name Var00001.

In a similar way (by first clicking a row) a new variable can be inserted into the Variable View.

   A *new case* is inserted into the Data View as follows:

1. Click the row that should be preceded by the new case.
2. Click the button Insert Cases. A new row will appear in which the value of all variables is system missing. SPSS renumbers the cases below the new case.

8.2.2 Moving variables or cases

A *variable* can be moved within the Data View in the following way:

1. insert a new variable at the destination position, as described above;
2. in the margin, click the name of the variable to be moved;
3. in the menu, select Edit > Cut. The variable disappears;
4. in the margin, click the name of the variable inserted in step 1;
5. in the menu, select Edit > Paste. The variable to be moved will now replace the inserted variable.

Cases can be moved in a similar way.

8.3 Searching the Data Editor

It is possible to search the Data View for a specific case, variable or value. These options are described in separate subsections.

8.3.1 Finding a case
You can find a case in the Data View in the following way:

1. click the button Goto Case

2. enter the number of the desired case;
3. click OK.

8.3.2 Finding a variable
When you are dealing with a large number of variables, it may be difficult to find a specific variable. You can find a variable as follows (analogous procedures apply in the Variable View and the Data View):

1. click the button Variables

2. from the list of variables, select the desired variable;
3. click the button Go To.

8.3.3 Finding a value
In several situations you may need to find a specific value of a variable. You could have encountered an extreme observation and you want to analyse why it deviates from the normal pattern, or you could have observed that the data file contains invalid values (e.g. the value 2 for a variable with coding 0 and 1) and you want to correct the error. You can find a specific value in the Data View as follows:

1. in the margin, click the name of a variable;
2. click the button Find

3. enter a value: you can specify a number or a value label;
4. click the button Find Next;
5. you can continue the search by repeatedly clicking Find Next;
6. exit the dialogue box by clicking the button Cancel.

8.4   Opening data files from other programs

In session 1 (Chapter 4) the point of departure in creating a data file was that no data had yet been entered. It often happens, however, that the data are already available in a different software format. In this section we discuss how to import data files created with an SPSS version other than SPSS for Windows, with a spreadsheet or database package and with ASCII files tab-delimited data.

Importing data from a database with the ODBC driver will be discussed in the next section, while Section 8.6 deals with reading ASCII files (txt files).

SPSS for Windows can open files created with various other software packages (and convert them to the SPSS for Windows format). Activate the dialogue box Open Data File by selecting from the menu

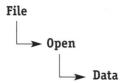

File
└──▶ **Open**
        └──▶ **Data**

In this dialogue box you can find (see 'Files of Type') the following list of file types:

- *SPSS (*.sav)*: this is the file format of SPSS for Windows;
- *SPSS/PC+ (*.sys)*: files stored as system files by SPSS for MS-DOS;
- *Systat (*.syd, *.sys)*: data files from the statistical package Systat;
- *SPSS portable (*.por)*: files stored as portable files with other versions of SPSS (e.g. SPSS for the Macintosh or OS/2);
- *Excel (*.xls)*: files in the format of the spreadsheet program Excel;
- *Lotus (*.w*)*: files in the format of the spreadsheet program Lotus 1-2-3;
- *SYLK (*.slk)*: files stored in the SYLK ('symbolic link') format;
- *dBASE (*.dbf)*: files in the format of the database programs dBASE II, III and IV;
- *SAS*: for files created with the SAS statistical software;
- *Text file with data (*.txt)*: to import ASCII data files, the Text Import Wizard is activated after selecting this option and specifying the file name (see Section 8.6);
- *Tab-delimited (*.dat)*: for in which the data values are separated by tabs.

Saving in other formats.

It is also possible to save a data file from SPSS for Windows in some other software format. In the dialogue box 'Save Data (As)' you find the same file formats that can be opened by SPSS (see 'Save as Type').

8.4.1 Opening Excel files

SPSS has two ways of importing spreadsheets, such as Excel files. In this subsection we discuss the Open Data command that can be used to import a (part of a) worksheet. The next subsection deals with the Open Database command for making more complex selections of parts of worksheets. Here we assume that the relevant data form a block in the spreadsheet.

With File > Open > Data you first specify the type of the data file, in this case 'Excel (*.xls)', and the filename. Normally, SPSS imports an entire worksheet, using the column letters as variable names. However, in the dialogue box you find the following options (see Figure 8.1):

- *Read variable names from the first row of data*: select this option when the first row in the spreadsheet (or in the range) contains the names of the variables. Any spaces included in a name are omitted. In that case SPSS creates a variable label with the original name.
- *Worksheet*: select the worksheet that contains the data.
- *Range*: to import a part of a worksheet. The range is specified by means of the cell coordinates, for instance C1:F100.

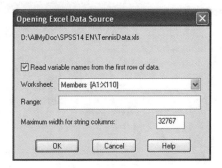

Figure 8.1   *The dialogue box in which you can specify which part of an Excel file SPSS has to open.*

SPSS will recognise the widths and formats of the spreadsheet columns. If a cell contains a formula, only the value in the cell will be copied. Empty cells and text in columns for numeric variables are converted into system missing values. An empty column in a worksheet will result in a variable with only system missing values.

SPSS assumes that the rows in the worksheet are the cases and the columns the variables. If your data is structured the other way round, you will have to use the Transpose command after opening the data file to rotate the data file (see Section 11.3.3).

8.5   Importing data with the Database Wizard

The File > Open Data command discussed in the previous section is used for opening a complete file. It can also be used to import part of an Excel worksheet, but when a more complex selection is required, you have to use the Database Wizard. This is used to import data into the SPSS Data Editor after specifying a query. Start the Database Wizard by selecting from the menu:

File
└──▶ **Open Database**
          └──▶ **New Query**

This will start up the Database Wizard (see Figure 8.2). You can select the desired data in a few steps:

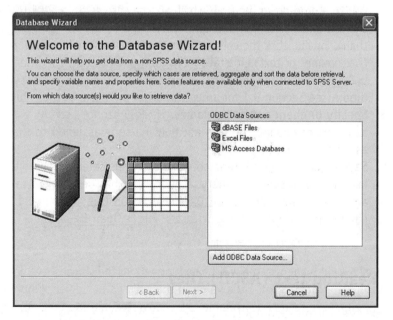

Figure 8.2   The Database Wizard for importing a selection of external data.

1. ***The data source.*** In the first step you have to state the format in which the data are stored, for example MS dBASE, Excel or Access. Click Next to specify the name of the data file. You may have to enter a password to obtain access to the database.
2. **The desired tables and fields.** SPSS will present a list of the tables and fields in the database (under 'Available Tables'). Select tables and fields by double-clicking, or drag them to the box 'Retrieve Fields In This Order'.
3. **Relationships between tables.** If you have selected more than one table, you have to specify the relationships between the tables. A relationship consists of a field available in both tables. If the field has the same name (and is of the same type) in both tables, SPSS will automatically indicate the relationship. You can also define a relationship yourself by dragging a field name from one of the tables to the other (releasing the button when in the field with which a relationship has to be established).

After you have completed these three steps, you can click the button Finish to import the data. Alternatively, you can press Next to continue with one of the following steps:

4. **Select cases.** Only those cases that meet the stated condition will be imported. You can specify a condition (in the dialogue box Limit Retrieved Cases) as follows. Click the first cell under Expression1. This will prompt an arrow that leads you to a drop-down list from which you have to select a field name. Next, click the cell under Relation, and specify the kind of relation (e.g. equals, or smaller than). Finally, click the cell under Expression2 to specify a field name or a value (i.e. number or text). To state more than one (partial) condition, click the cell under Connector to select AND or OR. You can also include functions in the condition (see Section 9.1 for a description of a number of these functions).
5. **Specify or change variable names.** If SPSS cannot literally use a field name as a variable name, the original field name is assigned to the new variable as a variable label.
6. **Save a query.** If you intend to make the same selection more than once, the last step is to save the query. A query that has been saved can be executed again with the File > Open Database > Run Query command. You can also change it at a later stage, with the File > Open Database > Edit command.

8.6   Reading text (ASCII) files

Text files, also called ASCII files, txt-files or DOS text, are the most elementary file type. If you cannot import a data file created with non-SPSS software in

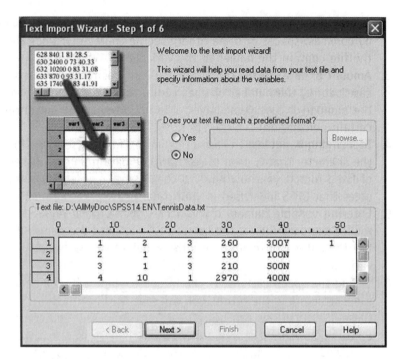

Figure 8.3   The Text Import Wizard for reading text data files.

any other way, it is usually still possible to import it in text format. Text files can be imported with the command:

File

└──▶ **Read Text Data**

Next, select the file you want to import, after which the Text Import Wizard is started (see Figure 8.3). With this function you can import text data in six steps as described below. In each step, the lower half of the window shows a preview of how SPSS will import the data.

1. **Retrieve a format.** If you have imported a similar text data file before and saved the specifications, enter the name of the file with these specifications. Otherwise, click Next to enter the specifications.
2. **Structure of the file.** SPSS needs to know two properties of the data file. Are the data in fixed format (each variable is located in the same columns for each case) or in delimited format (the variables are not necessarily

located in the same columns, but the data are separated from each other by commas, spaces or some other specific character)? Does the first row in the file contain the names of the variables?

3. **Amount of data.** In the third step you can specify the row in which the first case begins, the number of lines containing the data for a single case and the number of cases that have to be imported (all, a certain number, or a certain percentage).

4. **Identifying variables.** In case of delimited format (see step 2) you indicate the character that is used to separate the data from each other. In the case of fixed format you now have to check, and if necessary correct, the variables that SPSS identified in your data file.

5. **Entering variable names.** If the names of the variables are not in the first row of the data file (see step 2), SPSS has used the names V1, V2, etc. In the fifth step you can change these default names, and also specify the variable type (numeric or string variable, for example).

6. **Saving the specifications.** If you intend to import from a data file with the same structure in the future, you can save the specifications (the next time, these specifications can be retrieved in step 1). If you conclude from the Data Preview that the data are not being imported correctly, then return to a previous step with the button Back to change the specifications. If you are satisfied with the preview, click the button Finish to import the data.

9 Computation and classification of variables

In this chapter we deal with seven commands used to transform variables. These commands can be found in the Transform menu. The first is Compute and is used for computations involving variables. Variables can be added, multiplied or used in functions (see Section 9.1). The second command is Count, which is used to determine for each case how often a given value occurs within a group of variables (see Section 9.2).

Classification is necessary, for example, when making a crosstable that includes a variable with a very large number of different values (such as age or turnover). SPSS features two commands, called Visual Bander and Recode, for defining classifications. In most situations, Visual Bander is the more convenient to use, but Recode has some additional options, as explained in Section 9.3.

The Rank Cases command determines the ranking of the cases. This command creates a new variable whose values are the ranks (see Section 9.4). Next, the Automatic Recode command can be used to recode variables into a new, numeric variable with successive values. This command is often used to convert string variables into numeric variables (see Section 9.5). Finally, the Replace Missing Values command can be used to compute probable values for missing data in time series (see Section 9.6).

9.1 Compute a variable

With the Compute command you can perform a wide range of computations. Variables may be added and subtracted, but it is also possible to use a square root or logarithm function, to round numbers, to produce random numbers and to edit string variables. The command can be accessed from the menu by:

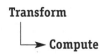

Transform
  └──▶ **Compute**

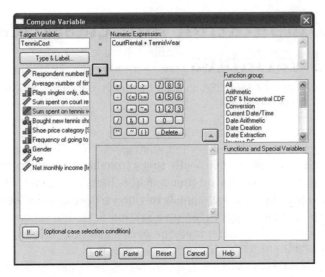

Figure 9.1 Computing the cost of playing tennis as the sum of the expenditures on court rental and tennis wear.

In the dialogue box Compute, two items must always be specified: the name of the variable to be computed and the type of computation. In the example of Figure 9.1 the cost of playing tennis is computed as the sum of the expenditures on court rental and tennis wear. The variable to be computed is the 'Target variable', named TennisCost in this example. The computation is specified under 'Numeric Expression' by clicking the respective items (the names of the variables and the plus sign in the keypad). After the command has been executed, the variable TennisCost is inserted in a new column, next to the last variable in the Data View. Always take a look at the values of the computed variable in order to verify that SPSS has performed the computation the way you wanted.

If one of the variables in the computation is missing, the target variable is assigned a system missing value for that case. (This does not apply when the computation involves a function; see below!)

In specifying a computation, the arithmetic operators can be clicked in the keypad. You find the arithmetic operators in the left-hand column of the keypad (see Figure 9.1). There are buttons for addition (+), subtraction (−), multiplication (*) and division (/), and it also contains the symbol for raising a number to a power, ** (e.g. 3**2 = 9).

Extensions.
The Compute command allows several extensions. For instance, you can use functions to perform more complex operations (see Section 9.1.1 for an overview of the many functions). By default the target variable is a numeric

variable; if you want a string variable, you have to define it yourself. The target variable is usually a new variable and therefore it is advisable to assign it a description. Both the variable type and the variable label are specified with the button Type&Label (see Section 9.1.2). SPSS will carry out the computation for all cases, but you can apply it only to a group of cases with the button If (see Section 9.1.3).

9.1.1 Functions in computations

Compute incorporates a very large number of functions that can be used in the expression. In the dialogue box these functions are divided into groups which are listed in alphabetical order under 'Function group'. We have classified the many groups in a logical manner into the following categories (the SPSS function group names are in parentheses):

1 arithmetic functions;
2 statistical functions;
3 search functions;
4 conversion and string functions;
5 missing values functions;
6 functions involving probability distributions (CDF & Noncentral CDF, Inverse DF, PDF & Noncentral PDF, Random Numbers and Significance);
7 date and time functions (Current Date/Time, Date Arithmetic, Date Creation, Date Extraction, Time Duration Creation and Time Duration Extraction);
8 other functions (Miscellaneous).

Each of these categories of functions is discussed below, but first we show how to specify a function with the menu.

Specifying a function.
First click under 'Function Group' the name of the relevant group and then select the function from the list under 'Functions and Special Variables'. When you click a function in the list, a description is displayed in the box to the left. Double-click a function to select it. SPSS then inserts it in the expression. Where a parameter has to be supplied, SPSS puts a question mark. In these places you have to insert a variable or a number. When entering the parameters, take good care to ensure that the cursor is always in the right position (that is, at the next question mark). This can easily lead to errors where SPSS writes variables one after the other (without commas in between). In that case SPSS is not able to recognise the variable and you have to insert the commas yourself.

1 Arithmetic functions
SPSS features the following arithmetic functions (see Table 9.1 for some examples):

Table 9.1   Examples of the use of arithmetic functions

Absolute value	Round	Truncate
ABS(4.5) = 4.5	RND(6.8) = 7	TRUNC(6.8) = 6
ABS(−6) = 6	RND(24.3) = 24	TRUNC(24.3) = 24
	RND(−6.8) = −7	TRUNC(−6.8) = −6
	RND(−24.3) = −24	TRUNC(−24.3) = −24
Modulo	*Square root*	
MOD(83,10) = 3	SQRT(9) = 3	
MOD(100,5) = 0	SQRT(8) = 2.8	
Raise e to power	*Natural logarithm*	*Logarithm (basis 10)*
EXP(1) = 2.72	LN(2.72) = 1	LG10(1000) = 3
EXP(2) = 7.4	LN(7.4) = 2	LG10(200) = 2.3
EXP(5) = 148.4	LN(148.4) = 5	LG10(1) = 0

- ABS: to determine the absolute value of a variable;
- RND: to round a number to the nearest integer;
- TRUNC: to truncate a decimal value, in other words, to round down;
- MOD: modulo, the remainder after division by a number x (insert a value for x);
- SQRT: to compute the square root;
- EXP: to raise the number e to the specified power (e is the basis for natural logarithms);
- LG10: to compute the logarithm to the base 10;
- LN: to compute the natural logarithm;
- trigonometric functions: ARTAN (inverse tangent), SIN (sine) and COS (cosine).

For all of the above, the name of the function is followed by a numeric expression in parentheses. This may be a variable, for example RND(A), or a computation, for example LG10(A/3) or SQRT(A*B).

A function may also contain other functions, as in the following far-fetched example:

TRUNC(SQRT(LN(X ** Y)))

which implies raising X to the power Y, taking the natural logarithm of this power, computing the square root of the logarithm and rounding down the result.

2. Statistical functions

The statistical functions compute for each case a statistic, e.g. average or variance, based on a number of variables. The statistic is computed *for each case*, in contrast to commands like Frequencies and Descriptives that produce statistics for a group of cases.

One of the most frequently used functions is:

MEAN: to compute the arithmetic average of a number of variables.

The name MEAN is followed by a number of variables, in parentheses and separated by commas, for example:

MEAN(A,B,C)

If A = 2, B = 3 and C = 4, the result of MEAN will be the number 3.

Instead of variables, one may also specify computations, for example:

MEAN(A*B,C*D)

Besides MEAN, other statistical functions are:

- CFVAR: to compute the coefficient of variation (the standard deviation divided by the mean) of a number of variables;
- MAX: to compute the maximum value of a number of variables;
- MIN: to compute the minimum value of a number of variables;
- SD: to compute the standard deviation of a number of variables;
- SUM: to compute the sum of a number of variables;
- VARIANCE: to compute the variance of a number of variables.

Missing values.

Some computations, like those with the functions MEAN and SUM, can also be defined with arithmetic operators, for example MEAN(A,B,C) is the same as (A+B+C)/3. An important difference, however, is the way these two expressions handle missing values. MEAN(A,B,C) will result in a system missing value only if all three variables are missing. (A+B+C)/3 results in a system missing value if at least one of the three variables is missing. Which command you should use depends on the reason why a value is missing, and on the purpose of the computation. Suppose that you have asked people how many kilometres they travelled by car during the months of January, February and March to compute, for each person, the average number of kilometres per month. Now suppose one of the respondents sold his or her car on 1 March. In that case the average should be computed only over the months of January and February, implying that

MEAN(January, February, March) is the appropriate command. Another example is that you want to compute the total number of kilometres travelled by each respondent in these months and that one respondent failed to record an entry for February. In that case the total distance should not be computed if one of the three variables is missing and therefore the appropriate command is: January + February + March.

With the statistical functions you can specify the minimum number of variables that need to have a valid value. This is done by adding a dot and a number immediately after the name of the function (i.e. preceding the opening parenthesis). The number indicates the minimum number of variables required to have a valid value.

Table 9.2 summarises the three different ways to compute the average of three variables. When plus signs are used, an average will only be computed in the first case, where all three variables have valid values. In the other two cases, NewVar gets the value system missing. The function MEAN computes an average in all three situations, in the third case even based on a single valid value. The last column shows an example of MEAN when a minimum number of valid values (in this case 2) is specified. The result is that no average is computed in the third case.

Table 9.2   Dealing with missing values in computations

NewVar = (A+B+C)/3				NewVar = MEAN(A,B,C)				NewVar = MEAN.2(A,B,C)			
A	B	C	NewVar	A	B	C	NewVar	A	B	C	NewVar
1	2	3	2	1	2	3	2	1	2	3	2
2	.	4	.	2	.	4	3	2	.	4	3
.	.	1	.	.	.	1	1	.	.	1	.

3. Search functions

SPSS includes search functions:

- ANY: to check whether a test variable equals one of the specified values. If this is the case, the function ANY returns the value 1; if not, ANY = 0 (see Table 9.3 for examples).
- INDEX: to find a given string (a letter or several characters) in a longer text.
- RANGE: to check whether a test variable is within a range of values (or variables). If this is the case, the function returns the value 1; if not, RANGE = 0 (see Table 9.3). It is possible to specify multiple ranges, see the third example

Table 9.3   Examples of the functions ANY and RANGE

NewVar = ANY(A,1,3)		NewVar = RANGE(A,1,3)		RANGE(Age,20,30,50,60)	
A	NewVar	A	NewVar	Age	NewVar
1	1	1	1	18	0
2	0	2	1	23	1
3	1	3	1	35	0
4	0	4	0	60	1

in Table 9.3, where two ranges, i.e. 20–30 and 50–60, have been specified for the variable Age.

- RINDEX: same as INDEX, but this function searches backward from the end of the string.

4. Conversion and String Functions

SPSS features many functions for transforming string variables; the most important ones are briefly discussed below (browse the list of functions for a more extensive overview).

- CONCAT: to concatenate (join) string variables;
- LENGTH: to compute the number of characters in a text (including any spaces);
- LOWER: to convert the upper case letters in a string to lower case;
- LPAD: to expand a string to a specified length by adding spaces (or other characters) on the left;
- LTRIM: to remove the blanks preceding a string (i.e. that are on the left of the string);
- NUMBER: to convert a string of digits into a numeric variable (Conversion);
- RPAD: same as LPAD, but adding characters on the right;
- RTRIM: same as LTRIM, but applies to the blanks following a string;
- STRING: to convert a numeric variable into a string variable consisting of digits (Conversion);
- SUBSTR: to return the substring found at a specified location within a longer string;
- UPCASE: converts the lower case letters in a string to upper case.

5. Missing values functions

SPSS has the following functions for missing values:

- NMISS: to count the number of variables in a series that have a missing value;
- NVALID: same as NMISS, but now counting the number of valid values;
- MISSING: returns 1 if the value for the specified variable is missing (user or system missing), otherwise 0;
- SYSMIS: returns 1 if the value for the specified variable is system missing value, otherwise 0;
- VALUE: to ignore user missing value definitions, the user missing values of the specified variable are treated as valid values.

6 Functions involving probability distributions
The following groups of functions use probability distributions (for each distribution you can specify the relevant parameters, such as mean, standard deviation or degrees of freedom):

- CDF: to compute the probability that a random number from a specified distribution is smaller than a variable. SPSS includes the many distributions, such as Bernoulli, binomial, Cauchy, chi-square, exponential, F, gamma, Laplace, log-normal, normal, Pareto, Poisson, t, uniform and Weibull.
- Inverse DF: to compute the value in a specified distribution that has a cumulative probability equal to a variable. See CDF for some of the available distributions.
- PDF: returns the probability density from a specified distribution. See CDF for the available distributions.
- Random Numbers: returns a random number from a specified distribution. See CDF for the available distributions.
- Significance: returns the cumulative probability that a value from a specified chi-square or F-distribution is greater than the specified variable.

Random numbers, that are used by some functions, can be applied for Monte Carlo experiments. SPSS uses pseudo-random numbers that are computed with a random number generator. This function uses a starting point. To repeat the same sequence of random numbers, one has to generate the series with the same starting point. This value is specified with the Random Number Generators command in the Transform menu. In the dialogue box you can specify a number under 'Set Starting Point' (see Figure 9.2).

7. Date and Time functions
SPSS has the following groups of function that are related to dates and time:

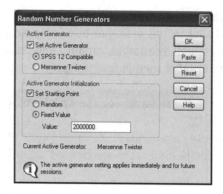

Figure 9.2   Specifying a new starting point for the random number generator.

- *Current Date/Time:* to store the current time and date in a variable.
- *Date Arithmetic:* to perform computations with dates (e.g. to compute the difference between two dates).
- *Date Creation:* to create a date variable based on variables that contain for example the day number, month number or year. Date variables in SPSS reflect the time that has elapsed since the beginning of the Gregorian calendar (15 October 1582).
- *Date Extraction:* returns for example a day, month or year from a date variable, so the opposite from the previous group of functions.
- *Time Duration Creation:* returns the time interval corresponding to a specified number of days, hours, minutes or seconds.
- Time Duration Extraction: returns the number of days, hours, minutes or seconds corresponding to a specified time interval (so the opposite from the previous group of functions).

8. Other functions (Miscellaneous)
Finally, SPSS has the following functions:

- Casenum: returns the current row number of a case in the Data View. This number changes when cases are inserted, deleted or sorted.
- LAG: returns the value of a variable in the previous case. If you have a file containing monthly sales, the increase in sales in a given month equals: Increase = Sales - LAG(Sales). In this example, the value of the first case becomes system missing. LAG can be used for both numeric and string variables and it is also possible to specify that a value of n cases earlier has to be used.
- Valuelabel: returns the value label of a variable.

9.1.2 Type and label of the target variable

The button Type&Label in the dialogue box Compute (see Figure 9.1) enables you to specify the type of the target variable and its label. SPSS distinguishes between two kinds of label (see Figure 9.3):

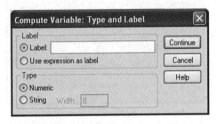

Figure 9.3   *Specifying the type and label of the target variable (the button
              Type&Label of the Compute command).*

- *A label* that you can type yourself.
- *The expression.* SPSS uses the content of the Expression block as a label for the target variable. This can be practical, for complex computations for example, or when you perform several similar computations with the same variable. The label of the target variable will then show the exact computation on which it is based.

In the lower half of the dialogue box you can specify the target variable type: numeric or text (string). For string variables you can specify the number of characters.

If you do not use the option Type&Label, the new target variable will have no label, and will be assigned the variable type of the previously computed target variable (the first one being numeric).

9.1.3 Conditional execution of the command

Normally, SPSS will carry out the Compute command, and the other commands discussed in this chapter, for all cases. With the button If you can apply the command to a certain group of cases only. You first have to indicate, in the dialogue box If Cases, that the command should only be executed for cases that satisfy a certain condition by clicking (see Figure 9.4):

Include if case satisfies condition

The next step is to specify the condition. Suppose that we want to select only players who bought new tennis shoes (NewShoe = Y). The various components of this condition can be specified by clicking them in the list of variables

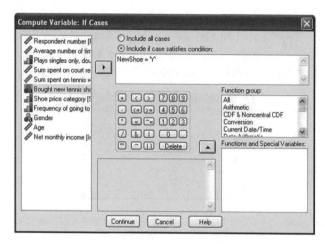

Figure 9.4   The dialogue box of If Cases to have the command executed for only those respondents that have bought tennis shoes (NewShoe = 'Y').

and the keypad, or by typing (see Figure 9.4). Because NewShoe is a string variable, the letter Y has to be placed in single quotation marks. Also remember that SPSS is case sensitive: it distinguishes between 'Y' and 'y'.

There are various ways of making the condition more complex. Besides 'equals', it may also contain 'greater than' (>) or 'smaller than' (<): these are called relational operators. For composite conditions the operators AND and OR are used (logical operators). It is also possible to specify that the cases should not satisfy a certain condition. All of these operators can be found in the keypad (see Table 9.4).

Table 9.4   The characters SPSS uses for relational and logical operators

Relational operators		Logical operators	
<	smaller than	&	AND: both conditions have to be met
>	greater than	|	OR: at least one of both conditions have to be met
<=	smaller than or equal	~	NOT: the condition has not to be met
>=	greater than or equal		
=	equal		
~=	unequal		

9.2   Count values in a group of variables

The Count command is used to determine the number of times a given value occurs in a group of variables. The command is rarely used, but can be very useful in some situations. Suppose that the tennis survey includes the following three statements concerning tennis on television:

- Statement 1. I watch a tennis match on television every week.
- Statement 2. When an important tennis match is on, I stay home to watch.
- Statement 3. I prefer watching tennis to watching football.

Each respondent is asked whether he or she agrees or disagrees with each of these statements. The Count command can be used to find out how many statements a person agrees with. Select:

Transform

└─► Count

In the dialogue box Count, shown in Figure 9.5, we first have to specify the target variable. This is a new variable, the variable Opinion in the example. We assign this variable the label Agree with Number of Statements. Next, we have to specify the variables whose values have to be counted. In this example, the variables are Statement1, Statement2 and Statement3.

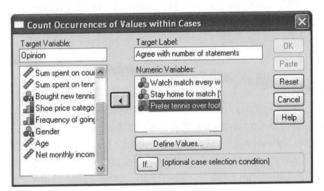

Figure 9.5 *Determining the number of statements with which a respondent agrees (with the Count command).*

The last step is to specify the value that has to be counted. Click the button Define Values; the corresponding dialogue box shown in Figure 9.6. Because the coding 0 = Disagree and 1 = Agree is used for the statements, we specify the value 1. By clicking the button Add, the number 1 is included in the list of values to be counted. This completes the command. After it has been executed, the new variable Opinion is added to the data file.

The variable Opinion has the value 0 if a respondent disagrees with all three statements. If someone agrees with one statement, Opinion will have the value 1.

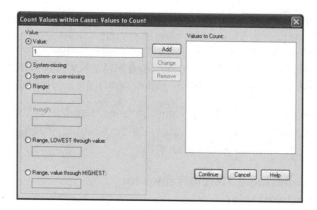

Figure 9.6   Specifying the values that have to be counted (the button Define Values of the Count command).

The value 2 results if a respondent agrees with two statements and, finally, Opinion has the value 3 when a respondent agrees with all three.

A variable computed with Count will never get a system missing value. Count interprets missing values as the absence of the desired value. If, in the example, a person does not answer any of the three statements (so that the values for Statement1, Statement2 and Statement3 are all missing), Opinion will have the value 0, the same as for a person who disagrees with all three statements.

Extensions

The Count command includes several further options. You can execute the command for a specific group of cases only (with the button If). Conditional execution of commands is discussed in Section 9.1.3.

In the example we have counted the number of occurrences of the value 1. You can also specify multiple values or a group of values (see Section 9.2.1). If the command is given via the menu, the same values will be counted for all selected variables. It is also possible to specify different values for different variables. In that case you have to switch to the syntax window (see Section 9.2.2).

9.2.1 Specifying values

There are six different ways to specify which value(s) SPSS has to count (see the left-hand part of Figure 9.6):

1. *Individual values,* by typing a value in the field next to 'Value'.
2. *System missing values.* In the list of values to be counted, SPSS adds the keyword SYSMIS.
3. *System or user missing values.* In the list of values to be counted, SPSS adds the keyword MISSING.

With the remaining options you can specify a range of values:

4. *From x through y*. Specify x and y under 'Range'.
5. *From the lowest value through x*. Specify x under 'Range'.
6. *From x through the highest value*. Specify x under 'Range'.

After having specified a value or range, use the button Add to include this specification in the list of values to be counted. You can also select an item in this list to change or remove it.

9.2.2 Counting different values for different variables

If you define the command via the menu, the specified values will be used for all variables. Sometimes this is not what you want. Suppose that for a number of people you know their monthly incomes as well as the values of their cars. You could then define a new variable Wealth with the values:

- 2 = If a person has both a high income and an expensive car.
- 1 = If a person has either a high income or an expensive car.
- 0 = If a person has a low income and a cheap car.

The range for 'high income' will be different from that for 'expensive car'. Specifying different ranges is not possible when using the menu, but can be achieved via the syntax window. The easiest way is to prepare the command in the dialogue box Count. This means that you specify the name and the label of the target variable and click the variables Income and Car in the list of variables. Then click the button Define Values to specify the range for the latter variable and transfer the command from the dialogue box to the syntax window by clicking Paste.

In the syntax window you can then type another range for the variable Income. The full command could be:

COUNT Wealth = Income(5 thru Highest) Car (8 thru Highest).

After you have clicked the execute button (the button with the arrow right, 'Run Current') the command is executed and the variable Wealth is computed.

9.3   Classify the values of a variable

To study the distribution of a variable with a very large number of different values, like age, or the amount spent on tennis wear, it makes sense first to classify such a variable. Instead of a frequency table with dozens of rows, you get a frequency table with a limited number of rows. Recoding may also be necessary for variables that have already been divided into classes, to limit the number of categories.

SPSS includes multiple commands for making classifications. The easiest one to use is Visual Bander, which we discuss first (Section 9.3.1). Visual Bander has only been included in SPSS since version 12; before that classifications were specified with Recode (see Section 9.3.2). Although less convenient to use than Visual Bander, Recode offers some options not available in Visual Bander, i.e. to specify classifications for string variables and to recode only some of the values. Suppose that most people went to see between 1 and 5 tennis tournaments, while a very small group visited 6, 7, 8, 10, 12 and 15 tournaments. With Recode you can then combine the values 6 and higher into a single category.

9.3.1 Visual Bander for interactive classification

The Visual Bander command can be accessed from the menu by

Transform

    └─▶ **Visual Bander**

Figure 9.7 shows the first dialogue box of this command. In this dialogue box you have to select the variable(s) that you wish to classify, the 'Variables to

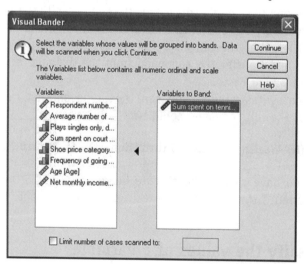

Figure 9.7   The dialogue box to specify which variables have to be classified (with the Visual Bander command).

Band'. In this example we select the variable TennisWear, which corresponds to the amount of money spent on tennis wear. Note that the dialogue box contains only numeric (ordinal and scale) variables; string variables can be classified with the command Recode.

In the next dialogue box the actual classification has to be specified (see Figure 9.8). Under 'Scanned Variable List', first click a variable for which you want to specify a classification. The histogram of this variable is then displayed, enabling you to see the exact distribution of the variable.

The next step is to specify the output variable, the banded variable. The new variable, TennisWearCategory in this example, is automatically assigned the same label as the original one, with the supplement '(Banded)'.

You can now specify the classification in the table. The cutpoints between the classes have to be typed in the column 'Value'. In this case the cutpoints have been specified as 250, 500 and 750. When you have defined a cutpoint, a vertical line appears in the histogram that corresponds to its position. You can also drag these lines; SPSS will then automatically change the cutpoints in the table. As you can see under 'Upper Endpoints', the highest value of each class has been defined as belonging to the class, 'Included (< =)'. The second class therefore comprises the values 251 *up to and including* 500 dollars.

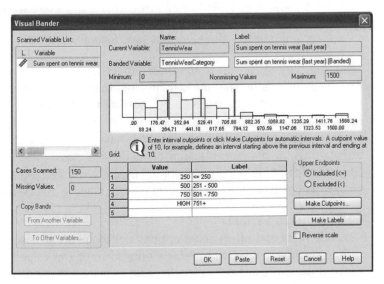

Figure 9.8   The dialogue box of Visual Bander to specify the classification.

In the bottom line of the table, the word HIGH indicates that all values above 750 dollars fall into the highest class. Without this, SPSS would assign all answers in excess of 750 dollars the value system missing value.

The final step consists of specifying the labels for the various classes (in the column 'Label'). You can specify your own labels, but it is easier to have SPSS generate them with the button Make Labels (as was done in this example).

Extensions.

Besides the above, the Visual Bander command includes the following options: assigning the same classification to multiple variables, specifying a descending classification and generating instead of specifying the cutpoints (with the button Make Cutpoints).

The same classification for multiple variables – If, in the first step, you have selected more than one variable to band, you can copy the classifications you have entered to other variables (under 'Scanned Variable List'). Copying takes place with the two buttons under 'Copy Bands', namely 'From Another Variable' and 'To Other Variables'.

Descending classification – Normally, the lowest values form class 1, the next group is class 2, and so on. This is an ascending classification. By clicking the option 'Reverse scale' you get a descending classification. Note that SPSS does not show this in the table in the dialogue box of Visual Bander.

Generating cutpoints – Instead of specifying the cutpoints, you can also have them generated by SPSS with the button Make Cutpoints. The dialogue box Make Cutpoints offers three options (see Figure 9.9):

- *Equal width intervals.* Out of the three properties that can be specified (the first cutpoint, the number of cutpoints and the interval), you have to enter two. The third property will then be computed by SPSS.
- *Equal percentiles.* Choose this option if you wish to have (approximately) equal numbers of cases in each class. You have to specify either the number of cutpoints, or the percentage of cases in each class.
- *Cutpoints derived from the distribution.* Cutpoints will be placed at the mean, and at the points x times the standard deviation above and below the mean.

9.3.2 Recoding a variable

The Recode command offers some options not available in Visual Bander, i.e. to recode string variables or to recode only some of the values of a variable. In these situations you have to use Recode; in many other cases you may prefer Visual Bander. Drawbacks of Recode are that you have to know the exact classification beforehand and that the dialogue box is less convenient to use.

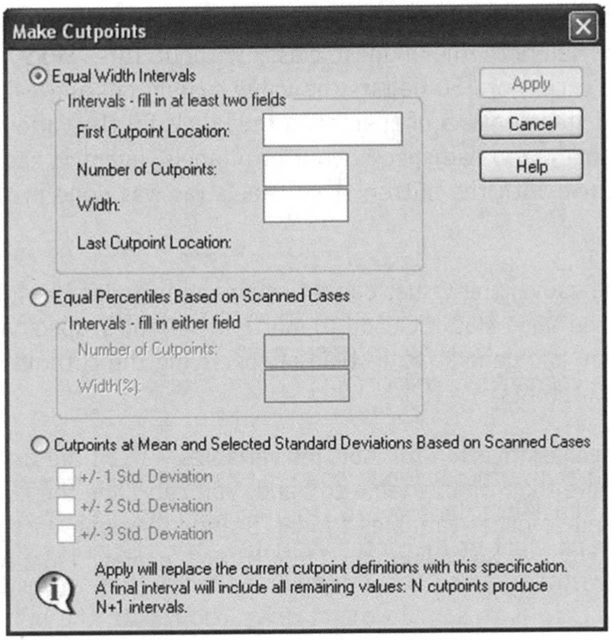

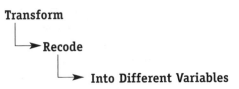

Figure 9.9   The dialogue box to have the cutpoints generated by SPSS (the button Make Cutpoints of the Visual Bander command).

There are two variants of the command, namely 'Recode into Different Variables' and 'Recode into Same Variables'. In the first of these, a new variable is introduced that contains the classification. In the second variant, the current values of a variable are overwritten. The dialogue boxes for the two commands are almost identical and for that reason we only discuss Recode into Different Variables.

In this subsection we discuss an example in which Recode is used to recode some of the values of a variable. Suppose that respondents were asked how many tennis tournaments they visit annually (an open question). It appears that most people visit between 1 and 5 tournaments and that a very small group watched 6, 7, 8, 10, 12 and 15 tournaments. We now show how to combine the values 6 and higher into a single class with Recode, without making any changes affecting the answers 1 to 5.

The command 'Recode into Different Variables' can be found as follows:

Transform
   └──▶**Recode**
          └──▶ **Into Different Variables**

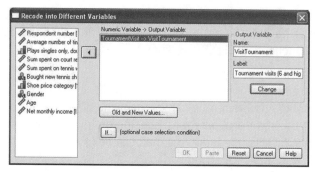

Figure 9.10   *The dialogue box to create a new variable containing the classification of another variable ('Recode into Different Variables').*

Figure 9.10 shows the dialogue box for this command, where you first have to select the variable to be recoded (TournamentVisit). The next step is to specify the name and label of the output variable. After you click the button Change, SPSS will write the name of the output variable in the rectangle in the centre.

The last step is to specify the classification, with the button 'Old and New Values' (see the dialogue box in Figure 9.11). In the left-hand part of the dialogue box you specify the old value(s) for each class (in the same way as for the Count command; see Section 9.2.1). When done, fill in the new value on the right and click the button Add to add the classification to the list of recodings.

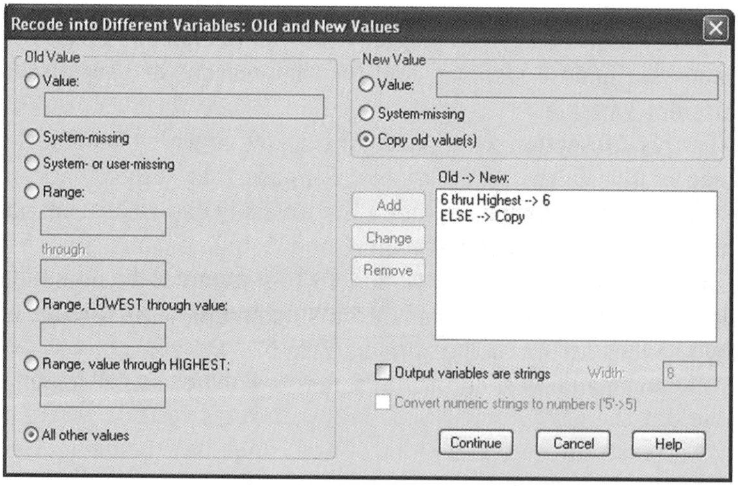

Figure 9.11   *The dialogue box for specifying the classification (the button 'Old and New Values' of the Recode command).*

In this example we have specified that the values 6 and higher ('6 thru Highest') have to be assigned the value 6 and that the other answers should remain unchanged ('ELSE —> Copy').

Extensions.

The Recode into Different Variables command offers various other options. You can execute the command only for a specific group of cases (with the button If; see Section 9.1.3). Furthermore, the dialogue box 'Old and New Values' contains a few additional options for string variables.

String variables – The dialogue box 'Old and New Values' contains two options for string variables:

- **Output variables are strings.** Click this option and specify the number of characters ('Width').
- **Convert numeric strings to numbers.** If the string variable consists of numbers in the form of text, for example '1' instead of 1, this option will convert the text '1' into the number 1.

9.4   Determine the ranking of cases

The output of the Rank Cases command is a variable that reflects the ranking of the cases. SPSS sorts the cases and assigns the first case the rank 1, the next case rank 2, and so on. Sorting takes place according to one or more variables, in ascending or descending order.

The Rank Cases command can be accessed via the menu as follows:

Transform
  └─► **Rank Cases**

The dialogue box Rank Cases is shown in Figure 9.12. At minimum, you have to specify the variable that will serve as the basis for the ranking. In the present example, this is the variable Age.

The assigned ranks are stored in a new variable. In this case the ranking variable has the name RAge (Rank Cases truncates variable names after the eighth character) and the label 'RANK of Age'. RAge has the value 1 for the youngest respondent, and equals the number of respondents for the oldest person. An overview of this variable will be displayed in the Viewer (because, by default, the option 'Display Summary Tables' is active; see Figure 9.12).

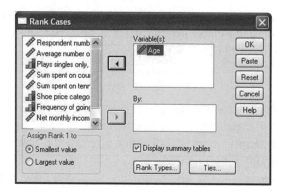

Figure 9.12   The dialogue box for determining the ranking of cases (the Rank Cases command).

Rank Cases can compute ranks only for numeric variables. If you wish to have ranks for a string variable, you first have to convert the string variable into a numeric variable with the Automatic Recode command (see Section 9.5).

Extensions.

The Rank Cases command offers great flexibility in determining ranks. In the dialogue box Rank Cases you can specify multiple variables, assign ranks within separate groups and change the order of sorting (see below). Further options are available with the buttons Ties and Rank Types, to determine the ranks for cases with equal ranking (see Section 9.4.1), and for the type of ranks to be computed (see Section 9.4.2).

Multiple variables – If you select multiple variables from the list of variables, SPSS will determine the ranking for each of these variables separately. For each ranking a new variable is created.

Ranks for groups – By specifying a variable in the dialogue box Rank Cases under 'By' you can calculate ranks for groups of cases. The respondents are first divided into different groups based on this variable and subsequently ranked within each group based on the variable specified under 'Variable(s)'.

Sorting order – By default, the cases are sorted in ascending order and the rank 1 is assigned to the lowest value. This can be changed in the dialogue box, under 'Assign Rank 1 to' by selecting:

- smallest value: to sort in ascending order;
- largest value: to sort in descending order.

9.4.1 Ranks for equal values (ties)

A problem occurs in ranking when cases have the same score (ties). SPSS offers various options for assigning ranks to such cases. The button Ties opens a dialogue box with the following four options (examples in Table 9.5):

Table 9.5   *Assigning ranks when multiple cases have the same value for the ranking variable ('ties')*

Observation	Value	Mean	Low	High	Unique value
1	11	3	2	4	2
2	7	1	1	1	1
3	11	3	2	4	2
4	13	5	5	5	3
5	11	3	2	4	2

- *Mean*: cases with the same score are assigned the average rank. This is the default option.
- *Low*: cases with the same score are assigned the lowest rank.
- *High*: cases with the same score are assigned the highest rank.
- *Sequential ranks to unique values*: only different (unique) values of a variable are assigned a new rank. If a variable has ten different values, the highest rank will be ten (even if there are a hundred cases).

9.4.2 Ranking methods

By default, Rank Cases computes normal ranks, but you can also compute different kinds of ranks. The button Rank Types in the dialogue box Rank Cases offers the following options (several of which may be selected):

- *Rank*: normal ranks (default option).
- *Savage score*: the scores are based on an exponential distribution.
- *Fractional rank*: the normal rank divided by the number of valid cases.
- *Fractional rank as %*: as above, but expressed as a percentage.
- *Sum of case weights*: the sum of the weights of the cases within a group. The new variable has the same value for all cases in a group.
- *Ntiles*: the cases are divided into n equal groups. The new variable has the same value for all cases in a group.
- *Proportion estimates*: the cumulative distribution of the corresponding rank is estimated.
- *Normal scores*: the z score corresponding to the estimated cumulative distribution. If the estimated cumulative distribution equals 0.50, the z score equals 0.

9.5   Automatic recoding

With the Automatic Recode command, a variable is recoded into a new, numeric variable with consecutive values. Recoding takes place automatically, in the sense that you do not have to specify which old value should be recoded into which new one. Automatic Recode sorts the values of the original variable and creates a new variable which is assigned the value 1 for the first value in the sorted series, 2 for the second value, and so on. The new variable is a numeric variable; the old one may be either a numeric or a string variable.

Automatic recoding is useful in the following situations:

1. *When string variables cannot be used*. In the analysis of variance, for example, the variable that determines the grouping has to be a numeric variable.
2. *When dealing with numeric variables having many empty categories*. Automatic recoding causes the empty categories to disappear. This not only produces better-looking output: for some commands it also saves memory space.

The Automatic Recode command can be found in the menu as follows:

Transform

└──▶ **Automatic Recode**

The dialogue box Automatic Recode is shown in Figure 9.13. In this box you need to specify the name of the original variable and the name of the new one. The original variable is selected from the list of variables (in this example Gender). In

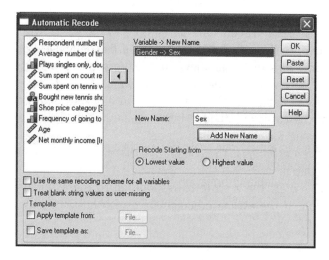

Figure 9.13   The dialogue box for automatic recoding of the string variable Gender (Y, N) into the numerical variable Sex (1, 2).

Table 9.6   *An overview of how SPSS has performed the recoding of Gender into Sex*

Gender into Sex		
Old Value	New Value	Value Label
F	1	Female
M	2	Male

the input field to the right of New Name you can enter the name of the new variable (Sex). Then click the button Add New Name to complete the command.

When the command has been executed, SPSS will show an overview of the recoding in the Viewer (see Table 9.6). The first value of the variable Gender ('F') has been recoded into the number 1 for the new variable Sex, while 'M' has become 2. The value labels of Gender are automatically assigned to Sex.

In the case where the original variable did not have value labels, the values of the original variable are used as value labels for the new variable. Likewise the variable label of the original variable is assigned to the new variable.

Extensions
By default Automatic Recode sorts the values of the original variable in ascending order. This can be changed with the options under 'Recode Starting from':

- *lowest value*: to sort in ascending order;
- *highest value*: to sort in descending order.

Finally, it is possible to recode multiple variables in the same way, by selecting the option 'Use the same recoding scheme for all variables'.

9.6   Replacing missing values

Missing data can affect your analyses. For time series data, SPSS can replace missing values by valid values. For each missing value SPSS computes a likely value based on the available information. For example, a missing value can be replaced by the average of the preceding observation and the following observation.

In most cases, it only makes sense to use this command for time series data, where each subsequent observation represents a measurement at a later point in time. For cross-sectional data this command cannot be used, with a few exceptions. By way of illustration we discuss the following two examples, each involving twelve measurements of a person's height, in which the fifth value is missing:

1. Time series data. A child's height is measured each month for one year. The value for May is missing. The average of the values for April and June will usually be an acceptable value for May. (It will not be acceptable if, for example, your research is aimed at detecting the presence of jumps in child growth.)
2. Cross-sectional data. Twelve people, randomly selected, were asked for their height, but the fifth person refused to answer. In this case there is no reason to assume that the average of the heights of the fourth and sixth persons will give a likely estimate of the height of the fifth person.

The command is found via the menu as follows:

Transform

  └─► **Replace Missing Values**

Replace Missing Values creates a new variable without missing values. In the dialogue box (see Figure 9.14) you have to specify:

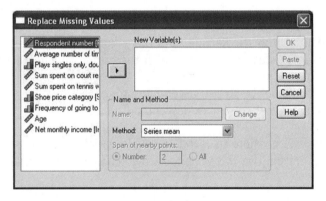

Figure 9.14   The dialogue box of the Replace Missing Values command.

1. *The old variable*: from the list of variables, select the variable for which missing values have to be replaced.
2. *The new variable*: in the input field next to 'Name', specify the name of the new variable. The default name used by SPSS is the old name extended by _1. Click Change after entering the name.
3. *The estimation method*. The following ways of estimating a likely value are available:

- *Series mean*: the mean of the entire series (the default method).
- *Mean of nearby points*: the mean of a number of neighbouring values. Under 'Span of nearby points' you specify how many values above and below the missing value have to be used.
- *Median of nearby points*: as above, but here the median is computed rather than the mean.
- *Linear interpolation*: linear interpolation between the preceding and the next valid value.
- *Linear trend at point*: based on all valid values, a linear trend is estimated. The missing values are then replaced by the predicted values on this trend.

10 Selecting, sorting and weighting cases

In this chapter we discuss four commands for transforming cases. The Split File command is used when several groups of cases are distinguished, for example men and women, and the same analyses are required for each group. With Split File you can specify the grouping and SPSS then performs each subsequent analysis for each group separately (see Section 10.1).

To select a group of cases, you can use the Select Cases command. Subsequent analyses are executed only for that specific group. The command offers several selection methods. You can select cases that meet a certain condition (see Section 10.2.1), make a random selection (see Section 10.2.2) or select based on the case numsber (see Section 10.2.3).

By default, SPSS assigns each case the same weight, but this can be changed with the Weight Cases command (see Section 10.3). The data file contains the cases in the order in which you have entered them. The Sort Cases command enables you to sort the cases based on one or more variables and in ascending or descending order (see Section 10.4).

10.1 Split File for analyses of groups

It often happens that you distinguish between groups and wish to carry out analyses for each group of cases separately. You may wish to analyse men and women as two separate groups, or veterans and young people, or people who spend a lot of money on tennis wear versus people who spend little. The Split File command is useful when you want to perform the same analyses for each group. In other words, use the same frequency table, the same bar chart or the same regression analysis for both men and women. You use Split File to specify which groups are to be distinguished and to instruct SPSS to perform each of the following analyses separately for each of the groups.

You find the Split File command in the menu by selecting:

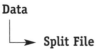

Data

$\quad\quad\longrightarrow$ **Split File**

The Split File dialogue box is shown in Figure 10.1. The first thing you now need to do is to 'switch on' Split File, by clicking either of the following options:

1. **Compare groups:** the output shows the results of all groups together, for example in one table containing all groups. Choose this option when you want to compare the groups with each other.
2. **Organize output by groups:** the results of each analysis are shown for each group separately. Choose this option if you wish to perform the same analysis for several groups.

In the next step you have to specify the variable(s) that determine the splitting. In this example we choose the variable Gender. After executing this command, SPSS will perform all subsequent analyses (frequency table, crosstable, correlation analysis, etc.) for men and women separately.

Extensions.
The Split File command can be extended in various ways. The command can be switched on and off, it is possible to specify more than one variable and you can indicate that the file has already been sorted.

Switching on and off. The command is effective only if switched on. When you switch it off again, SPSS will analyse the group of all cases as before. Split File is switched off or on by selecting one of the options in the dialogue box:

- *analyse all cases, do not create groups*: to switch off;
- *compare groups* or *Organize output by groups*: to switch on.

The bottom line in the dialogue box displays the current status of Split File (see Figure 10.1).

Several variables. If you specify more than one variable for the group classification, each combination of values of these variables forms a separate group.

Sorting cases. Split File requires that the cases have been sorted with respect to the variable(s) used for the grouping. There are two variants:

- *Sort the file by grouping variables*: if this option is selected, Split File will automatically sort the file in the proper way (default option).
- *File is already sorted*: click this option if the file has already been sorted. Especially when you are dealing with a very large data file this option saves time.

10.2   Select Cases for the selection of cases

You use Split File when you wish to analyse each group. Sometimes, however, you want to analyse only a single group. In such situations you can use the

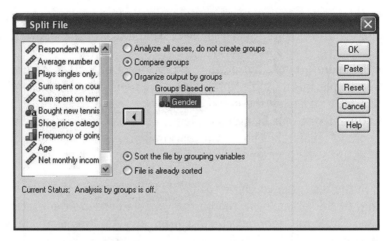

Figure 10.1   The dialogue box for splitting the data file into various groups where SPSS will perform each subsequent analysis for each group separately, in this example for both men and women (the Split File command).

Select Cases command. This command includes many ways of making a selection of cases, for example making a random selection and selecting based on a condition.

You find the Select Cases command as follows:

Data

Select Cases

The dialogue box Select Cases is shown in Figure 10.2. It contains the following selection methods:

- *All cases*: the analysis involves all cases (no selection, the default option).
- *If condition is satisfied*: only cases that meet one or more conditions are selected (see Section 10.2.1).
- *Random sample of cases*: SPSS selects a group of cases randomly (see Section 10.2.2).
- *Use filter variable*: for both conditional and random selections, SPSS automatically defines a new variable Filter_$ that indicates whether a case has been selected (value = 1) or not selected (value = 0). You may also define a filter variable yourself. SPSS selects all cases for which this variable has neither the value 0 nor a missing value.

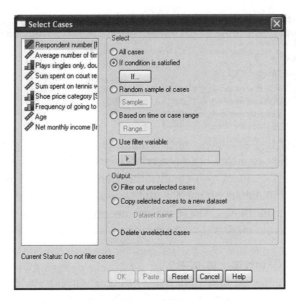

Figure 10.2   The dialogue box of the Select Cases command.

At the bottom of the dialogue box you can specify how SPSS has to deal with the cases not selected:

- *Filter out unselected cases*: the cases not selected remain available in the data file and can still be used later on (if you click 'All Cases', or make a new selection). The Data Editor identifies the cases not selected by crossing out their row numbers.
- *Copy selected cases to a new dataset*: the current dataset (the Active Dataset) remains unchanged.
- *Delete unselected cases*: the cases not selected are removed from the file (if you want to use them again, you have to reopen the data file, with File > Open).

10.2.1   Conditional selections

In conditional selections (If condition is satisfied) only those cases are selected that meet one or more conditions. The button If is used to open a dialogue box in which you can specify these conditions (see Section 9.1.3 for a discussion of this dialogue box).

Table 10.1 shows some examples of possible conditions. In the first example the persons selected are those who bought tennis shoes that fall into price category 1, the second condition will select respondents aged 30 years or over and in the third example only persons for whom the variable TournamentVisitdiffers from 2 will pass.

Table 10.1   Examples of conditions to select cases

1. ShoePrice = 1
2. Age >= 30
3. TournamentVisit ~= 2
4. (Gender = 'M') | (SingleDouble = 1)
5. (TennisWear > 500) & (CourtRental > 750)

The last two examples contain multiple conditions. The first of these leads to the selection of either male players or singles players. The final example requires respondents to meet two conditions: spending over 500 dollars on tennis wear and over 750 dollars on court rental. As you will note, the subconditions are contained in parentheses. These are not necessary, but they improve the readability and help avoid mixing up subconditions.

10.2.2   Random sampling

With random sampling (Random sample of cases) you either select a fraction of all cases or an exact number of cases. Clicking the button Sample in the dialogue box of Select Cases activates the dialogue box of Figure 10.3. This box offers the following two options:

- *Approximately*: state the percentage of cases you want to select. The actual selection as made by SPSS will be an approximation of this fraction.
- *Exactly*: state the exact number of cases you want to select and the number of cases from which the selection has to be made.

The selection is not purely random. SPSS uses a random number generator to select the cases. A series of random numbers is calculated based on a start value (a seed). Because the start value is different each time, the series of numbers is also different each time. If you wish to repeat the same random sample, you need to use the same seed. With the 'Random Number Seed' command from the Transform menu you can specify the seed (see Section 9.1.1).

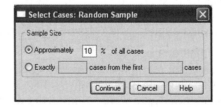

Figure 10.3   The dialogue box for selecting a random sample of, in this example, 10% of the cases (with Select Cases Random Sample).

10.2.3 Selection based on case number

Selecting on the basis of case numbers ('Based on time or case range') means that you select the cases with the row numbers x through y. The row numbers can be found in the margin of the Data Editor. Click the button Range and the dialogue box of Figure 10.4 will appear. In the present example, rows 1 to 25 are selected. This command can be useful to test the specification of a complex analysis when dealing with a very large data file. Another useful application is in combination with the Sort Cases command (see Section 10.4).

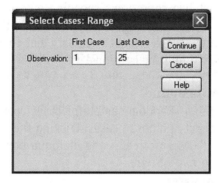

Figure 10.4   The dialogue box for selecting a fixed number of cases based on their row numbers (with Select Cases Based on Case Range).

10.3 Weight Cases for weighting cases

By default, all cases are assigned the same weight, but it may happen that one case in the data file does not represent just one case in reality. In such situations you can assign different weights to different cases with the Weight Cases command. This may be necessary when you have a non-representative sample, in which a certain group (for example, men) is overrepresented while another group (women) is underrepresented. By assigning each male respondent a weight smaller than 1 or each female respondent a weight larger than 1, the original distribution is restored.

Weight Cases is also applied when the distribution of a variable across various categories is known but the original data are not available. Suppose that the crosstable from Table 10.2 is included in a published report and you would like to perform a chi-square test to determine whether the variables Gender and Height are independent. If you were to enter the data in the normal way, you would have to enter 'M' for Gender and 1 for Height 30 times, followed by 'M' for Gender and 2 for Height 70 times, and so on. Using Weight Cases this can be done much easier. To use it, you need the data file from the right-hand side

Table 10.2   Data that are only available in a crosstable can be made available in SPSS with the Weight Cases command

Crosstable			Data file		
Gender	Height		Gender	Height	Number
Female	<= 1.70 m	> 1.70 m	F	1	65
	65	35	F	2	35
Male	30	70	M	1	30
			M	2	70

of Table 10.2, where you find four cases that each represent a cell in the crosstable. We show how these four cases can be weighted by the variable Number.

You find the Weight Cases command in the menu as follows:

Data

Weight Cases

The Weight Cases dialogue box is shown in Figure 10.5. By default, cases are not weighted, or rather each case has weight 1 ('Do not weight cases'). If you click 'Weight cases by', you can select a numeric variable that contains the weights that are to be assigned to each case. In this example, the weighting variable is Number. Each case is counted 'Number' times. Thus, the first case, a man shorter than 1.70 metres, is counted 30 times, etc.

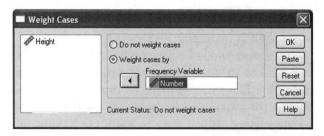

Figure 10.5   The dialogue box for weighting cases based on their score for the variable Number (the Weight Cases command).

10.4   Sort Cases

With the Sort Cases command you can change the order of the cases in the Data Editor. Sort Cases is particularly useful in combination with the command to select cases based on case numbers (see Section 10.2.3). Suppose that you want to analyse the fifty oldest respondents. You prepare this analysis by sorting the cases based on the variable Age and then selecting the first fifty cases.

To find the Sort Cases command in the menu, select:

Data

    Sort Cases

The Sort Cases dialogue box is shown in Figure 10.6. Only two items need to be specified, namely a variable and the way in which the cases are to be sorted (in ascending or descending order).

In order to select the fifty oldest respondents, you have to sort the cases in descending order. When this has been done, SPSS rearranges the cases in the Data Editor and changes the row numbers in the margin.

If you wish to restore the original order, have SPSS sort the cases in ascending order according to the respondent numbers (assuming that you have defined a variable containing them).

Multiple variables. It is also possible to sort cases based on multiple variables. If two cases have the same value of the first variable, the second variable will determine the order.

Missing values. SPSS treats a missing value as the lowest value. This means that when cases are sorted in ascending order, cases with a missing value will

Figure 10.6   *The dialogue box of the Sort Cases command in which the cases are sorted in descending order based on their score for Age (so the oldest respondent will be shown in the first row).*

be in front. Suppose that in the example above we wanted to perform an analysis on the fifty youngest respondents. We would then sort by Age in ascending order, followed by selecting the first fifty cases. These fifty cases also include the respondents without a valid value for Age. To avoid this, you first have to select the cases that are not missing. This is done with Select Cases > If, applying the condition:

~ MISSING(Age)

(the symbol ~ means 'not') and setting the option 'Unselected Cases Are' to 'Deleted'. You can then select the first fifty respondents.

11 Merging, aggregating and transposing data files

In the preceding two chapters we discussed the transformation of variables and cases. All of these resulted in changes within an existing data file. In this chapter we discuss transformations that result in a new data file.

Section 11.1 deals with the merging of data files. Two situations are distinguished, according to whether cases or variables are added. Both are illustrated with an example.

To change the level of detail of your analyses, you can combine cases. This is called aggregating and is discussed in Section 11.2.

SPSS assumes that the rows in a data file contain the cases and the columns the variables. However, for certain analyses it may be necessary to consider the rows as variables and the columns as cases. For such operations SPSS has the Restructure Data Wizard (see Section 11.3).

11.1 Merging data files

Sometimes there is a need to combine data files. An example is when three persons have separately entered the responses to a questionnaire. The three resulting data files then have to be combined into one overall data file. Another example is when you interview the same people before and after an event. In this case the data file with the information collected after the event needs to be merged with the data file created after conducting the interviews before the event. These two examples represent the two kinds of file merging operations that you can perform with the Merge Files command, namely:

- *Adding cases:* the two data files contain the same variables but different cases (see first example). To merge the files, SPSS has the Add Cases command (see Section 11.1.1).
- *Adding variables:* the two data files contain different variables but the same cases (see second example). To merge the files, SPSS has the Add Variables command (see Section 11.1.2).

11.1.1 Adding cases

When you merge two files containing the same variables but different cases, you add cases. For example, several persons each enter a part of the survey data, or you want to add information from a new time period to a file with data from previous periods.

You can find the Add Cases command in the menu as follows:

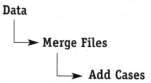

Data

└─▶ **Merge Files**

　　　└─▶ **Add Cases**

In the first dialogue box you have to specify which data file you want to merge with the current data file (the Active Dataset).

In the next dialogue box (see Figure 11.1) SPSS compares the variables in the two files. Variables that occur in both files are listed under 'Variables in New Active Dataset'. The other variables are listed under 'Unpaired Variables'. These include variables with different names, variables that are numeric in one file but string variables in the other, or string variables having unequal lengths in the two files. An asterisk (*) and a plus sign (+) refer to the files from which these variables originate. As you can see from the dialogue box (lower left), the asterisk indicates variables from the working file, while the plus sign refers to the file that is going to be added to it.

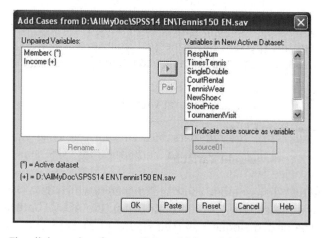

Figure 11.1   The dialogue box for specifying which variables have to be included in the new Active Dataset.

Extensions.
The Add Cases command offers four more options, namely: to include variables that are identical but have different names in the two files, to rename variables, to document the source of the case and to merge more than two files.

Identical variables with different names – When two variables are identical except for having different names in the two files, you have to click the two variables and then click the button Pair. This pair of variables is then added to the list of variables. The new variable is assigned the name of the variable in the Active Dataset.

Renaming variables – You can assign the unpaired variables a new name, with the button Rename.

Documenting the source of the case – By clicking 'Indicate Case Source as Variable' you can define a new variable indicating the file from which a case originates (the source of the case). The new variable, with the default name Source01, has the values 0 (zero) for cases from the Active Dataset and 1 for the other cases.

Merging multiple files – In the dialogue box Add Cases you can add one data file at a time to the Working Data File. If you want to add six data files, you have to repeat the same command six times. By copying the command to the syntax window with the button Paste, multiple files can be merged in one operation (the maximum is 50). For each file to be added you have to type the subcommand/File, followed by the file name in single quotation marks. You can then execute the command by clicking the button 'Run Current' (this is the button with the arrow right).

11.1.2 Adding variables

When you merge two files containing the same cases but different variables, you add variables. A well-known example is that where you have information on the same entities (persons or businesses) from several sources.

You can find the Add Variables command in the menu as follows:

Data

└─▶ **Merge Files**

└─▶ **Add Variables**

In the first dialogue box you have to specify which data file you want to merge with the file currently in the Data Editor, the Active Dataset.

In the next dialogue box (see Figure 11.2) SPSS compares the variables in the two files. Under 'New Active Dataset' you find all variables currently in the Data Editor, plus those variables from the file to be added that do not occur in

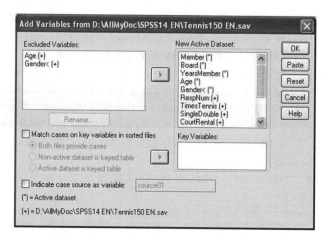

Figure 11.2   The dialogue box for specifying which variables have to be included in the new Active Dataset.

the Active Dataset. The variables from the file to be added that also occur in the Active Dataset are listed under 'Excluded Variables'. By clicking a variable and then clicking the button with the arrow, you can move variables from one list to the other.

By default, SPSS combines the first case from the Active Dataset with the first case from the other file, and so on. You can also specify that cases should only be combined if they have the same value for a key variable. You can specify this variable under 'Key Variables' (first click 'Match cases on key variables in sorted files'). In our example, RespNum could be used as a key variable. The procedure requires that both files have been sorted in ascending order of the key variable.

Extensions.
The Add Variables command offers three more options, namely: to rename variables in the list of 'Excluded Variables', to document the source of the case and to merge more than two files (see Section 11.1.1).

11.2   Combining cases with Aggregate

Aggregating means that groups of cases are combined in order to analyse them at a less detailed level. For example, a soup producer sells various tastes of soup, canned as well as dry, e.g. canned chicken soup, chicken soup in packets, canned tomato soup, tomato soup in packets, and so on. To analyse the sales of the various tastes, the sales of the different forms of packaging need to be combined. Alternatively, by aggregating according to taste, you can analyse the sales of both forms of packaging. Another example: if you have

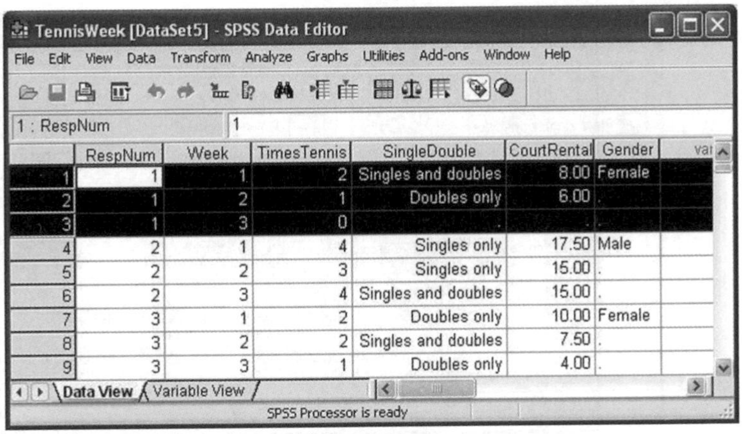

	RespNum	Week	TimesTennis	SingleDouble	CourtRental	Gender
1	1	1	2	Singles and doubles	8.00	Female
2	1	2	1	Doubles only	6.00	.
3	1	3	0	.	.	.
4	2	1	4	Singles only	17.50	Male
5	2	2	3	Singles only	15.00	.
6	2	3	4	Singles and doubles	15.00	.
7	3	1	2	Doubles only	10.00	Female
8	3	2	2	Singles and doubles	7.50	.
9	3	3	1	Doubles only	4.00	.

Figure 11.3 The dataset with weekly information on three tennis players.

measured medicine use for a number of patients during several periods, you can combine these observations into a single observation for each patient, reflecting the total medicine use of that patient.

Suppose that we have submitted a questionnaire to the same group of tennis players over a period of three weeks. Each week we asked them about the number of times they played that week, the type(s) of match played (singles, doubles or both) and the amount spent on court rental. An additional question about the respondent's gender was asked only in the first week. Figure 11.3 shows the data file for three players. The three cases for respondent 1 are highlighted in the Data Editor. To analyse the differences between the players, we need to combine these three cases into one new case. For this we use the Aggregate command.

You can find the Aggregate command in the menu as follows:

Data
└→ **Aggregate**

In the dialogue box you can specify how the cases have to be aggregated (see Figure 11.4). The two most important questions are: what will be the new cases? and which variables have to be aggregated in what way? You can answer the first question under Break Variable(s)'. Each value of the break variable identifies a new case. In this example, the break variable RespNum has three different values, so the aggregated file will contain three cases. (If you specify more than one break variable, every combination of the values of these variables identifies a new case.)

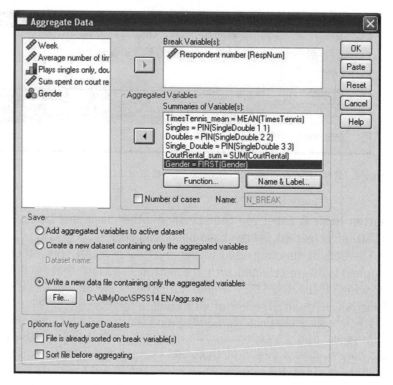

Figure 11.4   Aggregating the cases from the dataset in Figure 11.3.

Under 'Summaries of Variable(s)' you specify the variables you want to aggregate and how. In the example of Figure 11.4, the aggregated variables are defined as follows:

1. **TimesTennis_mean:** the mean of TimesTennis.
2. **Singles:** the percentage in the series of SingleDouble beginning with 1 and ending with 1 (in other words, the percentage of cases where SingleDouble equals 1, which is the percentage of weeks that the respondent played singles). Note that PIN is short for 'Percentage In'.
3. **Doubles:** as above, if SingleDouble equals 2.
4. **Single_Double:** as above, if SingleDouble equals 3.
5. **CourtRental_sum:** the sum of the observations for CourtRental, reflecting the total expenditure on court rental.
6. **Gender:** the first value in the series of observations for Gender.

By default, SPSS assigns the new variable the same name as the old one plus the applied function (see TimesTennis_mean and CourtRental_sum). With the

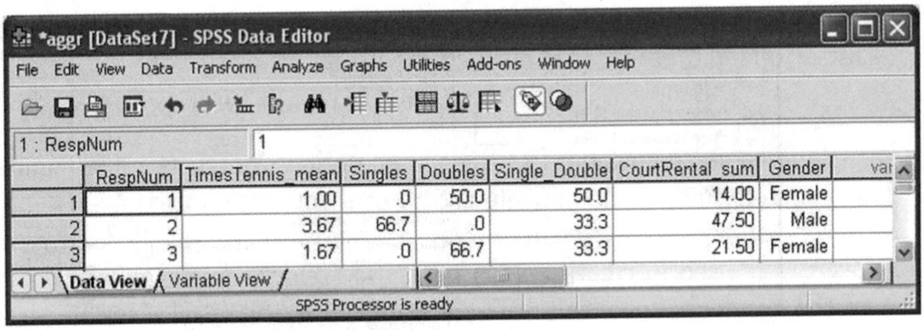

Figure 11.5   The aggregated dataset from Figure 11.3.

button Name & Label you can specify another name and label. In Figure 11.4 all variables except Gender have been renamed.

The default function used in aggregating is MEAN. The other functions in Figure 11.4 were selected with the button Function, that is, PIN (percentage in series), SUM and FIRST. Figure 11.6 shows the dialogue box of the button Function, with an overview of all available functions.

Figure 11.5 shows the aggregated data file. As you can see, the first respondent plays once a week on average (computed as 3/3) and the second respondent 3.67 times (11/3). The variables Singles, Doubles and Single_Double add

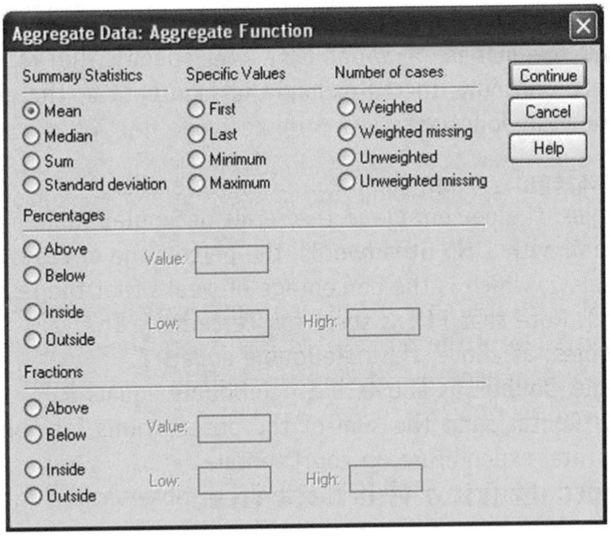

Figure 11.6   The dialogue box with the functions that can be used for aggregating cases (the button Function of the Aggregate command).

up to 100% for each respondent. Compare Figure 11.5 with Figure 11.3 for a better understanding of the functions used.

Extensions.

The Aggregate command offers three more options, i.e. to save the number of cases aggregated, to save the new file and to deal with string variables.

Number of cases aggregated – You can add a new variable to store how many cases were used in creating each new case (select the option 'Number of cases'). In the example above, this variable would have the value 3 for all cases.

Saving the new variables – The new (aggregated) variables can be:

- *Added to the active dataset.*
- *Stored in a new data file that is opened by SPSS*: this file only contains the aggregated variables; the active dataset remains unchanged ('Create a new dataset containing only the aggregated variables'). If needed you can save this file on disk.
- *Saved in a new file on disk*: the new data file is also opened as the next dataset; the active dataset remains unchanged ('Write a new data file containing only the aggregated variables').

String variables – In the dialogue box Aggregate, you can use string variables only as break variable, not as aggregated variable. If you want to aggregate string variables, like Gender in the example above, there are two solutions. You can either convert the string variable into a numeric variable (with the Automatic Recode command), or you can copy the command to the syntax window with the button Paste and then specify the string variable yourself (obviously, you can only use a function that can be executed for string variables). Suppose that you want to determine what fraction of the respondents in a group bought new tennis shoes (variable NewShoe, values Y and N). You then have to insert the following line in the Aggregate command:

/ PercShoe = PIN (NewShoe 'Y' 'Y')

The slash indicates that a new aggregate variable is being defined; the name of the variable in the aggregated file is PercShoe. You can then execute the Aggregate command by clicking the button 'Run Current' (this is the button with the arrow right).

11.3   Restructuring the data file

SPSS assumes that the rows in the data file contain the cases and the columns the variables. When this is not the case, you can use the Restructure Data Wizard to transform the file.

Data

└──▶ **Restructure**

The dialogue box Restructure Data Wizard (Figure 11.7) graphically illustrates the three applications of this command:

1. *To split cases*. Each case in fact comprises multiple cases. This is the first option 'Restructure selected variables into cases'.
2. *To convert cases into variables*, which can be used when several cases in fact represent several variables for the same case. This is the second option 'Restructure selected cases into variables' and forms the converse of the first operation.
3. *To transpose the data file*, which is necessary if the rows in your file contain the variables and the columns the cases.

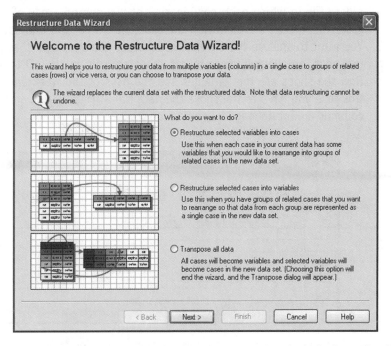

Figure 11.7   The dialogue box of the Restructure Data Wizard which shows the three applications of this command.

To decide which option you have to select, it is best to study the three pictures in Figure 11.7, by which you can determine which operation resembles what you intend to do. With a simple example we explain the three functions in greater detail below.

Suppose that five sports shops called A, B, C, D, E have kept a record of the sales of tennis shoes on each day of the week (Monday, Tuesday, and so on); see Figure 11.8. The type of analysis then determines the way the file data should be structured:

1. **You want to analyse the number of shoes sold on any given day in any given shop.** Each combination of a shop and a day of the week then constitutes a case, and the numbers of shoes sold is the variable to be analysed. Each row in Figure 11.8 would therefore have to be split up into six new rows (cases); see Section 11.3.1.
2. **You want to analyse the differences between the days of the week.** In this way you may find that, on average, more tennis shoes are sold on Saturdays than on Mondays. The days of the week are the variables and the shops are the cases. Therefore you need the file shown in Figure 11.8. In Section 11.3.2 we discuss the situation where you need the file of Figure 11.8, starting with a data file in which each combination of a shop and a day of the week is a case. This makes the operation the exact inverse of the one above.
3. **You want to analyse the differences between the shops.** In that way you may find that, on average, more tennis shoes are sold in shop D than in shop A. Now the shops are the variables and the days of the week are the cases. In this case you have to transpose the data file in Figure 11.8, so that rows and columns are interchanged; see Section 11.3.3.

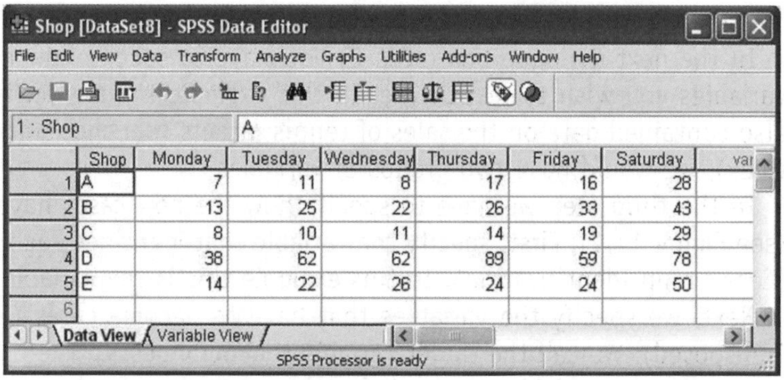

	Shop	Monday	Tuesday	Wednesday	Thursday	Friday	Saturday	var
1	A	7	11	8	17	16	28	
2	B	13	25	22	26	33	43	
3	C	8	10	11	14	19	29	
4	D	38	62	62	89	59	78	
5	E	14	22	26	24	24	50	
6								

Figure 11.8 The dataset with the sales of tennis shoes for each shop on each day of the week.

11.3.1 Splitting cases

The data file of Figure 11.8 is the starting point and we now want to analyse the number of shoes sold on any given day in any given shop. We need a file that contains the numbers of shoes sold for each combination of a shop and

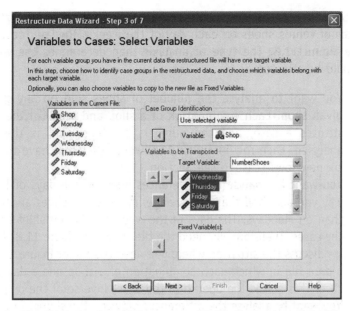

Figure 11.9   The third step in splitting cases with the Restructure Data Wizard.

a day of the week. We therefore have to split each of the rows in Figure 11.8 into six new rows, with a new case for each day of the week. In the dialogue box Restructure Data Wizard (Figure 11.7) we have to select the first option: 'Restructure selected variables into cases'.

In the next dialogue box (step 2) you have to specify how many groups of variables you wish to restructure. In this example the answer is 1. If the file also contained data on the sales of tennis rackets (per shop and per day of the week), we would have two groups of variables.

In the third step we have to specify how the new cases have to be formed (see Figure 11.9). First, specify the variable that identifies each group of cases (Case Group Identification). In this example this is the variable Shop.

Next, we specify the variables that have to become cases (Variables to be Transposed). We call the target variable NumberShoes. In the field below that, we specify the variables that will form the rows, i.e. Monday through Saturday.

In the fourth step one specifies the number of variables needed to form an index. The index is needed for tracing the new cases to the original variables. In this example, the days of the week become the cases and therefore a single index is sufficient.

Step 5 then asks what values this new index variable should have. You can choose numbers (1–6) or labels, that is, Monday to Saturday. In this example, the latter option is the obvious choice.

In step 6 you can specify how SPSS has to handle cases not selected and missing values. Both options are not relevant in this simple example. Finally, the restructuring of the data file takes place in step 7. The resulting data file is shown in Figure 11.10.

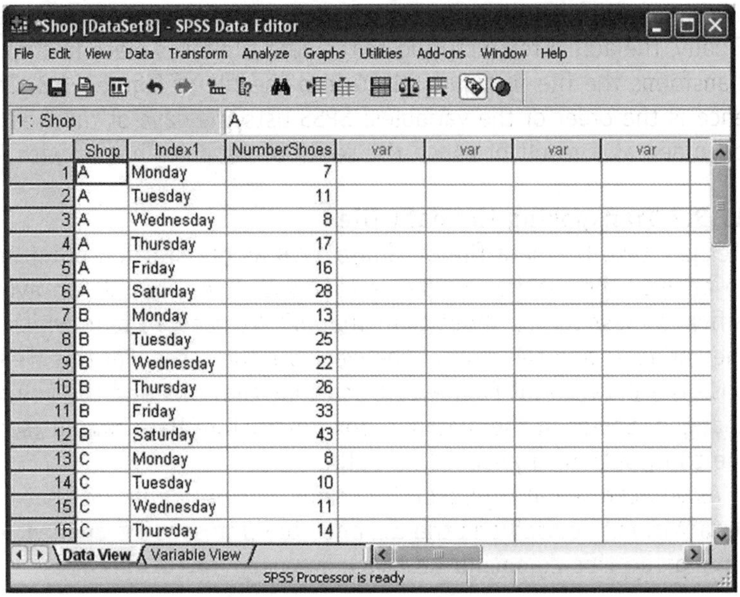

	Shop	Index1	NumberShoes	var	var	var	var
1	A	Monday	7				
2	A	Tuesday	11				
3	A	Wednesday	8				
4	A	Thursday	17				
5	A	Friday	16				
6	A	Saturday	28				
7	B	Monday	13				
8	B	Tuesday	25				
9	B	Wednesday	22				
10	B	Thursday	26				
11	B	Friday	33				
12	B	Saturday	43				
13	C	Monday	8				
14	C	Tuesday	10				
15	C	Wednesday	11				
16	C	Thursday	14				

Figure 11.10 *The dataset that has been created with the Restructure Data Wizard based on the dataset from Figure 11.8. In this case each combination of a shop and a day forms a separate case.*

11.3.2 Converting cases into variables

In this case we perform a data file transformation that is the exact inverse of the one discussed above. The starting point is the file in Figure 11.10 and we need the file of Figure 11.8. You need the file of Figure 11.8 if you intend to analyse the differences between the days of the week, for example. In that way you may find that, on average, more tennis shoes are sold on Saturdays than on Mondays. For this you need a file in which the days of the week are the variables and where the shops are the cases.

In the dialogue box Restructure Data Wizard (see Figure 11.7) you now have to select the second option: 'Restructure selected cases into variables'. In the next dialogue box (step 2) you have to specify which variable determines the division into cases in the new file, the 'Identifier Variable'. In this example this is the variable Shop, because we want a separate case for each value of Shop. In addition, you have to specify the 'Index Variable'. This is the variable whose values are going to form separate variables. In this example this is the variable WeekDay (called Index1 in Figure 11.10). Each value of WeekDay has to become a variable in the new file.

In step 3, SPSS asks whether the cases are already in the correct order or have to be sorted. In step 4 you can specify the order of the variables (with one Identifier Variable and one Index Variable, as, in this example, the result will be the same), and whether you want SPSS to count the number of cases aggregated. Finally, the actual restructuring of the data file takes place in step 5, where SPSS transforms the file in Figure 11.10 into the file of Figure 11.8. The only difference is the order of the variables: SPSS lists the days of the week in alphabetical order, as a result of which the series of variables begins with Friday.

11.3.3 Transposing the data file
We now take the data file of Figure 11.8 as our starting point and our goal is to analyse the differences between shops. Does shop A, on average, sell significantly less tennis shoes than shop D? We need a file in which the shops are the variables and the days of the week are the cases. For this we have to transpose the data file of Figure 11.8, so that the rows and the columns are interchanged. Select in the dialogue box Restructure Data Wizard (see Figure 11.7) the third option: 'Transpose all data'.

As you can see in Figure 11.7, clicking this option means that the Restructure Data Wizard is closed and the dialogue box Transpose is opened. You could also have given this command via the menu:

Data

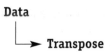

Transpose

In the dialogue box Transpose you have to specify which variables are to be transposed: in this example the variables Monday to Saturday (see Figure 11.11).

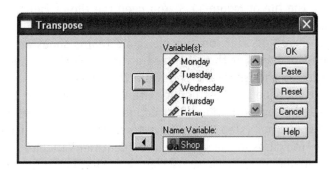

Figure 11.11   *The dialogue box of the Transpose command to transpose the dataset from Figure 11.8.*

Because each of these variables contains five cases, five new variables are created. By default these are named Var001 to Var005. If you specify the variable Shop under 'Name Variable', the new variables are renamed A to E, reflecting the values of Shop.

Figure 11.12 shows the transposed data file. With this file you can analyse differences between shops. As you can see, SPSS has also created a new variable Case_lbl (short for 'case label') that contains the names of the original variables.

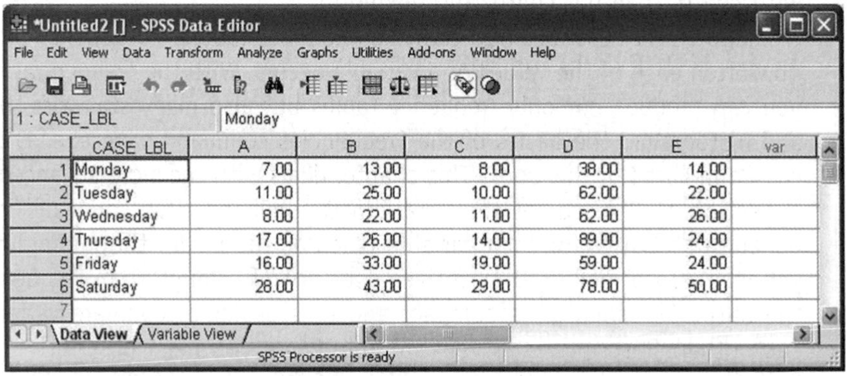

	CASE_LBL	A	B	C	D	E	var
1	Monday	7.00	13.00	8.00	38.00	14.00	
2	Tuesday	11.00	25.00	10.00	62.00	22.00	
3	Wednesday	8.00	22.00	11.00	62.00	26.00	
4	Thursday	17.00	26.00	14.00	89.00	24.00	
5	Friday	16.00	33.00	19.00	59.00	24.00	
6	Saturday	28.00	43.00	29.00	78.00	50.00	
7							

Figure 11.12 The transposed dataset from Figure 11.8.

12 Describing your data

In this chapter we discuss three commands that give information about the distribution of a variable. Variables can be described in three ways: in the form of a frequency table, with statistics (like mean and standard deviation) and with charts (like bar charts and boxplots).

Section 12.1 describes how to make frequency tables. A frequency table shows how often each of the values of a variable occurs. With the *Frequencies* command you can produce not only frequency tables but also many statistics, bar charts and histograms. The basics of the Frequencies command have already been discussed in Part I of this book. This chapter deals with the more advanced options.

Section 12.2 discusses the *Descriptives* command. This command is used to generate statistics for each variable (such as the mean, the minimum and the variance). In principle, Descriptives does not offer more than Frequencies, but the output is much more compact and it is easier to compare variables with each other. Descriptives is very suitable when you need descriptive statistics for a large number of interval or ratio variables.

The third command to describe a variable is *Explore* (see Section 12.3). Besides information that can also be provided by the other two commands, Explore can produce stem-and-leaf plots and boxplots.

12.1 Creating frequency tables

Frequency tables are used to provide an overview of the empirical distribution of a variable. The table shows how often each of the values occurs and what percentage of the total this represents. How many men and how many women took part in the survey? What percentage of players bought new tennis shoes last year? In many surveys, making frequency tables for all variables is the first step in a series of analyses, not only to include these tables in a report, but particularly to get a better understanding of your data.

Frequency tables can be made for all types of variables, from nominal to ratio variables. For continuous variables with a very large number of values, however, such a table will rapidly become too extensive (each value means another row in the table). That is why such variables are often first divided into categories, which turns them into ordinal variables.

You can make a frequency table with the menu as follows:

Analyze

→ **Descriptive Statistics**

→ **Frequencies**

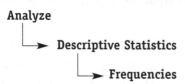

In the next dialogue box you can list the variable(s) for which you want to make a frequency table. For simple frequency tables, specifying the variables is all you have to do. Making a simple frequency table was one of the subjects in the sessions in Part I of this book (see Section 4.7 in particular). In this chapter we discuss the additional options.

Buttons – The dialogue box Frequencies contains three buttons for special options. With Statistics you can request statistics such as means, variances and percentiles (see Section 12.1.1). The button Charts enables you to create bar charts, pie charts and histograms (see Section 12.1.2), and with Format you can change the order of the rows and the layout of the table (see Section 12.1.3).

No table – With the buttons Statistics and Charts you can produce other output (statistics and charts) besides a frequency table. If you only require this output and you do not need the frequency table, you may switch off the option 'Display Frequency Tables' in the dialogue box Frequencies.

12.1.1 Statistics

With the button Statistics in the dialogue box Frequencies you can compute a wide range of statistics. In the dialogue box Statistics (see Figure 12.1) these

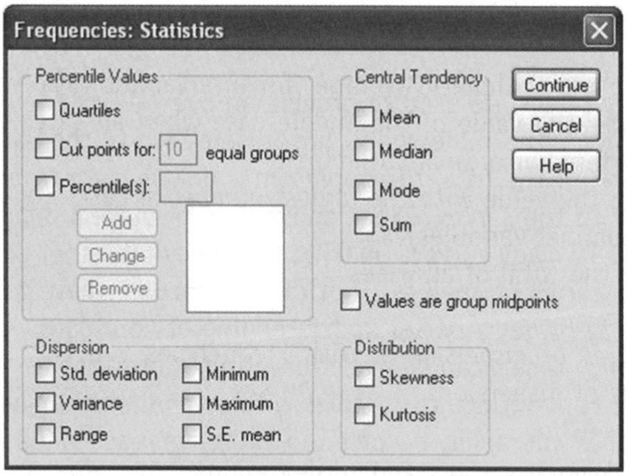

Figure 12.1 The dialogue box for requesting statistics with frequency tables (the button Statistics of the Frequencies command).

have been divided into four groups, i.e. percentiles, and measures of the central tendency, the dispersion and the distribution of a variable. We briefly discuss each of these groups.

Percentiles – Percentiles are values that indicate the percentage of all cases with a lower value. An example: 80 percent of the cases is lower than or equals the value corresponding to the 80th percentile. You can specify percentiles in three ways:

- *Quartiles*: the cases are divided into four groups of equal size (i.e. the 25th, 50th and 75th percentiles).
- *Cutpoints for x equal groups*: the cases are divided into x groups of equal size, where you have to specify the value of x (if x = 4, you obtain quartiles).
- *Percentile(s)*: you can enter the desired percentiles yourself and add them to the list (with the button Add); you can change or remove the percentiles entered.

Values representing intervals – For values that represent intervals you can compute the percentiles more accurately if these values refer to the midpoint of an interval. This means that if you have the age groups 20 to 30 and 30 to 40, the codes 25 and 35 have to be entered (and not 1 and 2). If this is the case, you can select the option 'Values are group midpoints'. SPSS then treats the values as interval midpoints and computes the percentiles (and the median) on that basis.

Averages – Under the heading 'Central Tendency' you find measures of the average of a variable:

- *Mean:* the arithmetic average (for interval and ratio variables).
- *Median:* the value of the middle case when all cases are sorted (especially important for ordinal variables).
- *Mode:* the value with the largest number of cases (of particular importance for nominal variables).
- *Sum:* the total of all cases.

Measures of dispersion – With Frequencies you can request the following measures of dispersion:

- *Std. deviation*: the standard deviation.
- *Variance*: the variance.
- *Range*: the difference between the highest and the lowest values.

- *Minimum*: the lowest value.
- *Maximum*: the highest value.
- *S.E. mean*: the standard error of the mean (i.e. the standard deviation divided by the square root of the number of valid observations).

Measures of the distribution – Finally, the dialogue box contains two statistics that provide information on the shape of the distribution:

- *Skewness of the distribution*. A positive value reflects that the distribution has a tail towards high values (a right tail). A skewness of 0 corresponds to a symmetric distribution, such as the normal distribution.
- *Kurtosis*: compares the top of the observed distribution to the normal distribution. A positive kurtosis reflects that the peak of the observed distribution is higher than that of a comparable normal distribution. The normal distribution has a kurtosis of 0.

12.1.2 Charts
You can use the button Charts in the dialogue box Frequencies to create bar charts pie charts or histograms. The dialogue box Charts offers the following options (see Figure 12.2):

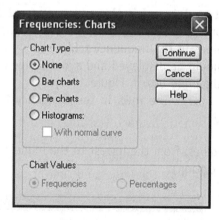

Figure 12.2   The dialogue box for requesting charts with frequency tables (the button Charts of the Frequencies command).

- *None*: no charts, the default option.
- *Bar charts*: for each variable a bar chart is created (see Figure 12.3).
- *Pie charts*: for each variable a pie chart is created.

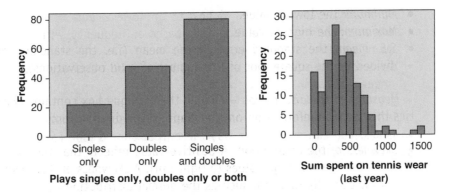

Figure 12.3   An example of a bar chart (left) and a histogram (right).

- *Histograms*: for each variable a histogram is created (see Figure 12.3). You can superimpose a normal distribution on the histogram (by selecting 'With normal curve').

For bar charts and pie charts you can specify the units on the vertical axis or the pie slices: the numbers of cases ('Frequencies') or the percentages of cases ('Percentages'). See Chapter 13 for a more detailed discussion of charts.

12.1.3 Format to determine the appearance of the table

With the button Format in the dialogue box Frequencies you can change the order of the values in the frequency table, specify how the statistics of multiple variables should be displayed and avoid tables with a very large number of rows (see the dialogue box in Figure 12.4).

Order of the rows – The rows in the frequency table can be sorted in four ways ('Order by'):

- *Ascending values*: from the lowest to the highest value of a variable (this is the default option).

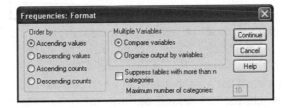

Figure 12.4   The dialogue box for changing the appearance of the frequency table (the button Format of the Frequencies command).

- *Descending values*: from the highest to the lowest value.
- *Ascending counts*: in ascending order based on frequency, with the least frequent value in the first row.
- *Descending counts*: in descending order based on frequency, with the most frequent value in the first row.

Statistics for multiple variables – When you request statistics for multiple variables, you can specify the way the output should look (see the dialogue box, under 'Multiple Variables'):

- *Combined table*: SPSS creates a single table containing the statistics for all variables specified ('Compare Variables', this is the default option).
- *Separate tables*: SPSS creates a separate table containing the statistics requested for each variable ('Organize output by variables').

Tables with many rows – By selecting Suppress tables with more than n categories you can ensure that a table will only be displayed for variables having fewer than n different values.

12.2   Descriptive statistics

You can use the Descriptives command to request statistics for one or more variables. Regarding the available options, this command does not add to the options available under Statistics with Frequencies (see Section 12.1.1). In fact, Frequencies can produce some statistics that are not available with Descriptives (these include mode, median and percentiles). Descriptives, however, is particularly useful in the following two situations:

- if you need statistics only (i.e. without frequency tables) for several variables; and
- if you want to sort the variables in the output (e.g. alphabetically, or based on their means).

The output of Descriptives is organised in a way different from that of Frequencies. Frequencies show a table with the statistics in the rows and the variables in the columns. This is convenient when you want an overview of the statistics for each variable, but less so when you want to compare variables. How much do people spend, on average, on court rental? How much on tennis wear? Are these variables comparable in terms of their variance? In such situations, the layout of the Descriptives output is more convenient. Descriptives shows a table with the variables in the rows and the statistics in the columns. In other words, if you ask for the means of five variables, the five means will be shown below each other, so that they can be easily compared. (Of course, columns and rows can be interchanged in both situations with the Pivot function; see Section 6.7.)

You can find the Descriptives command as follows:

Analyze
 └──▶ **Descriptive Statistics**
          └──▶ **Descriptives**

Figure 12.5 shows the dialogue box Descriptives. The only thing you have to do is to specify the variables for which you want to compute the statistics. Since statistics can only be computed for numeric variables, string variables are omitted from the list of variables.

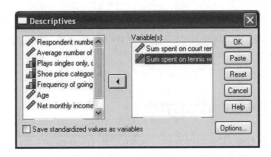

Figure 12.5   The dialogue box Descriptives for requesting statistics for the variables CourtRental and TennisWear.

Besides an overview of the data used (Notes and Active Dataset), the output of Descriptives consists of a table of statistics. The default statistics are the number of valid cases, the minimum and maximum, the means and the standard deviation (see Table 12.1). By default, the variables are listed in the order in which they were selected.

Table 12.1   Descriptive statistics for the variables CourtRental and TennisWear, generated with the Descriptives command

Descriptive Statistics

	N	Minimum	Maximum	Mean	Std. Deviation
Sum spent on court rental (last year)	150	80	2970	731.33	581.456
Sum spent on tennis wear (last year)	150	0	1500	393.33	282.526
Valid N (listwise)	150				

Extensions.

With the button Options you can specify the statistics and sort the variables in a different order. It is also possible to save z scores. Below we briefly discuss these options.

Statistics – With the button Options you can specify which statistics you require and in what order SPSS should present the variables in the output (see the dialogue box in Figure 12.6).

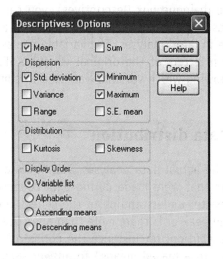

Figure 12.6   The dialogue box of the button Option of the Descriptives command (the selected options show the default output).

The following statistics can be requested (see Section 12.1.1 for more details on the meaning of the statistics):

- *the mean* (it is not possible to request the mode or the median) and the sum of all cases;
- *measures of dispersion*: standard deviation, variance, range, minimum value, maximum value and standard error of the mean S.E. mean);
- *measures of the distribution*: kurtosis and skewness, both with their standard errors.

Order of the variables – In the lower part of the dialogue box Options four ways of sorting the variables in the output are listed ('Display Order'):

- *Variable list*: in the order in which you selected the variables. This is the default sorting option.

- *Alphabetic*: in alphabetical order.
- *Ascending means*: in ascending order of the mean.
- *Descending means*: in descending order of the mean.

If you wish to sort the variables on the basis of another statistic than the mean, you can specify this in the syntax window.

Saving z scores – If you select the option 'Save Standardized Values as Variables' (in the dialogue box Descriptives), you can add the z scores of the selected variables to your data file. SPSS saves the z scores in new variables that you can use in later analyses. The variable names start with a Z, followed by the first seven letters of the original variable. SPSS automatically adds a variable label showing which variable was used in computing the z scores.

12.3 Explore data distribution

Before starting the actual data analyses, you have to examine your data. You might spot errors that were made during data collection or data entry and it will give you a better understanding of the collected data. Does the distribution have a single peak or is there more than one? Does the distribution match a theoretical distribution, for instance the normal distribution? Are there any outliers that lead to a biased means? To answer such questions, you can use frequency tables for nominal and ordinal variables. For continuous variables (interval or ratio) the Explore command is useful. This command not only produces statistics, but also graphs (histograms, boxplots and stem-and-leaf plots). You can get this output for all cases or separately for groups of cases.
You can find the command in the menu under:

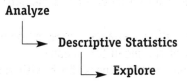

Analyze
⌐→ **Descriptive Statistics**
  ⌐→ **Explore**

Figure 12.7 shows the dialogue box Explore. Explore is a command with a large number of options, but we first consider the command in its simplest form. The minimum you need to specify is the variable that you want to examine. In this example we use the variable Age. We specify this variable under 'Dependent List'.
Besides the overview of the data used (Notes and Active Dataset), the Explore output consists of three parts: an overview of the numbers and

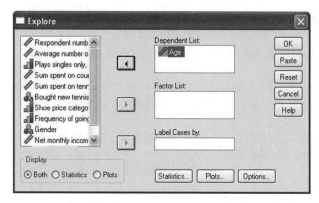

Figure 12.7   The dialogue box Explore for requesting statistics and charts for the variable Age.

percentages of valid cases, missing values and total cases (Case Processing Summary), a table of statistics (Descriptives) and two charts for each variable selected: a stem-and-leaf plot and a boxplot. The latter two, the statistics and the charts, are discussed below.

Descriptives – The 'Descriptives' table contains a number of statistics (see Table 12.2). Most of them have already been discussed in Section 12.1.1 with Frequencies. Three statistics are new:

Table 12.2   The default statistics of the Explore command

Descriptives

			Statistic	Std. Error
Age	Mean		33.20	.998
	95% Confidence Interval for Mean	Lower Bound	31.23	
		Upper Bound	35.17	
	5% Trimmed Mean		32.20	
	Median		30.00	
	Variance		149.477	
	Std. Deviation		12.226	
	Minimum		18	
	Maximum		75	
	Range		57	
	Interquartile Range		16	
	Skewness		1.179	.198
	Kurtosis		1.096	.394

- *95% Confidence Interval for Mean*: SPSS shows both the 'Lower Bound' and the 'Upper Bound' of this interval. Note that you can specify the percentage yourself (see Section 12.3.1).
- *5% Trimmed Mean*: the mean computed without the top 5% and the bottom 5% of all cases. By comparing this with the normal mean, you can detect a biased mean due to a few outliers.
- *Interquartile Range*: the difference between the 75th and 25th percentiles.

Stem-and-leaf plot – The first chart is a stem-and-leaf plot. A stem-and-leaf plot is similar to a histogram, but it contains more information and is therefore a bit more difficult to read. Like a histogram, it shows the cases combined into intervals, where the length of the stem (or the leaf) in the plot reflects the number of cases in an interval. Whereas a histogram only shows information for an interval, a stem-and-leaf plot also gives information on the distribution within an interval.

For further clarification we discuss Table 12.3, which shows the stem-and-leaf plot of the variable Age. The essence of a stem-and-leaf plot is that each value is divided into a stem and a leaf. The score of a respondent can be rewritten as:

Score = Stem * Stem Width + Leaf

Below the stem-and-leaf plot you can see that the 'Stem Width' is 10. For a respondent aged 35 years this means a stem of 3 and a leaf of 5 (3*10 + 5 = 35).

Consider, for example, the first line in Table 12.3. For this line, which has a frequency of 10, the stem equals 1, and the leaf consists of a series of 8s and 9s.

Table 12.3   The stem-and-leaf plot of the variable Age

Frequency	Stem & Leaf
10.00	1. 8888888999
28.00	2. 0000001111122222233333333344
32.00	2. 55555566666667777778888889999999
26.00	3. 00000000011111111222223444
16.00	3. 5555677777778889
14.00	4. 01112222222344
7.00	4. 5557779
6.00	5. 000024
3.00	5. 679
3.00	6. 114
5.00 Extremes	(>=65)
Stem width:	10
Each leaf:	1 case(s)

When we translate these into normal scores, we get the result: 1*10 + 8 = 18 and 1*10 + 9 = 19. Thus, the first line contains the respondents aged 18 or 19 years.

The first line contains seven 8s and three 9s. Below the plot you see that each leaf represents one case, meaning that the frequency 10 consists of seven 18-year-olds and three 19-year-olds.

This example shows the advantage over a histogram: a stem-and-leaf plot also gives information on the distribution within an interval. This enables you to understand the effect of an alternative grouping of values.

As shown by the last line in the plot, there are five extreme values, defined as respondents aged 65 and over (>=65).

Boxplot – The second chart is a boxplot (see Figure 12.8). Like a stem-and-leaf plot, a boxplot gives information on the distribution of a variable, but in more compact form. A boxplot shows the distribution of variable as a rectangle, a box, with whiskers. Here we give a brief explanation only; for further details of boxplots, see Section 13.8.

The upper and lower bounds of the box are formed by the 75th and 25th percentiles, respectively. The distance from top to bottom of the box therefore equals the interquartile range mentioned above. The horizontal line inside the box represents the median.

Below and above the box you see two horizontal lines, called *whiskers*. The whiskers are placed at 1.5 times the interquartile range below the first quartile

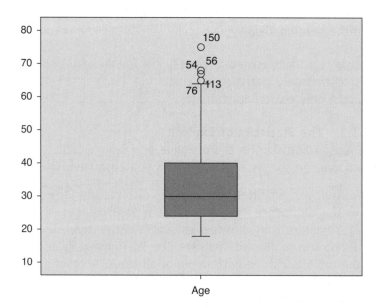

Figure 12.8   A boxplot of the variable Age.

(the bottom of the box) and above the third quartile (the top of the box). If such values do not occur, the whiskers are placed at the lowest or highest value (see the lower whisker in Figure 12.8, at the minimum age of 18 years). Cases falling outside the interval between the whiskers are either outliers or extremes. *Outliers* are those at more than 1.5 times the interquartile range from the top or the bottom of the rectangle and are designated by a circle. *Extremes* are still farther away (three times the interquartile range or more) and are designated by an asterisk.

Extensions.
Explore features many more options. In the dialogue box Explore you can distinguish between various groups. Furthermore, you can specify the desired output, namely both Statistics and Plots, or only one of these. These options are discussed below. The three following subsections each deal with one of the three buttons in the dialogue box Explore. With Statistics you can request additional statistics (see Section 12.3.1). With Plots you can specify the charts you want (see Section 12.3.2) and, finally, with Options you can specify how to treat missing values (see Section 12.3.3).

Group analyses – In many situations you are not only interested in the distribution of a variable across all cases, but you also want to explore whether differences between groups exist. By specifying a variable under 'Factor List' in the dialogue box Explore, you can obtain output for groups of cases. Each value of the factor variable defines a group.

Desized output – At the bottom left in the dialogue box Explore is a frame with the heading 'Display' in which you can specify the output you want:

- *both*: statistics as well as charts, this is the default option;
- *statistics*: only statistics, no charts;
- *plots*: only charts, no statistics.

12.3.1 The Statistics of Explore
The button Statistics in the dialogue box Explore leads to a dialogue box in which you can specify which statistics you want (see Figure 12.9):

- *Descriptives*: produces the statistics displayed in Table 12.2. You can specify the confidence interval (default is 95%).
- *M-estimators*: computes four estimates of the mean. The main purpose is to decide how to deal with outliers. The 5% Trimmed Mean, for instance, ignores the top 5% and the bottom 5% of all cases. Another approach is to assign different weights to cases that are farther removed from the median. Such an estimator is called an M-estimator Maximum likelihood estimator'). SPSS can display four such estimators, namely Andrew, Huber, Hampel and Tukey.

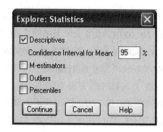

Figure 12.9   The dialogue box of the button Statistics of the Explore command.

- *Outliers*: provides an overview of the cases with the five highest and the five lowest values.
- *Percentiles*: shows the following percentiles: 5, 10, 25, 50, 75, 90 and 95.

12.3.2   The Plots command for creating charts

With the button Plots you can request various charts (see Figure 12.10):

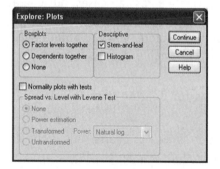

Figure 12.10   The dialogue box of the button Plots of the Explore command.

1. **Boxplots:** there are three options, the first two of which are relevant if you specify multiple dependent variables and also distinguish between different groups. Suppose that you specify the variables TennisWear (amount spent on tennis wear) and CourtRental (amount spent on court rental) as dependent variables and that you use Gender to distinguish between two groups (men and women). The various options then lead to the following boxplots:

   - *Factor levels together*: two boxplots, one for TennisWear and one for CourtRental. Both plots contain two boxes, one for men and one for women.

- *Dependents together*: one boxplot, containing two boxes for men, corresponding to expenses for tennis wear and court rental, respectively, plus two similar boxes for women. In total there are four boxes in one plot.
- *None*: no boxplot will be displayed.

2. **Stem-and-leaf:** whether or not to create a stem-and-leaf plot.
3. **Histogram:** whether or not to create a histogram.
4. **Normality plots with tests:** by applying the Kolmogorov–Smirnov test, SPSS shows whether a variable matches the normal distribution (see Section 19.4). SPSS also generates two charts showing to what extent the data approximate to a standard normal distribution (see Section 13.10 for more details on these two charts):

   - *Normal q–q plot*: the quantiles of an observed distribution are on one of the axes and the quantiles of the standard normal distribution on the other. A straight line represents a variable with a standard normal distribution. The curve shows the observed distribution. If the observed distribution matches the standard normal distribution closely, the curve approximates to the straight line.
   - *Detrended normal q–q plot*: this chart shows the deviations of the observed distribution from the standard normal distribution. If the sample was taken from a normally distributed population, the values will lie around the horizontal line that passes through zero, with only random deviations.

12.3.3   Options for dealing with missing values

With the button Options in the dialogue box Explore you can tell SPSS how to deal with missing values. There are three options:

- *Exclude cases listwise*: all cases are excluded for which a value for one of the variables (dependent variables or factor variable) is missing.
- *Exclude cases pairwise*: cases are only excluded if there is a missing value for the relevant dependent variable or factor variable.
- *Report values*: the missing values of the factor variable are treated as a separate category for which all requested output is shown.

13   Charts

As a result of the steadily increasing graphical capabilities of personal computers, charts are playing an ever more important role in statistics. Charts are no longer used only afterwards for presenting the results in a report or oral presentation. More and more, charts are being used while the analyses are still in progress, to get a better understanding of the available data and to detect possible relationships.

As charts are becoming more important, their variety is increasing. In this book we discuss eleven kinds of charts. Section 13.1 gives an overview of these, also indicating which type of chart is best suited for a given situation.

The five most common charts are bar, line, area, pie and scatter plots. These are the charts that you can create with the Chart Builder (see Sections 13.2–13.6). Section 13.7 deals with three kinds of high-low charts, namely high-low-close charts, range bar charts and difference line charts. The next three sections discuss charts that are useful when analysing the distribution of a continuous variable: boxplots (Section 13.8), histograms (Section 13.9) and normal distribution plots (Section 13.10).

The Chart Editor is used for changing charts. With the features in this window you can customise the various elements of a chart (see Section 13.11).

13.1   An overview of available charts

Charts serve two important purposes. They form a nice way of enlivening a report, to alternate with numeric information in tables. In addition, charts give compact and accessible insight into possible relations or the distribution of a variable. During the analyses, charts often serve the latter function, to determine whether it is worthwhile to perform some formal, statistical test. Scatterplots, for example, are often used to decide whether it makes sense to apply correlation and/or regression analysis, and histograms to see whether a variable is normally distributed.

With SPSS you can create many kinds of charts. We discuss the most important ones, namely: (1) bar charts, (2) line charts, (3) area charts, (4) pie charts, (5) scatterplots, (6) high-low-close charts, (7) range bar charts, (8) difference line charts, (9) boxplots, (10) histograms and (11) normal distribution plots (see

Table 13.1   Eleven kinds of charts you can create with SPSS

	1. Bar chart		7. Range bar chart
	2. Line chart		8. Difference line chart
	3. Area chart		9. Boxplot
	4. Pie chart		10. Histogram
	5. Scatterplot		11. Normal distribution plot
	6. High-low-close chart		

Table 13.1). Below we describe the use of each of these categories, also indicating the sections in which they are discussed.

1. ***Bar charts***. You can use bar charts to compare the *absolute values* of different groups or phenomena. The chart contains a bar for each element (group or phenomenon) (see Section 13.2).
2. ***Line charts***. You can use line charts to analyse *developments* or *trends* (and the relationship between various trends). Each measurement of a phenomenon is represented by a dot and successive dots are connected by a line (see Section 13.3).
3. ***Area charts***. Area charts provide information on the *development of a phenomenon and its components*. The simplest variant, with one component (or variable), equals a line chart in which the area between the line and the horizontal axis is coloured. In contrast to line charts, when there are several components, the area of each subsequent component is stacked on top of the previous one (see Section 13.4).
4. ***Pie charts***. With pie charts you can compare the *relative sizes* of a limited number of groups or phenomena (see Section 13.5).
5. ***Scatterplots***. Scatterplots give information on the *relation between variables*. In the simplest case, two variables are plotted, one on the horizontal axis and one on the vertical axis. The cases are represented by dots. The shape of the cluster of dots gives information on both the direction and the strength of the relationship. We discussed scatterplots in detail in Chapter 6 and therefore we only briefly discuss them in Section 13.6.
6. ***High-low-close charts***. High-low-close charts describe the development of a phenomenon by showing, for each time interval, the highest, the lowest and

the final value. This gives information on *both the overall trend and the fluctuations within each measuring period*. For each period the chart contains a vertical line. The upper endpoint represents the highest value, the lower endpoint represents the lowest value, while a dot is placed on the line at the final value. High-low-close charts are often used to show the developments and fluctuations in stock prices and temperatures, among other things (see the introduction in Sections 13.7 and 13.7.1).

7. **Range bar charts.** You can use range bar charts to obtain insight into the *absolute values of two phenomena and the difference between these*. The chart contains a number of observations for both phenomena (or groups). A requirement is that one group always has a lower score than the other group. For each measurement, SPSS shows a bar that begins at the low score and ends at the high score. The length of the bar thus represents the difference between the two groups (see the introduction in Sections 13.7 and 13.7.2).

8. **Difference line charts.** Besides presenting the information contained in range bar charts, difference line charts can also deal with *reversals* (points where the phenomenon that initially was the smallest becomes the largest). A difference line chart is a line chart with two lines, in which the area between them is coloured. This area reflects the difference between the two phenomena or groups. After a reversal, the colour changes. Compared with range charts, you use difference line charts when there are reversals and/or to present a large number of observations (see the introduction in Sections 13.7 and 13.7.3).

   The following three types of charts give information on the distribution of a continuous variable; in other words, an interval or a ratio variable.

9. **Boxplots.** Boxplots give information on various aspects of the distribution of a continuous variable. The plot shows a rectangle, the box, that contains the cases (50% of the total) that lie within the interquartile range. A boxplot gives information on the *median, the interquartile range, the skewness and the extreme values* of a variable (see Section 13.8).

10. **Histograms.** Histograms are bar charts for continuous variables and are used to study the *shape of a distribution*. Because continuous variables often have many different values, bar charts are not appropriate. A histogram shows a bar for each interval of values. By superimposing a normal distribution in the histogram you can see how well the observed distribution matches the normal distribution (see Section 13.9).

11. **Normal distribution plots.** Normal distribution plots give insight into the *match between the observed distribution of a variable and the normal distribution*. In these plots, the cumulative distribution of a variable is plotted against the normal distribution. We discuss two variants, a normal quantile plot and a normal probability plot (see Section 13.10).

Creating charts – The easiest way to create charts is by using the Chart Builder. This is how we did it in Chapters 5 and 6. However, the Chart Builder only contains the most common kinds of charts, namely bar, line, area, pie and scatterplots. For other kinds of charts you have to use the (old) SPSS commands in the Graphs menu. Some statistical procedures also create charts as a by-product. This applies for example to Frequencies (bar charts and histograms), Explore (boxplots, histograms and normal distribution plots) and Linear Regression (various charts for analysing the residuals). SPSS displays charts in the Viewer where you can view, save and print them.

Changing charts – To change a chart you double-click it in the Viewer. SPSS then transfers the chart to a separate window, the Chart Editor. This window contains commands to change the various elements of a chart according to your own preferences and requirements. We discuss the Chart Editor in Section 13.11.

13.2 Bar charts

In Section 5.2 we discussed creating a simple bar chart with the Chart Builder. In this section we discuss more advanced bar charts. The Gallery (see Figure 13.1) contains the following six variants of a bar chart (the name is displayed when you point at a picture in the Gallery):

- *Simple Bar*: this is the variant we created in Chapter 5. A bar is shown for each value of the (nominal or ordinal) variable on the horizontal axis.
- *Clustered Bar*: a group of bars is shown for each value of the (nominal or ordinal) variable on the horizontal axis. Each group of bars contains a bar for each value of the cluster variable (which has to be either nominal or ordinal).
- *Stacked Bar*: similar to a clustered bar, but in this case the bars in a group are stacked on top of each other.
- *Simple 3-D Bar*: a group of bars that are displayed behind each other is shown for each value of the (nominal or ordinal) variable on the horizontal axis (three dimensional). Each group of bars contains a bar for each value of the variable on the Z-axis (which has to be either nominal or ordinal).
- *Clustered 3-D Bar*: similar to a clustered bar chart, but in this case each bar is split into a group of bars displayed behind each other, based on the variable on the Z-axis (which has to be either nominal or ordinal).
- *Stacked 3-D Bar*: similar to a stacked bar chart, but in this case each stacked bar is split into a group of bars displayed behind each other, based on the variable on the Z-axis (which has to be either nominal or ordinal).

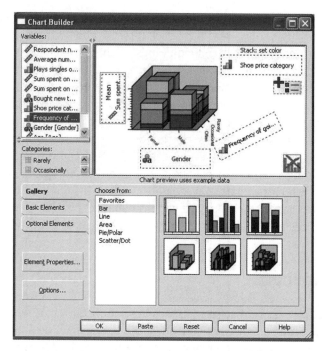

Figure 13.1   The Chart Builder shows a preview of a Stacked 3-D Bar Chart.

Figure 13.1 shows an example of a Stacked 3-D Bar Chart. On the horizontal axis the variable Gender determines that two groups of bars are shown. The stack variable ShoePrice has three values: this is why each bar consists of three stacked parts. The Z-axis, this is the axis giving depth to the bar chart, contains the variable TournamentVisit. A stacked bar is made for each of the three values of this variable (Rarely, Occasionally and Often).

The vertical axis in a bar chart often shows the number or percentage of cases. You can also select a continuous (scale) variable for this axis and request a statistic. In the example of Figure 13.1 the vertical axis shows the mean of the court rental expenditures. Figure 13.2 shows the statistics you can select, with the button Element Properties.

Extensions.
The three most important extensions when you create a chart with the Chart Builder concern adding titles and footnotes (Optional Elements), specifying the properties of the various axes (Element Properties) and how SPSS has to deal with missing values (Options). We briefly discuss each of these.

Titles and footnotes – With the tab Optional Elements you can specify multiple titles and footnotes. The position in the chart and the font are fixed; if needed you can change these afterwards in the Chart Editor.

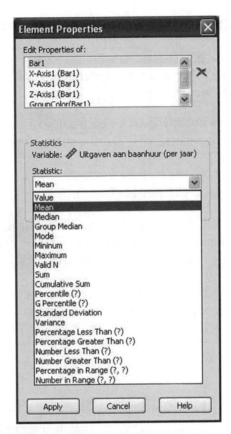

Figure 13.2 The dialogue box Element Properties with an overview of the statistics from which you can select.

Element properties – With the button Element Properties you specify the properties of the various elements in the chart. For example, for each axis you can determine the order of the values (e.g. in Figure 13.1 you can switch the groups Female and Male), whether certain values have to be excluded and how SPSS has to display categories with a very low number of cases. For continuous (scale) variables you can specify the minimum, maximum and increment. You first have to select the element you intend to change under 'Edit Properties of'. Do not forget to click the button Apply after changing properties to have the changes applied to the chart.

Missing values – With the button Options you can specify how SPSS has to deal with user missing values. They can be excluded or included as a separate category. SPSS can exclude all cases that have a missing for at least one of the variables (exclude listwise), or maximise the use of the available valid cases (exclude variable-by-variable).

13.3   Line charts

Creating line charts with the Chart Builder is very similar to creating bar charts (see Section 5.2). The Chart Builder contains the following two variants of a line chart (see Figure 13.3):

- *Simple Line*: a dot is shown for each value of the (nominal or ordinal) variable on the horizontal axis, and the subsequent dots are connected with a line.
- *Multiple Line*: see the example in Figure 13.3, where a separate line is shown for each value of the variable Gender.

The vertical axis in Figure 13.3 shows the number of cases. You can also select a continuous (scale) variable for this axis and request a statistic (see Figure 13.2 for an overview of available statistics).

The *extensions* of a line chart are similar to those of a bar chart (see Section 13.2). In addition, you can specify (under Interpolation) how the dots have to be connected: with a straight line (as in Figure 13.3), a spline, or with steps or jumps.

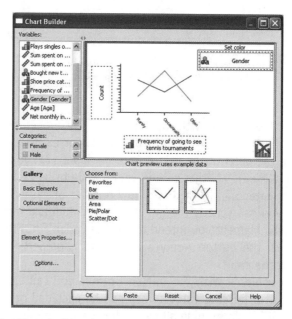

Figure 13.3   The Chart Builder shows a preview of a Multiple Line Chart.

13.4   Area charts

Creating area charts with the Chart Builder is very similar to creating bar charts (see Section 5.2). The Chart Builder contains the following two variants of an area chart (see Figure 13.4):

- *Simple Area*: a dot is shown for each value of the (nominal or ordinal) variable on the horizontal axis. The subsequent dots are connected with a line and the area between the line and the horizontal axis is coloured.
- *Stacked Area*: see the example in Figure 13.4, where a separate area is coloured for each value of the variable TournamentVisit. The differences between the lines reflect the number of cases in a category.

The vertical axis in Figure 13.4 shows the number of cases. You can also select a continuous (scale) variable for this axis and request a statistic (see Figure 13.2 for an overview of available statistics).

The extensions of an area chart are similar to those of a bar chart (see Section 13.2). In addition, you can specify (under Interpolation) how the dots have to be connected: with a straight line (as in Figure 13.4), a spline, or with steps or jumps.

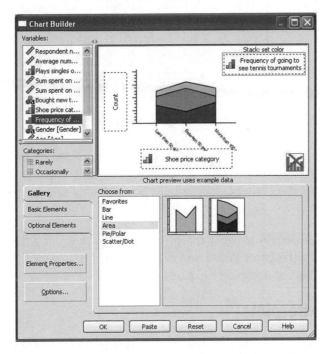

Figure 13.4   The Chart Builder shows a preview of a Stacked Area Chart.

13.5   Pie charts

Creating pie charts with the Chart Builder is very similar to creating bar charts (see Section 5.2). The variable that determines the number of slices is shown under the pie chart in Figure 13.5; in this case the chart consist of three slices. This variable has to be nominal or ordinal.

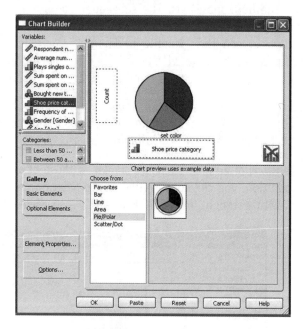

Figure 13.5   The Chart Builder shows a preview of a pie chart.

In this example the size of the slices is determined by the number of cases in the categories (Count). You can also select a continuous (scale) variable for this and request a statistic. Surprisingly, you can only select between the value and the sum.

The *extensions* of a pie chart are similar to those of a bar chart (see Section 13.2). In the Chart Editor you can explode slices (click a slice, click the right mouse button and select explode slice).

13.6   Scatterplots

Creating scatterplots with the Chart Builderis very similar to creating bar charts (see Section 5.2). The Gallery (see Figure 13.6) contains the following five

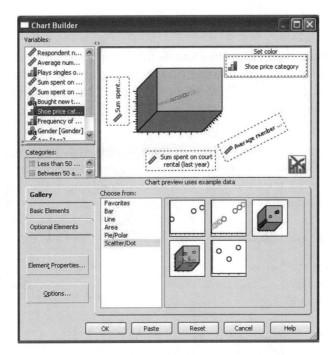

Figure 13.6   The Chart Builder shows a preview of a Grouped 3-D Scatter Plot.

variants of a scatterplot (the name is displayed when you point at a picture in the Gallery):

- *Simple Scatter*: each case is shown as a dot which is placed at the intersection of its values for the variables on the horizontal and vertical axis.
- *Grouped Scatter*: similar, but in this case the dots are coloured depending upon the value of a third variable (which has to be either nominal or ordinal).
- *Simple 3-D Scatter*: similar to Simple Scatter, but in this case three axes are used.
- *Grouped 3-D Scatter*: similar to Simple 3-D Scatter, but in this case the dots are coloured depending upon the value of a fourth variable (which has to be either nominal or ordinal); see the example in Figure 13.6.
- *Summary Point*: similar to Simple Scatter and Grouped Scatter, but in this case you can specify for the vertical axis a statistic of the variable on the horizontal axis (such as the number or percentage of cases).

The vertical axis in Figure 13.6 shows the tennis wear expenditures, the horizontal axis the court rental expenditures and the depth axis (Z-axis) the number of times played. The dots are coloured based on the value for ShoePrice.

The *extensions* of a scatterplot are similar to those of a bar chart (see Section 13.2).

13.7   High-low charts

High-low charts show the differences between groups (and/or variables). Each point in the chart is determined by at least two values: a high value and a low value. Sometimes a third value is used as well, the final (close) value or the mean value. For example, you might represent the daily temperature by the maximum, the minimum and the mean (or the temperature at noon). Another well-known application is stock prices. In that case usually the highest, lowest and closing price are shown.

You can create a high-low chart by selecting from the menu:

Graphs

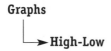
➤ **High-Low**

The first dialogue box is shown in Figure 13.7. SPSS distinguishes between the following variants of high-low charts:

- *Simple high-low-close*: for each point three values are shown: a high value and a low value, in the form of horizontal bars connected by a vertical line, plus a closing value in the form of a dot on the vertical line (see Section 13.7.1). For example: the highest, lowest and closing prices of a stock for a number of days.
- *Clustered high-low-close*: as above, but for two groups (or variables). For example: the highest, lowest and closing prices of two stocks for a number of days.

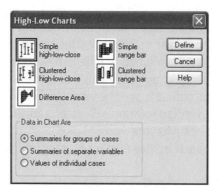

Figure 13.7   The dialogue box showing the variants of high-low charts.

- *Simple range bar*: a range bar chart that shows the difference between a high value and a low value for each measurement, in the form of a bar (see Section 13.7.2). It is required that the same group or variable always has the highest score. For example: the difference in the sums spent on tennis wear by men and women, broken down by age category.
- *Clustered range bar*: as above, but for two groups or variables. For example: the difference between the sums spent on tennis wear and court rental by men and women, broken down by age category.
- *Difference area*: a difference line chart. This shows the difference between two values in the form of a coloured area; it is not required that the same group always has the highest score (see Section 13.7.3).

A measurement in a high-low chart can represent three items: a group of cases, a separate variable or an individual case. You specify this in the lower half of the dialogue box.

13.7.1 High-low-close charts

You can use high-low-close charts for phenomena for which a highest value, a lowest value and an intermediate value have been measured. Stock prices are a well-known example, as are temperatures. Suppose that you have measured the maximum, minimum and mean temperatures on five summer days. The data are shown in Table 13.2.

Table 13.2   The temperature measured on five different days (in degrees Celsius)

Day	Maximum temperature	Minimum temperature	Average temperature
Monday	32	15	23
Tuesday	29	17	24
Wednesday	28	16	22
Thursday	30	18	25
Friday	31	17	24

The data file contains five observations for the variables Day, MaxTemp, MinTemp and MeanTemp. Since the chart has to show individual cases, we choose in the dialogue box with the basic settings for 'Simple-high-low-close' and 'Values of individual cases'. In the next dialogue box you can specify the

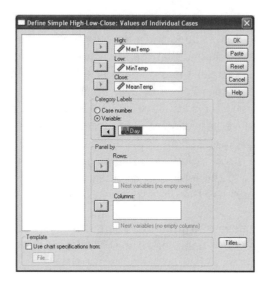

Figure 13.8   The dialogue box of a high-low-close chart, using the data from Table 13.2.

various variables (see Figure 13.8). Under 'Category Labels' we have specified the variable Day as the label.

Figure 13.9 shows the corresponding high-low-close chart. From this chart you can see that the largest difference between the maximum and the minimum temperature was measured on Monday. The highest mean occurred on Thursday.

13.7.2 Range bar charts

A range bar chart shows the difference between two groups of cases (or variables) in the form of a bar. Suppose you have found that men systematically spend more on court rental than women. A range bar chart is useful to analyse whether the magnitude of this difference is influenced by the type of play practised.[1] You can create a range bar chart by selecting from the menu:

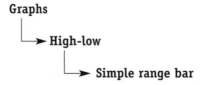

Our chart has to show groups of cases, based on type of play and broken down by gender. We therefore choose 'Summaries for groups of cases' in the dialogue box with the basic settings. In the next dialogue box you can specify the variables (see Figure 13.10).

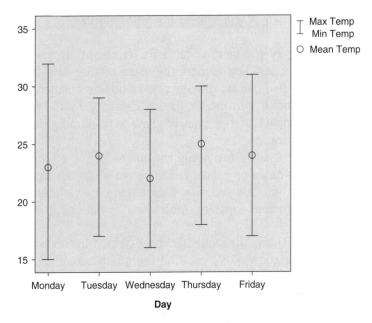

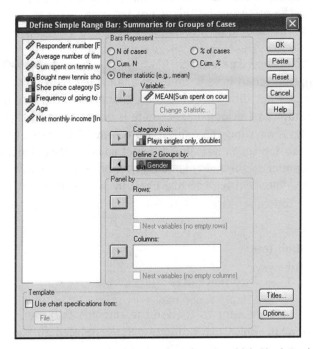

Figure 13.9   The high-low-close chart created with the command in Figure 13.8

Figure 13.10   The dialogue box of a range bar chart in which SingleDouble determines the first grouping and Gender the subsequent subgrouping. The chart shows the mean values of CourtRental.

In the dialogue box you specify the following items:

- *The meaning of the bars*, under 'Bars Represent'. In this case click 'Other summary function' and request the mean of the variable CourtRental. The button Change Summary gives access to a large number of statistics.;
- *The classification into groups*, under 'Category Axis'. Because we want to study the impact of the type of play, SingleDouble determines the first group classification.
- *The classification into two subgroups*, under 'Define 2 Groups by'. The second breakdown is based on gender and therefore we specify this variable here. The classification into subgroups must be based on a variable with only two values (a dichotomous variable), otherwise it is not possible to make bars.

Figure 13.11 shows the range bar chart created in this way. On the horizontal axis, the 'Category Axis', you find the group classification. The lower end of each bar is determined by the mean for women and the upper end by the mean for men. As you can see, the difference in mean expenditure on court rental is by far the largest for the category of singles players. For those who only play doubles the difference between men and women is smallest.

The range bar chart assumes that one of the variables (or groups) is *always* larger than the other one. If this is not the case, you can use a difference line chart (that can also show reversals).

13.7.3 Difference line charts

A difference line chart is very similar to a range bar chart. There are three important differences. A difference line chart shows the difference between two values in the form of a coloured area. There is no requirement that the same group (or variable) always has the highest score. When the lowest group becomes the highest, that is, after a reversal, a different colour is used. Finally, difference line charts are preferred for a very large number of measurements.

You can create a difference line chart by selecting from the menu:

Graphs
∟➤ **High-low**
　　∟➤ **Difference Area**

Suppose that we want to analyse the amounts that men and women spend on tennis wear. These expenditures may be related to the expenditures on

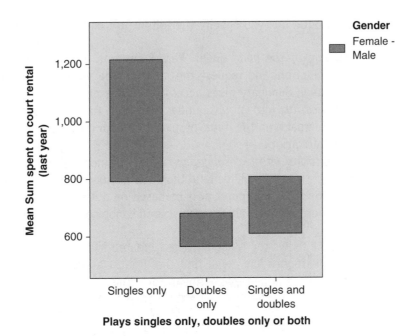

Figure 13.11   The range bar chart created with the command in Figure 13.10.

tennis shoes (measured as the price of new shoes, ShoePrice). We can use a difference line chart to explore this relationship. The chart has to show groups of cases based on ShoePrice and broken down by gender. In the dialogue box with the basic settings we therefore choose for 'Difference Area' and 'Summaries for groups of cases'. In the next dialogue box you can specify the variables.

This dialogue box is very similar to the dialogue box discussed in the preceding subsection (refer to that subsection for a more detailed treatment). Under 'Lines Represent' we specify that we want to analyse the expenditure on tennis wear and request the mean of this variable. The variable under 'Category Axis', in this case ShoePrice, determines the classification into groups. Under 'Define 2 Groups by' we specify the classification into two subgroups, with the variable Gender.

Figure 13.12 shows the difference line chart created in this way. The chart contains two lines, and the difference between the lines has been coloured. As you can see, within the group of players who buy cheap shoes, men spend more money on tennis wear than women. This difference has become very small in

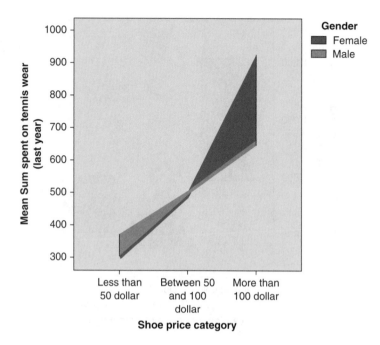

Figure 13.12   The difference line chart in which ShoePrice determines the grouping and Gender the division in subgroups.

the middle category (with shoes between 50 and 100 dollars) and then reverses. In the category with the most expensive tennis shoes, women spend considerably more money on tennis wear than men. Note that the exact position of the reversal point has no meaning, because ShoePrice is an ordinal variable.

13.8   Boxplots

A boxplot gives information on the distribution of a variable. The values of a variable are on the vertical axis, while the horizontal axis shows the variables or groups for which the boxplot is requested. Each variable (or group) is represented by a rectangle in the chart, a box. This rectangle gives information on the dispersion of the variable. To simplify the explanation, we first discuss an example of a boxplot and then explain how you can create a boxplot.

Figure 13.13 contains a boxplot of the variable TennisWear, the amount spent on tennis wear. The rectangle, the box, is the basic element of the chart.

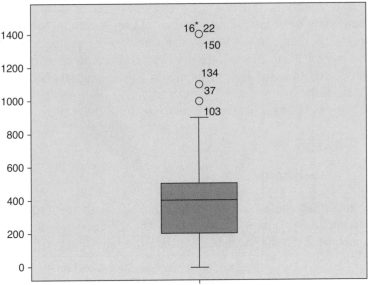

Figure 13.13   The boxplot for the variable TennisWear.

The top of the box is formed by the 75th percentile and the bottom by the 25th percentile. The difference between the top and bottom of the box equals the interquartile range. In other words, half of all cases of TennisWear lie in the box.

The horizontal line in the box refers to the median, the value of the middle case. On the vertical axis you can read the value of the median, in this case 400.

Above and below the box you see horizontal lines called whiskers. The whiskers are placed at 1.5 times the interquartile range below the first quartile (the bottom of the box) and above the third quartile (the top of the box). If there are no such cases, the whisker ends at the highest or the lowest value (see the lower whisker in Figure 13.13 at the minimum of 0). The cases above and below these whiskers are very far removed from the median. SPSS distinguishes between outliers and extremes:

- *Outliers* are values more than 1.5 times the interquartile range above the 75th percentile (or below the 25th percentile). SPSS marks their positions by a circle and the case number. In Figure 13.13, case 134, among others, is an outlier.
- *Extremes* are values at least 3 times the interquartile range above the 75th percentile or below the 25th percentile. SPSS marks their positions by an asterisk (*) and the case number. In Figure 13.13, case 22 is an extreme.

When multiple outliers and extremes have values lying close together, SPSS shows only one case number. If you transfer the chart to the Chart Editor, by double-clicking it in the Viewer, you can view the numbers in this window with the button Point Identification. (First click Point Identification ('Data Label Mode') and then the relevant points in the boxplot; see Section 6.5 for a more detailed discussion of point identification.)

You can create a boxplot by selecting from the menu:

Graphs

  ➤ Boxplot

Note that you can also create a boxplot with the Explore command (see Section 12.3). Figure 13.14 contains the dialogue box of the Graphs Boxplot command. SPSS distinguishes between the following two boxplot variants:

Figure 13.14   The dialogue box for specifying the basic settings of a boxplot.

- *Simple*: a boxplot for one or more variables or a boxplot for one or more groups of cases. When multiple variables or groups are specified, the boxplot contains a box for each variable or group. For example: the boxplot of TennisWear in Figure 13.13, or a boxplot of the variable Age broken down into the groups of men and of women, or a boxplot of the variables CourtRental (expenditure on court rental) and TennisWear (expenditure on tennis wear).
- *Clustered*: a boxplot in which multiple variables as well as multiple groups of cases are shown. For example: a boxplot with boxes for the variables CourtRental and TennisWear, both broken down into men and women.

A box can refer to a group of cases or to a variable. You can specify this in the lower half of the dialogue box:

- *Summaries for groups of cases*: select this option if the basic division involves groups. For example: a boxplot of the variable Age broken down into the groups of men and of women (variant: Simple), or a boxplot with boxes for the variables CourtRental and TennisWear for men, and then boxes for the same variables for women (variant: Clustered).
- *Summaries of separate variables*: select this option if the basic division involves variables. For example: the boxplot of TennisWear in Figure 13.13 (variant: Simple), or a boxplot of the variables CourtRental and TennisWear (variant: Simple), or a boxplot that first shows the variable CourtRental broken down into men and women, and then the variable TennisWear broken down into men and women (variant: Clustered).

After you have specified the basic settings, you specify the content of the boxplot in the next dialogue box (Figure 13.15 shows an example of this). Here you specify:

- *The variable to be shown in the box*. You specify this variable under 'Boxes Represent' (or 'Variable'). Depending on the boxplot variant you can specify one or more variables.
- *The groups to be distinguished* (if relevant). You specify the grouping variable under 'Category Axis'. It is not possible to further distinguish between subgroups.

By default, the outliers and extremes are labelled with the case number. If you specify a variable under 'Label Cases by' SPSS identifies these cases with the value of this variable.

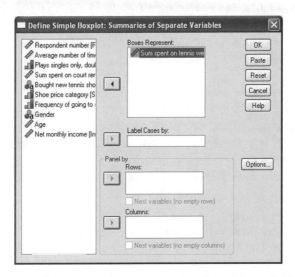

Figure 13.15 *The dialogue box for creating a boxplot of the variable Tennis Wear (with the basic settings 'Simple' and 'Summaries of separate variables').*

13.9   Histograms

In simple terms, a histogram is a bar chart for continuous variables. Continuous variables often have many different values, like Age in years and CourtRental in dollars. In that case, bar charts, in which a bar is shown for each value, are not appropriate. A histogram shows a bar for groups of values.

You can create a histogram by selecting from the menu:[2]

Graphs

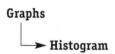

Histogram

Figure 13.16 shows the next dialogue box. Here you specify a variable and indicate whether you want to superimpose a normal distribution in the histogram (by checking the option 'Display normal curve').

SPSS automatically determines the intervals (the groups of values). These are displayed on the horizontal axis (see Figure 13.17); the vertical axis shows the numbers of cases. To the right of the chart you find the standard deviation, the mean and the total number of cases. A normal distribution is superimposed on the histogram, indicating a reasonable match between the distribution of TennisWear and a normal distribution.

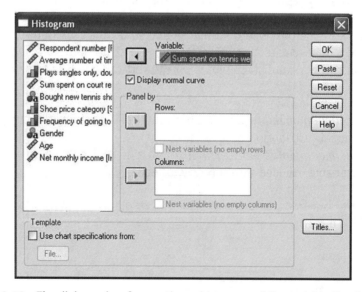

Figure 13.16   The dialogue box for creating a histogram of the variable TennisWear (with a normal distribution superimposed).

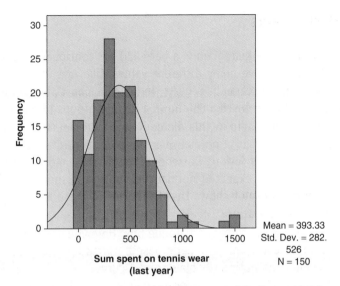

Figure 13.17   The histogram created with the command in Figure 13.16.

13.10   Normal distribution plots

Normal distribution plots show to what extent the observed distribution of a variable approximates the normal distribution. The plot shows the observed distribution as a string of points and the standard normal distribution as a straight line. The closer the points are to the straight line, the better the match between the observed distribution and the normal distribution.

SPSS can create two kinds of normal distribution plots. In both cases the standard normal distribution is on the vertical axis. The horizontal axis varies, namely:

- *normal probability plot*: the horizontal axis contains the cumulative proportional distribution of a variable;
- *normal quantile plot*: the horizontal axis contains the observed values of a variable, divided into intervals of equal widths.

You can find the commands for both plots as follows: for the normal probability plot:

and the normal quantile plot:

Graphs

└─▸ **Q-Q**

Because the dialogue boxes of the two commands are identical, we only discuss the dialogue box for the normal quantile plot. In the simplest case you only specify a variable in this dialogue box (see Figure 13.18). SPSS then produces two variants of a normal quantile plot, a normal plot see Figure 13.19) and a plot with deviations Detrended normal Q-Q plot'; see Figure 13.19). In the first plot, the expected normal distribution is shown on the vertical axis, while the second plot shows the deviations of the observed distribution from the normal distribution.

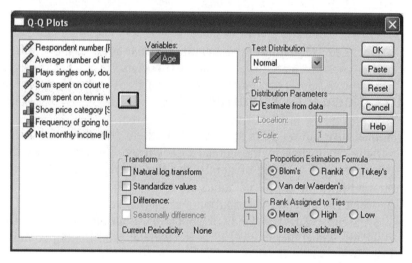

Figure 13.18   The dialogue box for creating a normal quantile plot of the variable Age.

For both variants of the normal quantile plot, the closer the points are to the straight line, the closer the observed distribution is to the normal distribution. As Figure 13.19 shows, the observed distribution of Age rather strongly deviates from the normal distribution. Initially the observed frequency is higher, then it becomes lower and then again considerably higher than that of the standard normal distribution.

The Normal P-P command creates two comparable variants of the normal probability plot.

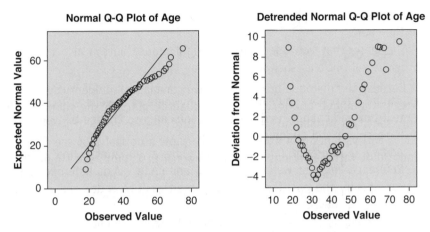

Figure 13.19 The normal (left) and detrended (right) normal quantile plots, both created with the command in Figure 13.18.

If you conclude from the normal distribution plots that the observed distribution does not match the normal distribution, this means that your data do not meet an important assumption of many statistical techniques. Perhaps you can then transform the variable in such a way that it becomes normally distributed. SPSS offers various options, listed in the dialogue box under 'Transform' (see Figure 13.18).

13.11   The Chart Editor

You can use the commands in the Graphs menu to specify which type of chart you want and what information it should show. To change an existing chart, you double-click the chart in the Viewer. The chart is then transferred to the Chart Editor. This window offers many options for changing the elements composing the chart. The use of the Chart Editor in general has been discussed in the session chapters (see Sections 5.6 and 6.5 in particular).

Each chart is composed of various elements (such as bars, a title and a horizontal axis) and each of these elements has a number of properties (like size, colour and lines). You can change the properties of an element in the Properties window. The Properties window is opened by double-clicking an element, or by clicking an element and then pressing the right mouse button (in the next menu, Properties is the first option). The Properties window contains the properties divided into a number of tabs. By going through these tabs, you can easily find the property that you want to change. Do not forget to click

Apply after you have changed a property: only then will the change be implemented in the chart.

The menu that you open with the right mouse button also contains some other useful options, such as:

- *Adding a text box*: you can add text anywhere in the chart. You can drag the text box and change its dimensions; you can also change text properties like font, colour and alignment.
- *Adding a reference line*, which may be a horizontal line ('Add X Axis Reference Line') as well as a vertical line ('Add Y Axis Reference Line'). You can specify the position and the properties (like width and colour) of the line.
- *Interchanging the axes*, with the option 'Transpose Chart'.

Notes

1 In the tennis survey, we distinguished the following types of play: (1) singles only, (2) doubles only and (3) both singles and doubles.
2 You can also create histograms with the Frequencies and Explore commands (see Chapter 11).

14   Crosstables

Crosstables provide an insight into the relationship between two variables, mostly nominal and ordinal variables. Each combination of values yields a cell. This cell usually displays the number of cases that have the corresponding combination of values.

In Section 14.1 we discuss how you can make a simple crosstable with the Crosstabs command. The following sections deal with more advanced options. By default, SPSS displays the number of cases in each cell. However, you can also request other statistics, such as the row percentage or column percentage (see Section 14.2). The chi-square test is often used to determine whether the two variables in the crosstable are independent of each other. Section 14.3 discusses the output of this test. The chi-square test is an independence test that gives little information on the strength and direction of the relationship. For that purpose, several other tests exist that are discussed in Section 14.4. The final section (Section 14.5) deals with the options for changing the format of the table.

14.1   A simple crosstable

Crosstables provide an insight into the relationship between two variables. Do men and women, on average, buy tennis shoes equally often? Do players who play both singles and doubles visit tennis tournaments more often than players who practise only one type of play? To answer this type of question, crosstables are very useful. Their strength is both simplicity (anyone can understand a crosstable) and power (crosstables yield a great deal of information but do not require advanced statistical analyses).

You can use crosstables for category variables in particular, in other words, for nominal and ordinal variables. Continuous variables with many different values often have to be classified (recoded; see Section 9.3) before you can use them in a crosstable.

You can find the Crosstable command in the menu as follows:

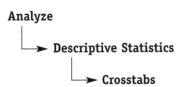

Analyze
  └──▶ **Descriptive Statistics**
          └──▶ **Crosstabs**

In the next dialogue box you specify which variable you want as row variable and which one as column variable. Suppose you are interested in the question whether men and women bought new tennis shoes equally often during the last year. In that case the table has to contain the variables Gender and NewShoe (with the values yes and no). The question then is which variable to use for the rows and which one for the columns. The usual approach is to specify *the independent variable (the cause) as the row variable* and *the dependent variable (the effect) as the column variable*. The reason is that it is easier to compare a series of numbers listed one below the other than next to each other. In this case the independent variable is Gender. The dependent variable is the behaviour that you want to study, in this example buying tennis shoes. After you have specified Gender as the row variable and NewShoe as the column variable, the command is complete (see Figure 14.1).

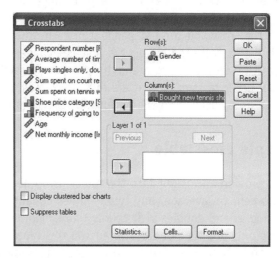

Figure 14.1   The dialogue box of the Crosstabs command, to make a crosstable of the variables Gender and NewShoe.

Besides the overview of the data used (Notes and Active Dataset), the output of Crosstabs consists of two items: an overview of the valid, missing and total cases (Case Processing Summary) and the crosstable itself.

The cells in the crosstable display the numbers of cases and, at the end of each row (and column), the total number of cases in that row (or column; see Table 14.1). As you can see, 42 women reported to have not bought new tennis shoes last year and 29 have. In all, 71 women were interviewed and 79 men. The table shows that both men and women answered No more often than Yes. More women bought new tennis shoes (29) than men (22), although fewer

Table 14.1   The crosstable of Gender and NewShoe, made with the command in Figure 14.1

Gender * Bought new tennis shoes last year? Crosstabulation

Count

| | | Bought new tennis shoes last year? | | Total |
		No	Yes	
Gender	Female	42	29	71
	Male	57	22	79
Total		99	51	150

women were interviewed (71 versus 79, respectively). Therefore, it appears that, on average, women bought new tennis shoes more often than men.

Extensions.
SPSS offers several options for showing more information in the crosstable, or testing whether the variables are independent. Above the crosstable, on the left, you can see how to read the content of the cells. This heading of Table 14.1 displays 'Count', that is, the counted number of cases. With the button Cells you can also display, for example, the row or column percentages in a cell (see Section 14.2).

From Table 14.1 it appears that women buy new tennis shoes more often than men. With a chi-square test you can determine whether this difference is significant (see Section 14.3). Besides this test, Crosstabs offers many more that can be requested with the button Statistics (see Section 14.4). You can change the appearance of the table and the order of the rows with the button Format (see Section 14.5). Finally, the dialogue box Crosstabs offers four more options, namely making multiple crosstables, making a table for each group of cases, requesting bar charts and the option of suppressing a table. We briefly discuss these four options below.

If you only have a crosstable at your disposal but no original data, you can import the table with the Weight command (see the example in Section 10.3).

Multiple crosstables – If you specify more than one variable under Rows and Columns in the dialogue box Crosstabs, SPSS makes crosstables for each row variable with each column variable.

Crosstables for groups – If you specify a variable under Layer in the dialogue box Crosstabs, SPSS makes a separate crosstable for each value of this variable.

Clustered bar chart – Check the option 'Display clustered bar charts' in the dialogue box Crosstabsto request a clustered bar chart with each crosstable.

The command in Figure 14.1 produces a bar chart with four bars: first, two bars for women, corresponding to women who did not and women who did buy new tennis shoes, respectively, and then two bars for men (see Section 13.2 for more information on bar charts).

Suppress crosstable – When you are not interested in the crosstable itself, but only in the bar chart or in the tests specified with the button Statistics, you can avoid displaying crosstables by checking 'Suppress tables' in the dialogue box Crosstabs.

14.2   The cells content

By default, SPSS displays the number of cases in each cell of the crosstable. However, we often need more information. What fraction of the women bought new tennis shoes? What percentage of those who bought tennis shoes are men? With the button Cells you can specify the information displayed in each cell.

Figure 14.2 contains the dialogue box Cells, in which both the number of cases (observed counts) and the row percentages are requested. Table 14.2 shows the output of this command. It turns out that 40.8% of the women and 27.8% of the men bought new tennis shoes last year.

You can display the following information in a cell:

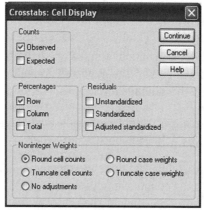

Figure 14.2   The dialogue box for determining the cell contents (the button Cells of the Crosstabs command).

Table 14.2 The crosstable of Gender and NewShoe, made with the command in Figure 14.2

Gender * Bought new tennis shoes last year? Crosstabulation

			Bought new tennis shoes last year?		Total
			No	Yes	
Gender	Female	Count	42	29	71
		% within Gender	59.2%	40.8%	100.0%
	Male	Count	57	22	79
		% within Gender	72.2%	27.8%	100.0%
Total		Count	99	51	150
		% within Gender	66.0%	34.0%	100.0%

1. *Number of cases (Counts)*

   - *Observed*: the default content;
   - *Expected*: the expected or theoretical frequency used for the chi-square test.

2. *Percentages*

   - *Row*: the number of cases in a cell divided by the number of cases in the corresponding row;
   - *Column*: as above for a column;
   - *Total*: the number of cases in a cell divided by the total number of cases in the entire crosstable.

3. *Residuals*

   - *Unstandardized*: the normal residual, that is, the difference between the observed frequency and the expected frequency;
   - *Standardized*: the unstandardised residual divided by an estimate of its standard error;
   - *Adj. standardized*: the standardised residual expressed in standard deviation units above or below the mean.

4. *Weighting.* The crosstable contains the weighted number of cases. If the weighting is not integer, the counts are not integers either. Under 'Noninteger Weights' you can specify how SPSS should then display the counts. SPSS can round or truncate either the number of cases or the weights, or report a non-integer number ('No adjustments').

14.3   The chi-square test

The chi-square test is used to determine whether two nominal variables are *independent* (unrelated). In the example with the variables Gender and NewShoe, the *null hypothesis H$_0$* is that there is no relationship between a respondent's gender and buying tennis shoes. The *alternative hypothesis H$_1$* states that there is a relationship between the two variables (without specifying what this relationship is like).[1] The chi-square test is an independence test that gives little information on the strength or direction of the relation (other tests are available for this; see the following section).

You can request the chi-square test with the button Statistics (the next section shows the dialogue box Statistics). Table 14.3 shows the output of the chi-square test. SPSS computes several chi-squares; the one normally used, the 'ordinary' Pearson chi-square, is shown in the first row.

Table 14.3   *The chi-square test for determining whether Gender and NewShoe are independent*

Chi-Square Tests

	Value	df	Asymp. Sig. (2-sided)	Exact Sig. (2-sided)	Exact Sig. (1-sided)
Pearson Chi-Square	2.815[b]	1	.093		
Continuity Correction [a]	2.265	1	.132		
Likelihood Ratio	2.818	1	.093		
Fisher's Exact Test				.120	.066
N of Valid Cases	150				

a. Computed only for a 2x2 table

b. 0 cells (.0%) have expected count less than 5. The minimum expected count is 24.14.

The first column displays the value of the computed chi-square and the next column the degrees of freedom (df). This number is computed as follows:

(number of rows - 1) * (number of columns - 1)

In the example with two rows and two columns the degrees of freedom therefore equals 1. The column 'Asymp. Sig.' contains the probability that, if two variables are independent, a random sample yields the chi-square computed. This is the significance level, also called the p-value. A value of 0.05 is commonly used as threshold value. The significance level in this example equals 0.093. This means that we *cannot* reject the null hypothesis, which states that there is no relationship between the two variables. Although the crosstable showed that women buy new tennis shoes more often than men, this difference is not large enough to be statistically significant.

The chi-square test compares the observed frequency with the expected or theoretical frequency (SPSS uses the term'. Whether or not the chi-square test may be applied depends, among other things, on the expected frequencies. The chi-square test can be used if the following two assumptions are met:

- all expected frequencies at least equal 1; and
- no more than 20% of the expected frequencies are lower than 5.

To check whether these assumptions are met, SPSS displays the number and percentage of cells with an expected count of less than 5 (below the table, in footnote b) as well as the minimum of the expected count (24.14 in this example). Therefore, in this example the conditions for the chi-square test are met.

With the button Cells you can specify the cell contents; one of the options is the expected frequency (see Section 14.2).

The three other tests in Table 14.3 are called Continuity Correction, Likelihood Ratio and Fisher's Exact Test. The first test refers to the Yates correction for continuity, in which positive differences between observed and expected frequencies are reduced by 0.5 and negative differences increased by 0.5. The Likelihood Ratio chi-square is based on the maximum likelihood theory and for large numbers of cases this leads to results similar to the Pearson chi-square. Fisher's Exact Test is mainly used for very small samples.

14.4   The statistics of crosstabs

With the button Statistics in the dialogue box Crosstabs you can request a large number of statistics. The best known of these is the chi-square discussed in the previous section. Because the chi-square test is only an independence test that gives little information on the strength and the direction of the relationship between two variables, other tests have been developed for this purpose. You can request these tests in the dialogue box Statistics (see Figure 14.3).
For each test, SPSS displays the value of the coefficient and the corresponding significance level. The dialogue box Statistics offers the following options:

- *Chi-square*: the Pearson chi-square and the Likelihood Ratio chi-square (see Section 14.2). For a 2 × 2 table the Yates correction for continuity and Fisher's Exact Test are also computed. If both variables are numeric, the Mantel–Haenszel chi-square is displayed (indicated as 'Linear-by-linear association test'). This is a measure of the strength of linear correlation between two ordinal variables (and is computed as the square of the Pearson correlation coefficient multiplied by the number of cases minus 1).

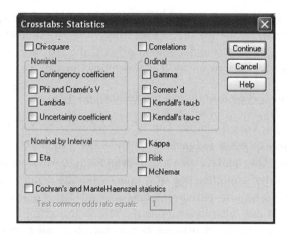

Figure 14.3   The dialogue box for requesting statistics that provide information on the strength and direction of the association between two variables (the button Statistics of the Crosstabs command).

- *Correlations*: the Pearson correlation coefficient, the measure of linear correlation used for interval and ratio variables, and the Spearman correlation coefficient for ordinal variables.

The following measures provide information about the strength of correlation between two nominal variables:

- *Contingency coefficient*.
- *Phi and Cramér's V*.
- *Lambda*: SPSS displays the lambda, both symmetric and asymmetric, and the Goodman & Kruskal tau. First one variable is treated as the dependent variable and then the other.
- *Uncertainty coefficient*: symmetric and asymmetric.

Besides the Mantel–Haenszel chi-square and the Spearman correlation coefficient mentioned above, you can request the following measures to obtain an insight into the strength of association between two ordinal variables:

- *Goodman & Kruskal's gamma*;
- *Somer's d*: symmetric and asymmetric;
- *Kendall's tau-b*: can return the extremes −1 and +1 only for square tables;
- *Kendall's tau-c*: can return the extremes −1 and +1 for any table.

If the dependent variable is interval and the independent variable nominal or ordinal:

- *Eta*.

Finally, you can request the following tests:

- *Kappa*: Cohen's kappa coefficient reflects the agreement between two raters who express a judgement on the same object.
- *Risk*: the relative risk ratio expresses to what extent there is association between the presence of a factor and the occurrence of an event.
- *McNemar*: non-parametric test for two dichotomous variables, often used in situations with measurements before and after.
- *Cochran's and Maentzel statistics*: provide insight into the association between two dichotomous variables, particularly useful when you distinguish several groups.

14.5   Format for specifying the order of the rows

With the button Format you can change the order of the rows. The dialogue box offers the following two options:

- *Ascending*: the rows are displayed in ascending order, from the lowest to the highest value (default);
- *Descending*: the rows are displayed in descending order, from the highest to the lowest value.

Note

1 You can also use the chi-square analysis to test whether a sample is representative with respect to a certain variable (see Section 19.1).

15 Analysing multiple responses

Multiple response data occur when you have asked a question for which respondents can choose multiple answer categories. Suppose that you are studying the attendance to cultural manifestations. The questionnaire contains a list of manifestations like exhibitions, concerts, theatrical and ballet performances, and the respondents are asked to indicate which type of cultural manifestation they attend. Each respondent can then give more than one answer. Another example is that you submit a large number of statements to respondents and ask them whether they agree with these. Analysing multiple responses often ends up in a (too) large number of frequency tables and crosstables. With the Multiple Response command you can make one compact frequency table (or crosstable), showing the frequency of a single category for each of a series of variables. Usually, this is the category 'Yes' or 'Agree'. This results in compact and convenient information.

To carry out multiple response analyses, you first need to specify a set of variables. The set contains all variables that you want to analyse together (see Section 15.1). If you entered the data with Data Entry, SPSS has automatically made a set (see Section 7.1.1). With sets of variables you can perform two types of analysis, that is, make frequency tables and crosstables. These are discussed in Sections 15.2 and 15.3, respectively.

15.1 Specifying a multiple response set

Suppose that the tennis survey contains three statements concerning tennis on television. For each statement, the respondent is asked whether he agrees or disagrees. The statements are the following:

- Statement 1. I watch a tennis match on television every week.
- Statement 2. When an important tennis match is on, I stay home to watch.
- Statement 3. I prefer watching tennis to watching football.

The answers are coded as 0 (disagree) and 1 (agree). You can combine the three statements (variables) into a multiple response set with the Multiple Response command.

You can find the command for defining Multiple Response sets in the menu as follows:

Analyze

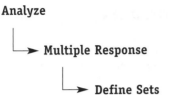

In the next dialogue box you can define the set (see Figure 15.1). The definition consists of three parts. Under 'Variables in Set' you specify the names of the variables that belong to the set (in this example Statement1, Statement2 and Statement3). Under 'Variables Are Coded As' you specify the value(s) of a variable that you want to count. There are two possibilities: for dichotomous variables, having only two values, you specify the value to count. In the example this is the value 1, the code for agreeing with a statement. For non-dichotomous variables you specify the range of the values to be included. The third and last part of the definition concerns the name and label of the set.

When you have specified the complete definition, click the button Add to include the set in the list of defined sets. The name of the new set is shown in the list, preceded by a dollar sign.

If you wish to define more sets, you may do so; if not, exit the dialogue box with the button Close. In the next two sections we discuss the use of multiple response sets.

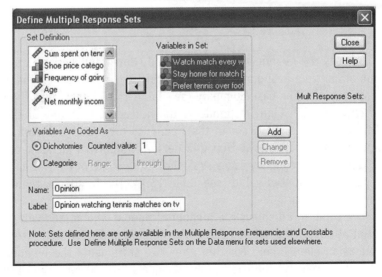

Figure 15.1   The dialogue box for defining multiple response sets.

15.2   Making a frequency table for a set

To obtain a compact overview of the answers to the various questions in a multiple response set, a frequency table is a useful tool. You can make this as follows:

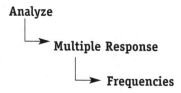

Analyze

⌞➤ **Multiple Response**

⌞➤ **Frequencies**

In the dialogue box Multiple Response Frequencies you indicate for which set you require a table (see Figure 15.2). You find the list of defined sets under 'Mult Response Sets'. The sets for which you require a frequency table appear under 'Table(s) for'. In this case we request a frequency table for the only available set, $Opinion.

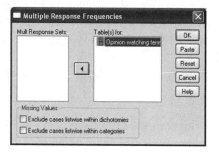

Figure 15.2   The dialogue box for requesting a frequency table of a multiple response set.

Besides the overview of the data used (Notes and Active Dataset), the output of Multiple Response Frequencies consists of a Case Summary and the frequency table. The Case Summary (see Table 15.1) shows that the total number of cases is 150. Eight respondents did not agree with any of the statements. This group does not occur in the frequency table and is therefore reported as missing cases. It follows that 142 persons agree with at least one statement.

Above the frequency table SPSS shows the name of the set and the footnote reports the counted value (see Table 15.2). The frequency table contains one row for each variable.

The column N displays the number of people who agreed with a given statement. In all, 98 people agreed with the statement 'I watch a tennis match on television every week'. For the other two statements the numbers are 78 and 105, respectively. The total under N equals 281; at maximum this could have been 450 (3*150).

Table 15.1   The Case Summary showing the numbers of valid and missing cases, made with the command in Figure 15.2

Case Summary

	Cases					
	Valid		Missing		Total	
	N	Percent	N	Percent	N	Percent
$Opinion [a]	142	94.7%	8	5.3%	150	100.0%

[a]. Dichotomy group tabulated at value 1.

Table 15.2   The frequency table made with the command in Figure 15.2

$Opinion Frequencies

		Responses		Percent of Cases
		N	Percent	
Opinion watching tennis matches [a] on tv	Watch match every week	98	34.9%	69.0%
	Stay home for match	78	27.8%	54.9%
	Prefer tennis over football	105	37.4%	73.9%
Total		281	100.0%	197.9%

[a]. Dichotomy group tabulated at value 1.

The column 'Percent' shows the percentage of people who agreed with a statement compared with the total number of times that respondents agreed with a statement. For the first statement, therefore, the percentage 34.9% is computed as 98/281. If this percentage exceeds 33% for any of the three statements, agreement with that statement is above average.

The column 'Percent of Cases' displays the percentage with respect to the total number of valid cases. For the first statement, 69.0% is computed as 98/142.

15.3   Making a crosstable with a set

You can also relate the answers to the various components of a multiple response set to another variable in a crosstable. You can make such a table as follows:

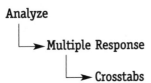

Analyze
→ Multiple Response
→ Crosstabs

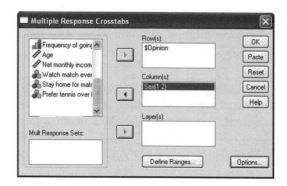

Figure 15.3   The dialogue box for requesting a crosstable of the multiple response set $Opinion and the variable Sex.

In the dialogue box Multiple Response Crosstabs you specify which set you want to relate to which variable (see Figure 15.3). The left-hand part of the dialogue box shows the list of variables and the list of defined sets. You have to specify at least one item (variable or set) for the rows and one item for the columns. In this example, we select the set $Opinion for the rows and the variable Sex for the columns. Note that you can only include numeric variables in the crosstable.[1] String variables are therefore omitted from the list of variables.

Next, you specify the range of values of Sex you want to include in the table with the button Define Ranges. In this example the range runs from 1 (Female) to 2 (Male).

Besides the overview of the data used (Notes and Active Dataset), the output of Multiple Response Crosstabs consists of a Case Summary (similar to Table 15.1) and the crosstable (see Table 15.3). In the crosstable the numbers of persons agreeing with a statement are broken down into women and men. The table shows that the group that agrees with the first statement (98 persons) con-

Table 15.3   The crosstable made with the command in Figure 15.3

$Opinion*Sex Crosstabulation

			Sex		Total
			Female	Male	
Opinion watching tennis matches[a] on tv	Watch match every week	Count	48	50	98
	Stay home for match	Count	42	36	78
	Prefer tennis over football	Count	47	58	105
Total		Count	67	75	142

Percentages and totals are based on respondents.

[a] Dichotomy group tabulated at value 1.

tains about equal numbers of women and men, namely 48 and 50. The two other statements show larger differences between women and men. Below the table you see that a total of 67 women agree with at least one of the statements, as against 75 men.

The button Options in the dialogue box Multiple Response Crosstabs offers various options for customising the content of the table (see Figure 15.4). Besides the number of cases you can also display percentages in the cells, based on the row totals (Row), the column totals (Column) and the table totals (Total). These numbers are based on the number of cases (142 in our example) or on the number of responses counted (98 + 78 + 105 = 281 in this case).

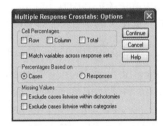

Figure 15.4   *The dialogue box for displaying percentages in the cells (the button Options of the Multiple Response Crosstabs command).*

Note

1 If you intend to use a string variable you can transform this variable into a numeric variable with Automatic Recode. In this example this has been done for the string variable Gender, resulting in the new numeric variable Sex.

16   Describing groups and testing the differences

In this chapter we discuss four commands useful for investigating differences between groups of cases, for example between men and women. All applications involve differences in interval or ratio variables. Means, discussed in Section 16.1, is particularly suitable for describing groups. This command produces a variety of statistics for each group, such as the mean, minimum, maximum and variance.

The other three commands are variants of the t-test, the technique that tests for the significance of a difference between two groups. (For more than two groups you can use analysis of variance; see Chapter 17.) In the first variant the sample mean is tested against another mean with *One-Sample T Test* (see Section 16.2). The other two variants of the t-test are based on two random samples. The first assumes that the cases belong to two independent random samples, the *Independent-Samples T Test* (see Section 16.3). Sometimes the two samples are not independent, but the cases form pairs. In that case you use the *Paired-Samples T Test* (see Section 16.4).

16.1   Describing groups with Means

Many studies distinguish between groups and you then investigate how these groups score on a number of variables. Groups can be men and women, or people who bought tennis shoes from the price categories 1, 2 or 3. It could be interesting to find out how often these groups play tennis, how much they spend on tennis wear, how old they are, and so on. The Means command is particularly suitable for presenting group summaries. The command produces statistics like the mean and variance for each group.

The variable that determines the grouping is called the *independent variable*; in the examples above, the independent variables are Gender and ShoePrice. The independent variable is almost always a nominal or ordinal variable. The variables for which you request statistics are called the *dependent variables*; in the examples above TimesTennis, TennisWear and Age. The dependent variables are almost always interval or ratio variables. (If the dependent variable is nominal or ordinal, you use a crosstable.)

You can find the Means command in the menu as follows:

Analyze

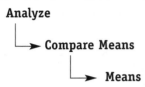

In the next dialogue box you specify the dependent and independent variables. Suppose that you want to study the relationship between the type of play (singles, doubles, or both) and the amount of money spent on tennis wear. In that case, the variable SingleDouble is the independent variable and TennisWear the dependent variable (see Figure 16.1).

Figure 16.1   *The dialogue box of the Means command for requesting statistics of the variable TennisWear for each value of the variable SingleDouble.*

Besides the overview of the data used (Notes and Active Dataset), the output of Means consists of two parts: an overview of valid, missing and total cases (Case Processing Summary), and a table containing the statistics (Report) (see Table 16.1).

Table 16.1   *The table with the group statistics made with the Means command in Figure 16.1*

Report

Sum spent on tennis wear (last year)

Plays singles only,	Mean	N	Std. Deviation
Singles only	368.18	22	216.875
Doubles only	433.33	48	309.655
Singles and doubles	376.25	80	282.056
Total	393.33	150	282.526

For each group SPSS shows the mean, the number of cases and the standard deviation. In this example there are three groups: singles only, doubles only and both types of play. As you can see, the mean expenditure on tennis wear in the group who only play doubles (433 dollars) clearly exceeds the amounts spent by the other two groups (368 and 376 dollars, respectively). The bottom row contains the statistics for all cases ('Total'). You see that the mean expenditure on tennis wear per person equals 393 dollars.

Extensions.

Means includes three extensions. If you specify multiple dependent variables, SPSS computes the statistics for each dependent variable based on the same grouping. You can also distinguish between subgroups (see Section 16.1.1) and request statistics other than the mean and the standard deviation, with the button Options (see Section 16.1.2).

16.1.1 Distinguishing between subgroups

You can further split up the groups into subgroups by specifying a second independent variable. In the example above you may wonder whether the respondent's gender influences the amount spent on tennis wear. You specify the division into subgroups as follows. In the dialogue box you indicate that you want another layer, by clicking Next Layer. Then you select a variable for the second layer, in this case the variable Gender. Table 16.2 shows the output of this command.

Table 16.2   A table with both group statistics and subgroup statistics made with the Means command

Report

Sum spent on tennis wear (last year)

Plays singles only.	Gender	Mean	N	Std. Deviation
Singles only	Female	360.00	10	201.108
	Male	375.00	12	237.888
	Total	368.18	22	216.875
Doubles only	Female	500.00	23	386.123
	Male	372.00	25	207.204
	Total	433.33	48	309.655
Singles and doubles	Female	439.47	38	304.506
	Male	319.05	42	250.110
	Total	376.25	80	282.056
Total	Female	447.89	71	321.096
	Male	344.30	79	234.109
	Total	393.33	150	282.526

The output first shows the statistics for each subgroup, then for each group and finally for all cases. Within each group, there are two subgroups (female and male). You see that the mean expenditure on tennis wear by women who only play singles is 360 dollars, while men who only play singles spend 375 dollars. The table shows that the high mean for the group who only play doubles only (433 dollars) is entirely due to the women in this group. The mean for men (372 dollars) is even below the overall mean (393 dollars), while women who only play doubles spent, on average, 500 dollars on tennis wear.

When you specify the variable that defines the subgroup (in this example Gender), it is essential that you first click the button Next Layer. If you do not, SPSS places the variable Gender in the list of independent variables below SingleDouble. In that case, SPSS assumes that you want statistics for TennisWear based on two separate groupings (SingleDouble and Gender). You will then get two tables, similar to the output in Table 16.1.

16.1.2 Requesting statistics with Options

With the button Options you can specify which statistics the output should contain. The dialogue box Options consists of two parts: the upper part shows a list of statistics, and below that you see two overview tables that can only be requested for the first layer (that is, at group level) (see Figure 16.2).

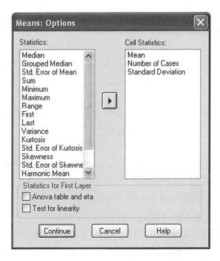

Figure 16.2   *The dialogue box for determining which group statistics you want (the button Options of the Means command). The selected statistics are the default ones.*

The statistics for each (sub)group are the following:

- *Mean* (default)
- *Number of Cases*: number of valid cases (default)
- *Standard Deviation* (default)
- *Median*: the middle case
- *Grouped Median*: the median in case the data have been coded as the central value of a group (e.g. 15 as the code for the group from 10 to 20)
- *Std. Error of Mean*: the standard error of the mean
- *Sum*
- *Minimum*
- *Maximum*
- *Range*: the difference between maximum and minimum
- *First*: the first value in a group
- *Last*: the last value in a group
- *Variance*
- *Kurtosis*
- *Std. Error of Kurtosis*: the standard error of the kurtosis
- *Skewness*: the measure of asymmetry of the distribution
- *Std. Error of Skewness*: the standard error of the skewness
- *Harmonic Mean*: estimate of the mean group size for groups with unequal numbers of cases
- *Geometric Mean*: computed as the nth root of the product of all values (n is the number of cases)
- *Percent of Total Sum*: the group sum divided by the overall sum (that is, the sum of all cases), expressed as a percentage
- *Percent of Total N*: the number of cases in a group divided by the total number of cases, expressed as a percentage.

Statistics at group level. These are the statistics that SPSS displays only for the first layer, that is, the group level:

- *ANOVA table and eta*: an analysis of variance with one independent variable. The output is similar to that of the One-Way ANOVA command (see Chapter 17) and also contains an eta (that measures the degree of association between the dependent and the independent variable).
- *Test of linearity*: similar output, assuming a linear relationship between the two variables. The table also contains a Pearson correlation coefficient and an R^2.

16.2   Testing the sample mean against a specified value

You can use the t-test for one sample to determine whether *the sample mean matches some other value*. That other value could be a norm, the national mean or the outcome of another survey. By analysing whether the mean age in the sample differs from the mean age of all members of a tennis club you obtain information on the representativeness of the sample. In a steel factory where sheets of steel are cut, the mean length of a sheet should not deviate from the specified norm. With the t-test for one random sample you can determine whether this is the case. This test always involves the mean of an interval or ratio variable, assuming that the cases come from a random sample from a normally distributed population. The *null hypothesis* H_0 states that the sample mean equals the specified value. The *alternative hypothesis* H_1 states that the mean differs from this value. However, if you suspect that the sample mean differs from the specified value in some direction, the alternative hypothesis is that the sample mean is higher (or lower) than the specified value.

Comparable tests. The one-sample t-test can give information on the representativeness of the sample. If the sample is representative, its mean has to equal the mean of the population. However, if the means do not differ, the sample is not necessarily representative. Also important is whether the distribution of the sample matches the distribution of the population. You can determine this with the chi-square test, where you can test whether the observed distribution matches an expected distribution that you specify yourself (see Section 19.1).

If your data do not meet the assumptions of the t-test (interval or ratio variables and normally distributed), you have to switch to a non-parametric test. With the sign test, for example, you can determine whether the median of the sample matches a specified value; see Section 19.7.

You can find the command for the t-test for one sample in the menu as follows:

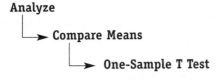

Analyze
    → **Compare Means**
        → **One-Sample T Test**

In the next dialogue box you specify two items, namely the variable whose mean you want to test (the 'Test Variable') and the value to be compared with

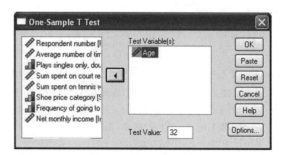

Figure 16.3   The dialogue box of the One-Sample T Test command for testing whether the mean of Age matches 32.

the sample mean (the 'Test Value'). Suppose that we know from a large nation-wide study that the mean age of tennis players is 32 years. Figure 16.3 shows the test to determine whether the sample mean matches this value.

Besides the overview of the data used (Notes and Active Dataset), the output of One-Sample T Test consists of a description of the analysed variable (One-Sample Statistics; see Table 16.3) and the results of the t-test (One-Sample Test; see Table 16.4).

The top row in this table shows that the sample mean is tested against the specified value of 32. Below this you see the results of the t-test. These include the t-value (1.202), the degrees of freedom (the number of cases minus 1; in this example 150 − 1) and the significance level for a two-tailed test. This significance level, or p-value, (0.231) in this example is higher than the usual threshold value 0.05. This means that we cannot reject the null hypothesis. In other words, there is no reason to assume that the sample mean differs from 32.

The last part of the table gives further information on the differences between the sample mean and the test value. The mean difference is 1.20 (computed as 33.2 − 32). The 95% confidence interval of the differences, which ranges from −0.77 to 3.17, is another way to find out whether we can

Table 16.3   The first part of the output of the One-Sample T Test command that describes the test variable

One-Sample Statistics

	N	Mean	Std. Deviation	Std. Error Mean
Age	150	33.20	12.226	.998

Table 16.4   The second part of the output of the One-Sample T Test command with the results of the t-test

One-Sample Test

	Test Value = 32					
					95% Confidence Interval of the Difference	
				Mean		
	t	df	Sig. (2-tailed)	Difference	Lower	Upper
Age	1.202	149	.231	1.200	-.77	3.17

accept or reject the null hypothesis. Since this interval includes the value 0, we do not reject the null hypothesis.

Extensions.
One-Sample T Test has two extensions. If you specify more than one test variable, SPSS performs a t-test for each test variable, compared with the same test value. With Options you can specify the confidence interval and define how SPSS has to treat missing values (see Section 16.2.1).

16.2.1 Preferred settings with Options
The button Options offers the following (see Figure 16.4):

- *Confidence interval*: to specify the preferred confidence interval (default is 95%).

To specify how SPSS should treat missing values when you request t-tests for multiple test variables:

- *Exclude cases analysis by analysis*: for each t-test, SPSS separately determines which cases have valid values for the variable in question.
- *Exclude cases listwise*: SPSS only uses those cases that have valid values for all specified test variables. The same set of cases is used for each t-test.

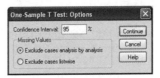

Figure 16.4   The dialogue box of the button Options of the One-Sample T Test command. The selected statistics are the default settings.

16.3   Testing means for two groups: the t-test

You can use the t-test for two groups to determine whether the *means of two groups are equal*. Do men and women, on average, spend equal amounts of money on tennis wear? Do people who only play singles on average pay equal amounts for court rental as people who only play doubles? With the t-test you can obtain the answer to these questions. The test always involves the means of an interval or ratio variable, where the assumption is that, for both groups, the cases belong to random samples from a normally distributed population. The *null hypothesis* H_0 states that the two means are equal. The *alternative hypothesis* H_1 can be formulated in two ways. In the first case we assume that the means are not equal. In the second case we assume that the mean for one of the groups is higher and the alternative hypothesis explicitly states that the mean of group 1 is higher (or lower) than that of group 2.

Comparable tests. In the examples above, the two groups were independent of each other. Sometimes, however, there is a relationship between the groups. Suppose that you interviewed couples who play tennis. You can then investigate whether, on average, the husbands spend the same amount of money on tennis wear as their wives. In that case, you have to use the *paired t-test* (see Section 16.4). This is also true in situations where the same persons have been interviewed at two different times, for example before and after a certain event, and where you are interested whether the means of the two measurements are equal.

If your data do not meet the assumptions of the t-test (interval or ratio variables and normally distributed), you have to use other tests. For nominal variables you can use the *chi-square test* (see Section 14.3) and for ordinal variables the *Mann–Whitney test* or the *Kolmogorov–Smirnov test* (see Section 19.5).

You can find the command for the t-test for two independent groups in the menu as follows:

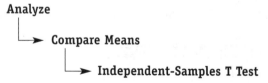

Analyze
    └─▶ **Compare Means**
            └─▶ **Independent-Samples T Test**

In the next dialogue box you specify the variable whose means you want to test and the one that determines the grouping. Suppose you assume that people who only play singles spend more money on court rental than people who only play doubles. After all, when playing singles, two persons pay for the court rental, for doubles the same cost is split among four persons. In this example the variable CourtRental is the test variable and SingleDouble the grouping variable (see Figure 16.5).

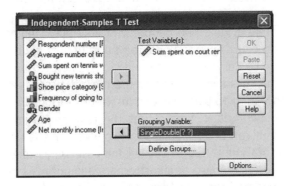

Figure 16.5 *The dialogue box of the t-test for two independent groups.*
The mean expenditures of CourtRental are tested for two groups
determined by the variable SingleDouble.

The next step is to specify which two groups you distinguish (in Figure 16.5 you see that SingleDouble is still followed by two question marks). The button Define Groups leads to a dialogue box in which you can specify the two groups. Singles only is code 1, doubles only is code 2 (see Figure 16.6). The command is now ready to be executed.

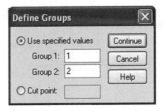

Figure 16.6 *The dialogue box for specifying the two groups (the button*
Define Groups of the Independent-Samples T Test command).

Besides the overview of the data used (Notes and Active Dataset), the output of Independent-Samples T Test consists of a description of the two groups (Group Statistics) and the results of the t-test (Independent Samples Test).

Table 16.5 shows that, on average, people who only play singles spend 1023 dollars on court rental, while people who play doubles spend 626 dollars. This is a difference of almost 400 dollars. Together with the standard deviations of the two means and the numbers of cases in the groups, the difference between the means determines the outcome of the t-test.

Table 16.5   Descriptive statistics for the two groups that are compared

Group Statistics

	Plays singles only, doubles only or both	N	Mean	Std. Deviation	Std. Error Mean
Sum spent on court rental (last year)	Singles only	22	1022.73	776.060	165.456
	Doubles only	48	626.25	463.133	66.847

Table 16.6 shows whether the difference between the means is significant. As you can see, SPSS performs two different t-tests, depending on the assumption about the variances of the groups. You can assume that the variances in the two populations are equal, or that they are not. SPSS tests this assumption with the Levene test. The null hypothesis H0 of the Levene test is that the variances of the two populations are equal. This test computes the difference between each case and the group mean and then performs an analysis of variance on the differences. The result of the test is shown as an F-value with a corresponding significance level. A very low significance level, lower than 0.05, leads to the rejection of the null hypothesis of equal variances. In this example the significance level equals 0.003. We therefore reject the null hypothesis of equal variances and use the results of the t-test that does not assume that the variances are equal (the Unequal Variance method). Note that the difference between the results of the Equal Variance and Unequal Variance methods becomes progressively smaller for larger samples.

Table 16.6   The output of the t-test (for two independent groups)

Independent Samples Test

		Levene's Test for Equality of Variances		t-test for Equality of Means					95% Confidence Interval of the Difference	
		F	Sig.	t	df	Sig. (2-tailed)	Mean Difference	Std. Error Difference	Lower	Upper
Sum spent on court rental (last year)	Equal variances assumed	9.635	.003	2.664	68	.010	396.477	148.851	99.451	693.504
	Equal variances not assumed			2.222	28.081	.035	396.477	178.450	30.986	761.968

The output of the Unequal Variance method is shown in the bottom row of Table 16.6. First you see the t-value (2.22). The t-value is computed based on the variances within the two groups.[1] The variances within the two groups are also used to compute the degrees of freedom.[2]

Next you find the significance level for a two-tailed test. The alternative hypothesis determines the choice between one-tailed and two-tailed testing. The null hypothesis in both cases states that the two sample means do not differ. The alternative hypothesis states that, for one-tailed testing, the mean in one group is higher than in the other group. For two-tailed testing the alternative hypothesis states that the means of the two groups differ, without stating a priori which group has a higher mean. The significance level computed by SPSS relates to two-tailed testing; for a one-tailed test you have to divide this value by 2.

In this example we compare the amounts spent on court rental by people who play only singles and by those who play only doubles. It seems plausible that, on average, people who play only doubles spend less on court rental, because the doubles players can split the cost of court rental among four persons. In this case we therefore perform a one-tailed test, and divide the significance level of 0.035 by 2. This leads to a one-tailed significance level of 0.0175.

The significance level (or p-value) is the probability that the observed difference between the two groups is found for random samples of this size if in reality both population means are equal. This probability therefore refers to wrongly rejecting the null hypothesis. It is common practice to reject the null hypothesis of equal group means if the significance level is below 0.05. In this example the significance level is clearly lower than 0.05 and we therefore reject the null hypothesis of equal means. Because, moreover, the mean for the singles players (1023) is higher than that for the doubles players (626), we accept the alternative hypothesis: on average, people who play only singles spend significantly more money on court rental than people who play only doubles.

The last three columns contain information on the differences between the two groups, namely the standard error (Std. Error Difference) and the 95% confidence interval for the difference between the means. If we use an a of 0.05, this confidence interval forms an alternative way of assessing the outcome of the t-test: we accept the null hypothesis of equal means in the two populations if the 95% confidence interval contains the value zero. (You can specify the confidence interval with Options; see Section 16.2.1.)

If the Levene test leads to acceptance of the null hypothesis of equal variances in the two populations, you have to use the t-test according to the Equal Variance method. This method does not use the variances of the two separate groups in computing the t-value, but the 'pooled' variance instead. This variance is computed based on the variances in the two groups, each weighted by the number of cases in the group. In this case you can easily compute the number of degrees of freedom as the sum of the numbers of cases in the two groups minus 2 (22 + 48 − 2 = 68).

Extensions.
The t-test command includes various extensions. If you specify more than one test variable, SPSS performs a t-test for each test variable. You can also use continuous variables for the specification of the two groups that you distinguish (see Section 16.3.1). Finally, you can use the button Options to specify the confidence interval and how SPSS should treat missing values (see Section 16.2.1).

16.3.1 Specifying the groups

With the button Define Groups in the dialogue box 'Independent-Samples T Test' you can specify the two groups (see Figure 16.6). There are two ways of specifying a group classification:

- *Use specified values:* specify which value of the grouping variable forms the first group and which value forms the second group. Cases with other values of the grouping variable are excluded.
- *Cut point:* specify the value of the grouping variable that separates the two groups (the cutoff value). Group 1 is formed by the values higher than or equal to the cut point. Group 2 consists of the values below the cut point.

16.4   The paired t-test

Like the ordinary t-test, the paired t-test determines whether *the means of two groups are equal*. The difference is that with the paired t-test the two groups do not form independent random samples. The cases in the two groups are related. A good example is when you have interviewed couples who play tennis and want to analyse the differences between husbands and wives. Another application of the paired t-test is when you are dealing with before and after measurements. For example, the same persons are asked the same questions before and after an event. You can then use the paired t-test to find out whether (on average) respondents have changed their opinions. The paired t-test is similar in many respects to the t-test for independent random samples. Therefore, the discussion in this section is considerably shorter.

Suppose that you want to test the hypothesis that, on average, wives spend more money on tennis wear than their husbands. The null hypothesis H_0 states that the two means are equal. In this case the alternative hypothesis H_1 states that the mean for the wives is higher than that for their husbands. In other words, this is a form of one-tailed testing (see Section 16.3). (In a two-tailed test, the alternative hypothesis would have been: the means for husbands and wives are different.)

You can find the command for the paired t-test in the menu as follows:

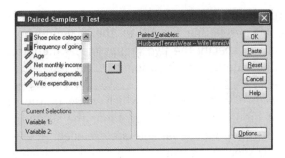

Figure 16.7 *The dialogue box of the Paired Samples T Test command. The test is whether the mean tennis wear expenditures of husbands and wives are equal.*

In the next dialogue box you specify the two variables that form a pair. In this example the variable HusbandTennisWear contains the sums spent by the husbands on tennis wear, while WifeTennisWear contains the same information for the wives. When you click a variable in the list of variables it is displayed under 'Current Selections'. When you have selected two variables, the arrow button will be highlighted and you can place the pair in the overview of 'Paired Variables'. The command is now ready for execution (see Figure 16.7).

Besides the overview of the data used (Notes and Active Dataset), the output of Paired-Samples T Test consists of a description of the two groups (Paired Samples Statistics), the Pearson correlation coefficient between the two variables (Paired Samples Correlations) and the results of the t-test (Paired Samples Test).

Table 16.7 contains an overview of the differences between husbands and wives. In all, 150 couples were interviewed and, on average, husbands spend almost 365 dollars on tennis wear and wives 422 dollars. From Table 16.8 it appears that there is a strong correlation between spouses: the correlation coefficient between HusbandTennisWear and WifeTennisWear is as high as 0.996. In other words, for couples where the husbands spend a lot of money

Table 16.7 *The first part of the output of the paired t-test with descriptive statistics for the two groups.*

Paired Samples Statistics

		Mean	N	Std. Deviation	Std. Error Mean
Pair 1	Husband expenditures tenniswear	364.8933	150	280.84358	22.93078
	Wife expenditures tenniswear	422.0067	150	282.95752	23.10338

Table 16.8   The second part of the output of the paired t-test showing the correlation between the two groups

Paired Samples Correlations

		N	Correlation	Sig.
Pair 1	Husband expenditures tenniswear & Wife expenditures tenniswear	150	.996	.000

on tennis wear (on average, compared with other husbands), the wives on average also spend a lot on tennis wear (compared with other wives). The significance level (0.000 under 'Sig.') shows that the correlation coefficient clearly differs from zero. The correlation coefficient indicates of the effectiveness of applying the paired t-test. If the correlation between the two variables is low, you might as well have considered each observation of a husband and his wife as separate cases (and applied a t-test for independent samples; see Section 16.3). The closer the correlation coefficient is to 1, the greater the advantage of conducting a paired t-test.

Finally, Table 16.9 contains the results of the paired t-test. The first part describes the differences found within pairs. As you can see, the mean difference between husbands and wives amounts to 57 dollars. The minus sign (−57.11) indicates that the first group (husbands) has a lower score than the second group (wives). SPSS also reports the 95% confidence interval of the difference. This gives a good indication of the outcome of the paired t-test: if this interval contains zero we will accept the null hypothesis that there are no differences between the spouses.

Table 16.9   The third part of the output of the paired t-test with the results of the t-test

Paired Samples Test

		Paired Differences							
				Std. Error Mean	95% Confidence Interval of the Difference		t	df	Sig. (2-tailed)
		Mean	Std. Deviation		Lower	Upper			
Pair 1	Husband expenditures tenniswear - Wife expenditures tenniswear	-57.11333	25.09647	2.04912	-61.16242	-53.06425	-27.872	149	.000

The last part of the output contains the result of the paired t-test. The t-value is computed based on the mean difference between the two variables, the standard deviation of the differences and the number of pairs. The degrees of freedom equal the number of pairs minus 1. Finally, the table contains the significance level for two-tailed testing (see Section 16.3 for the interpretation).

In this example we have to divide the significance level by 2 because we apply a one-tailed test. Given the displayed significance level (0.000) it is clear that we reject the null hypothesis of equal means. We conclude that wives spend significantly more money on tennis wear than their husbands.

Extensions.

By specifying multiple pairs in the list of paired variables, you can perform a number of paired t-tests. Furthermore, the dialogue box of the paired t-test contains the button Options. You can use this button to specify the confidence interval and how SPSS should treat missing values (see Section 16.2.1).

Notes

1 In the Unequal Variance method, the *t*-value is computed as follows:

$$t = \frac{\bar{x}_1 - \bar{x}_2}{\sqrt{\dfrac{S_1^2}{N_1} + \dfrac{S_2^2}{N_2}}}. \text{ In the example: } t = \frac{1023 - 626}{\sqrt{\dfrac{776^2}{22} + \dfrac{463^2}{48}}} = 2.22$$

$\bar{x}_1, \bar{x}_2 =$ the means of groups 1 and 2, respectively
$S_1^2, S_2^2 =$ the variances of groups 1 and 2, respectively
$N_1, N_2 =$ the numbers of cases in groups 1 and 2, respectively

2 In the Unequal Variance method, the degrees of freedom are computed as follows (see preceding footnote for the meanings of the symbols):

$$\text{Degrees of freedom} = \frac{\left(\dfrac{S_1^2}{N_1} + \dfrac{S_2^2}{N_2}\right)^2}{\dfrac{\left(\dfrac{S_1^2}{N_1}\right)^2}{N_1 - 1} + \dfrac{\left(\dfrac{S_2^2}{N_2}\right)^2}{N_2 - 1}}. \text{ In the example: } \frac{\left(\dfrac{776^2}{22} + \dfrac{463^2}{48}\right)^2}{\dfrac{\left(\dfrac{776^2}{22}\right)^2}{22 - 1} + \dfrac{\left(\dfrac{463^2}{48}\right)^2}{48 - 1}} = 28.08$$

3 In the Equal Variance method, the 'pooled' variance S_p and the *t*-value are computed as follows (see preceding footnote for the meanings of the symbols):

$$S_p^2 = \frac{(N_1 - 1) \times S_1^2 + (N_2 - 1) \times S_2^2}{N_1 + N_2 - 2}; \quad t = \frac{\bar{x}_1 - \bar{x}_2}{\sqrt{\dfrac{S_p^2}{N_1} + \dfrac{S_p^2}{N_2}}}$$

In the example:

$$S_p^2 = \frac{(22 - 1) \times 776^2 + (48 - 1) \times 463^2}{22 + 48 - 2} = 334133; \quad t = \frac{1023 - 626}{\sqrt{\dfrac{334133}{22} + \dfrac{334133}{48}}} = 2.66$$

4 The paired *t*-value is computed as follows:

$$t = \frac{\bar{D}}{S_D/\sqrt{N}}$$

$\bar{D}$: the mean difference between the two groups
S_D: the standard deviation of the differences
N: the number of pairs

In the example: $t = \dfrac{-57}{25/\sqrt{150}} = -27.9$

17   Analysis of variance

Analysis of variance, like the t-test, tests the hypothesis that the means of several groups are equal. One of the most important differences is that in a t-test only two groups are distinguished, whereas analysis of variance usually compares three or more groups.

In this chapter we discuss two SPSS commands for analysis of variance. Because the assumptions and hypotheses for the two commands are similar, the first section (Section 17.1) contains a general description of analysis of variance. This section also deals with the differences between the two commands for analysis of variance. The first, One-Way ANOVA, distinguishes between groups based on one variable (factor) (see Section 17.2). *Univariate* is used when we distinguish groups based on two or more variables (see Section 17.3).

17.1   The use of analysis of variance

You can use analysis of variance to determine whether the *means of a number of groups are equal*. Do people who play only singles, only doubles, or both, on average spend equal amounts of money per year on tennis court rental? Or suppose that you distinguish between three age groups, young (younger than 25 years), adult (from 25 to 45) and veteran (over 45). Do all age groups play equally often, on a monthly basis? Do all age groups, on average, spend equal amounts of money on tennis wear? Analysis of variance answers these kinds of questions.

Assumptions. Analysis of variance, like the t-test, compares the group means of an interval or ratio variable. The assumption is that the cases in the groups belong to independent, random samples from normally distributed populations. Another assumption is that the variances within the groups are equal.

Hypotheses. The *null hypothesis* H_0 states that the means of all groups are equal. The *alternative hypothesis* H_1 states that not all means are equal. Analysis of variance compares the variance between the groups with the variance within the groups. When you divide the former variance by the latter, you get the F-value. Therefore, instead of analysis of variance the term F-test is also used (by analogy with the t-test for two groups).

Factors. Analysis of variance uses two types of variables: variables whose group means are compared and variables that determine the grouping. SPSS calls the first group the *dependent variables*. The variables that define the grouping are called the factor variables, *factors* for short. Based on the number of factors we distinguish two forms of analysis of variance:

- *One-factor analysis of variance*: with One-Way ANOVA[1] the grouping is based on one variable (see Section 17.2). Examples are: distinguishing between singles players, doubles players and players who practise both, or between the age groups young, adult and veteran. For this command the factor must always be a numeric variable. If you want to use a string variable as factor, you first have to transform that variable into a numeric variable with Automatic Recode (see Section 9.5).
- *Multiple-factor analysis of variance*: with Univariate analysis of variance the grouping is based on multiple variables (see Section 17.3). Example: the age groups young, adult and veteran, broken down according to gender. In that case, you distinguish six groups (young–male, young– female, adult–male, and so on).

Comparable tests. You can use analysis of variance to compare the means of three or more groups. If you distinguish only two groups, the t-test is a more natural choice. If the assumptions underlying analysis of variance, a normal distribution and interval or ratio variables, are not met, you can use a nonparametric test. If the samples are independent of each other and the test variable is at least ordinal, the Kruskal–Wallis test and the median test are suitable (see Section 19.6).

17.2   One-factor analysis of variance

In one-factor analysis of variance we distinguish groups based on one variable. The corresponding SPSS command is One-Way ANOVA. The background of analysis of variance has been described in Section 17.1 and therefore we now focus the discussion on the specification and the output of One-Way ANOVA.

You can find the command in the menu as follows:

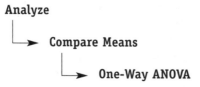

Analyze
  └──▸ **Compare Means**
        └──▸ **One-Way ANOVA**

In the next dialogue box you specify the variable whose means you want to test, and the grouping variable. Specify the first variable under 'Dependent List', the second under 'Factor'. In the tennis survey, people were asked about the price of the tennis shoes they had bought, where a distinction into three price categories was made. They were also asked how much they had spent on tennis wear. The question now is whether people who bought tennis shoes from one price category spend as much on tennis wear as players with shoes from another price category. Expensive shoes might occur in combination with expensive tennis wear, if we assume that these are purchased by people with higher incomes. The opposite could also be true: if people set aside a certain budget for tennis and can spend their money either on expensive shoes or on expensive tennis wear. Because both arguments are plausible, we test the hypothesis of equal mean expenditure on tennis wear for the three price categories. In this example the variable TennisWear is the dependent variable and ShoePrice the factor (see Figure 17.1).

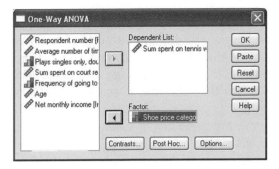

Figure 17.1   The dialogue box for analysis of variance with one factor (One-Way ANOVA). It is tested whether the mean expenditures for tennis wear are equal for each category of ShoePrice.

Besides the overview of the data used (Notes and Active Dataset), the output consists of a table (see Table 17.1) showing the results of the analysis of variance (ANOVA). The analysis of variance involves only those 51 respondents who bought new tennis shoes. The first column contains the Sum of Squares. The *total sum of squares* is computed as the sum of the squared differences between an observation and the overall mean (the mean of all cases). This sum of squares is found in the bottom row, labelled as Total. The total sum of squares is divided into 'between' and 'within' the groups.

- The *sum of squares between the groups* is computed as the sum of the squared differences between a group mean and the overall mean multiplied by the number of cases in that group. If the null hypothesis of equal group means were entirely true, the sum of squares between the groups would be zero.

Table 17.1   The output of the analysis of variance with one factor (One-Way ANOVA)

ANOVA

Sum spent on tennis wear (last year)

	Sum of Squares	df	Mean Square	F	Sig.
Between Groups	1487875	2	743937.255	11.676	.000
Within Groups	3058400	48	63716.667		
Total	4546275	50			

- The *sum of squares within the groups*, sometimes called the 'error' or residual, is computed as the sum of the squared differences between an observation and its corresponding group mean.

The second column shows the degrees of freedom. SPSS reports the degrees of freedom between the groups, within the groups and overall. Between the groups, this is the number of groups minus 1 (that is, $3 - 1 = 2$), and within the groups the total number of cases minus the number of groups (that is, $51 - 3 = 48$). For the Total row, it equals the total number of cases minus 1 ($51 - 1 = 50$).

For each row, *the mean sum of squares* equals the sum of squares divided by the degrees of freedom.

The last two columns show the results of the *F-test*. The F-value, in this example 11.676, is computed as follows:

$$F = \frac{\text{Mean sum of squares between groups}}{\text{Mean sum of squares within groups}}$$

Finally, SPSS displays the significance level corresponding to the F-value and the degrees of freedom. In this example the significance level, or p-value, equals 0.000. If we use a critical a of 0.05, this leads to the rejection of the null hypothesis of equal means. We therefore conclude that not all group means are equal. In other words, at least two group means differ from each other.

Extensions.
By specifying multiple dependent variables you can perform a number of analyses of variance with the same grouping. The dialogue box One-Way ANOVA contains three buttons leading to additional features. With Options you can, among other things, request statistics for each group, test whether the variances within the groups are equal and specify how SPSS has to treat missing values (see Section 17.2.1).

A disadvantage of analysis of variance is that it only tests whether or not the means of all groups are equal. If the null hypothesis of equal means is rejected, you only know that not all means are equal. With the button Post Hoc you can determine which groups differ from each other (see Section 17.2.2). The last button, Contrasts, offers the option of testing specific hypotheses about group means. In the corresponding dialogue box you can specify your hypothesis.

17.2.1 Requesting statistics with Options

The button Options in the dialogue box One-Way ANOVA gives access to the following three options: you can request statistics and alternative tests, create a line chart of the group means and specify how SPSS has to treat missing values (see the dialogue box in Figure 17.2).

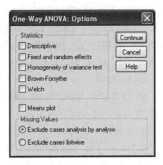

Figure 17.2   The dialogue box of the button Options of the One-Way ANOVA command.

Statistics and alternative tests – Under the heading Statistics you find the following options:

Descriptive – To request statistics for each group as well as for the total. SPSS shows the number of cases, mean, standard deviation, standard error, 95% confidence interval of the mean, minimum and maximum.

Fixed and random effects – For both the fixed effects model and the random effects model, SPSS presents the standard deviation, standard error and 95% confidence interval.

Homogeneity of variance test – One of the assumptions in analysis of variance is that the group variances are equal. With the Levene test you can check whether your data meet this assumption. The null hypothesis states that the group variances are equal. SPSS displays the Levene statistic and the corresponding significance level. It is questionable how important it is that the Levene test should lead to acceptance of the null hypothesis of equal group variances. Analysis of variance is not extremely sensitive to unequal group variances. Therefore, sometimes the rule of thumb is used that it is sufficient if the ratio of the largest standard deviation to the smallest is smaller than 2. (You can request the standard deviations with Descriptive.)

Brown–Forsythe and Welch – These two tests are alternatives to the normal F-test. You can use them if the assumption of equal group variances is not met (which may appear from the results of the Levene test, see above).

Chart of group means – With the option 'Means plot' you get a line chart of all group means. This is useful to get a quick overview of whether there are large differences among the group means and which groups stand out (high or low).

Missing values – The last option relates to the question how SPSS has to treat missing values if you specify multiple dependent variables:

- *Exclude cases analysis by analysis*: for each analysis separately, SPSS determines which cases have valid values for the two relevant variables (the dependent variable and the factor).
- *Exclude cases listwise*: SPSS uses only cases that have valid values for the factor as well as for all dependent variables. In this situation, the same set of cases is used for all analyses of variance.

17.2.2   Post Hoc to determine which group means are different

Analysis of variance determines whether the means of all groups are equal. This null hypothesis is rejected even if only two group means differ. That is why analysis of variance alone often does not yield enough information. We also want to know which group means differ significantly. With the button Post Hoc in the dialogue box One-Way ANOVA you can perform several tests for this purpose (see Figure 17.3). These tests are called multiple comparison tests.

The dialogue box consists of three parts: (i) multiple comparison tests that assume equal group variances, (ii) multiple comparison tests that do not make this assumption and (iii) the option of specifying a significance level.

Equal variances assumed – SPSS offers a large number of multiple comparison tests that you can use, assuming equal group variances. We discuss the three best-known tests:

- *LSD*: Least significant difference performs t-tests to compare each group mean with each of the other group means. A disadvantage of the LSD test is that, as the number of groups grows, the number of comparisons rapidly increases, which enhances the likelihood of falsely finding significant differences between groups. The following multiple comparison tests control for the error rate of multiple comparisons, which means that, as the number of groups becomes larger, the observed differences between the group means

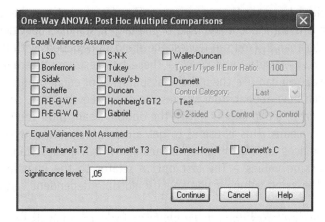

Figure 17.3   The dialogue box of the button Post Hoc of the One-Way ANOVA command for testing which groups have different means.

have to be progressively larger in order to be considered significant. For each test SPSS reports the magnitude of the difference between two group means that is required so that this difference is considered significant by the test.

- *Bonferroni*: ensures that the probability of false rejection of the null hypothesis of equal means for any two groups among all comparisons does not exceed 0.05. The LSD method uses a probability of 0.05 for each individual comparison of two groups. The Bonferroni test controls by dividing the significance level by the number of comparisons.
- *Scheffé*: this is the most conservative of all multiple comparison tests, which means that this test requires the largest difference between two means before the difference is considered significant.

Equal variances not assumed – If the Levene test (see Section 17.2.1) shows that the group variances are not equal, you can choose among four multiple comparison tests: Tamhane's T2, Dunnett's T3, Games–Howell and Dunnett's C.

Significance level – By default, SPSS uses a significance level of 5%. If desired, you can specify another percentage.

17.3   Analysis of variance with multiple factors: Univariate

In analysis of variance with multiple factors we use more than one variable to form groups. For this purpose SPSS has several commands. In this chapter we briefly discuss only the simplest variant, called Univariate.

Because we have already described the background to analysis of variance in Section 17.1, we now focus on the specification and output of Univariate. You can find the command in the menu as follows:

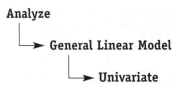

Analyze
> **General Linear Model**
> > **Univariate**

As in the case of One-Way ANOVA, the next dialogue box lets you specify the variable whose means you want to test (the dependent variable), and the grouping. The grouping in this case is based on multiple variables, specified under 'Fixed Factor(s)'. In the example of Figure 17.4, the dependent variable is TimesTennis, the number of times per month a person plays tennis. The groups are formed by both Gender and SingleDouble (the types of play practiced: singles, doubles, or both).

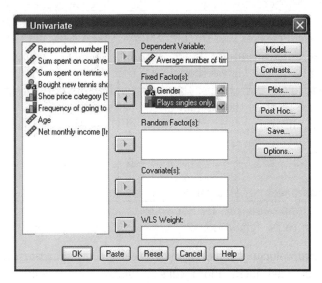

Figure 17.4   The dialogue box for analysis of variance with multiple factors (Univariate). It is tested whether the means of TimesTennis are equal for each combination of the values of Gender and SingleDouble.

Besides the overview of the data used (Notes and Active Dataset), the output of Univariate consists of an overview of the groups (Between-Subjects Factors; see Table 17.2), and the results of the analysis of variance (Tests of Between-Subjects Effects, see Table 17.3).

Table 17.2 The first part of the output of the analysis of variance with multiple factors showing the sample sizes of the various factors

Between-Subjects Factors

		Value Label	N
Gender	F	Female	71
	M	Male	79
Plays singles only, doubles only or both	1	Singles only	22
	2	Doubles only	48
	3	Singles and doubles	80

Table 17.3 The second part of the output showing the results of the analysis of variance

Tests of Between-Subjects Effects

Dependent Variable: Average number of times played (per month)

Source	Type III Sum of Squares	df	Mean Square	F	Sig.
Corrected Model	96.700[a]	5	19.340	2.251	.052
Intercept	1892.334	1	1892.334	220.224	.000
Gender	44.105	1	44.105	5.133	.025
SingleDouble	44.572	2	22.286	2.594	.078
Gender * SingleDouble	1.037	2	.518	.060	.941
Error	1237.360	144	8.593		
Total	3905.000	150			
Corrected Total	1334.060	149			

a. R Squared = .072 (Adjusted R Squared = .040)

In the first column of Table 17.3 you find the sums of squares. The total sum of squares (Corrected Total, 1334) consists of two components, namely the part accounted for (Corrected Model, 96.7) and the part not accounted for (Error, 1237.36).

In this case, the sum of squares accounted for consists of three components: the two factors (Gender and SingleDouble) and the interaction term. The interaction term refers to the combined effect of Gender and SingleDouble and is indicated in the table as Gender*SingleDouble. There is interaction between both factors if practising another type of play leads to playing more (or less) often and if this effect is not the same for men as for women.

Note that the displayed sum of squares accounted for (Corrected Model) does not simply equal the sum of the three components, because not all categories of the two factors contain the same number of cases. SPSS adjusts the sum on the basis of the number of cases.

The second column shows the degrees of freedom for the various effects. These are computed as follows:

- *for each factor*: the number of groups minus 1 (Gender: 2 − 1; SingleDouble: 3 − 1);
- *for the interaction term*: the degrees of freedom for the first factor, multiplied by that for the second factor (that is, 2 * 1);
- *for the full model (Corrected Model)*: the sum of all factors (main effects) and the interaction terms (that is, 1 + 2 + 2 = 5);
- *for the error term (the residual)*: the number of cases, minus the degrees of freedom for the full model, minus 1 (that is, 150 − 5 − 1);
- for the *total sum of squares (Corrected Total)*: the number of cases minus 1.

The next column contains the mean sum of squares. For each category this is the sum of squares divided by the degrees of freedom.

Finally, an *F-test* is carried out for each effect. The F-values are computed as follows:

$$\text{F-value} = \frac{\text{Mean sum of square effect}}{\text{Mean sum of squares residual}}$$

The best way to determine the relative importance of the three components (Gender, SingleDouble and the interaction term), is to inspect the F-values (or the significance level in the last column). The component with the highest (or the lowest significance level) has the strongest influence.

For each F-value and the corresponding degrees of freedom, SPSS computes the significance level (p-value). If we use a critical a of 0.05, we conclude that only the effect of Gender (0.025) is significant. Neither the effect of SingleDouble nor the interaction term is significant.

Extensions.

Instead of using two factors, you can also perform Univariate analysis of variance with more factors. SPSS does not limit the number of factors: your data are more likely to. After all, each combination of values of the factors leads to a new group. With three, four or more factors, the number of groups therefore rises fast. You then need very large numbers of cases in order to perform an analysis that remains meaningful.

The dialogue box Univariate contains several more options and buttons to tailor the analysis of variance. For example, you can control for the influence of covariates, test less common models (button Model), explore interactions with graphical analyses (Plots), perform multiple comparison tests to determine the significance of differences between groups (Post Hoc) and save the results in the form of new variables (Save). We briefly discuss each of these options below.

Controlling covariates – If the dependent variable also depends on another (continuous) variable that does not occur as a factor in the analysis of variance, you can control for this variable, called a covariate. You can do this by specifying one or more variables under 'Covariate(s)' in the dialogue box Univariate.

Testing other models – By default, SPSS tests a 'full factorial' model, which is a model in which the main effects of all factors and covariates are estimated, as well as the interactions between the factors. SPSS tests all possible interactions, to a maximum of five levels. With the button Model you can specify the model SPSS has to use (see Figure 17.5). First click 'Custom' at the top of the dialogue box. Next you specify which factors, covariates and interactions

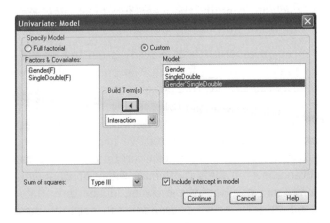

Figure 17.5   The dialogue box of the button Model of the Univariate command.

you want to consider in the analysis. You can define the exact model, but also specify a number of interactions. This can be done with the drop-down list in the centre of the dialogue box Model. To find out which specification best suits your situation, you can create 'profile plots', as discussed below.

Graphical analyses – With profile plots you can get an insight into the proper specification of the model. A profile plot, which you can create with the button Plots in the dialogue box Univariate, is a line chart that shows the group means based on two factors. Figure 17.6 contains an example of a profile plot.

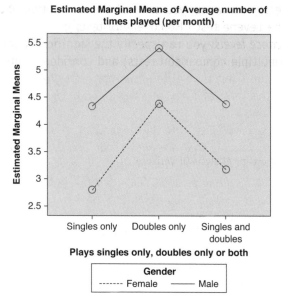

*Figure 17.6   A profile plot for detecting interaction between factors
(button Plot of the Univariate command).*

The group mean (number of times played) is plotted on the vertical axis. The upper line shows the average for men who practise only singles, only doubles or both types, respectively. The lower line shows the same information for women. Because in this example the two lines are approximately parallel, this indicates that there is no interaction between these two factors. Non-parallel lines are an indication of interaction.

Multiple comparison tests – You can carry out multiple comparison tests in order to determine afterwards (post hoc) which group means differ from each other. The button Post Hoc in the dialogue box Univariate leads to a large number of possible tests. We have discussed some of these under One-Way ANOVA (see Section 17.2.2).

Saving results – The values predicted by the model, the residuals and a number of other diagnostics can be saved as variables. To do this, click Save in the dialogue box Univariate and then specify which data you want to save. You can specify that the variables have to be included in a new and opened dataset ('create a new dataset') or saved in a new file on disk ('write a new data file').

Additional statistics – The button Options in the dialogue box Univariate enables you to request all kinds of additional information, such as:

- *descriptive statistics* for each group (numbers of cases, means and standard deviations);

- *equal group variances*: you can test the assumption of equal group variances with the Levene test ('Homogeneity tests');
- *significance levels*: you can specify the significance levels used for post hoc tests (multiple comparison tests) and confidence intervals.

Note

1 ANOVA is short for ANalysis Of VAriance.

18 Correlation and regression

Correlation and regression are two useful techniques to explore a (linear) correlation between two (or more) interval or ratio variables. Correlation analysis provides information about the relationship between two variables, if necessary you can control for the effect of a third variable. Regression analysis results in numerical explanation of a dependent variable by one or more independent variables.

The first two sections focus on correlation analysis. Section 18.1 discusses the bivariate, to be requested with the SPSS command *Bivariate Correlations*. This command can also produce the Kendall's tau and the Spearman correlation coefficient. You can use these measures if the assumptions of the Pearson correlation coefficient are not met. It is possible that the relationship between two variables is obscured by the influence of a third variable. With the command *Partial Correlations* you can investigate the true relationship between two variables by controlling for the effects of other variables (see Section 18.2).

In the last two sections we discuss two forms of regression analysis. The *Linear Regression* command is the subject of Section 18.3. In the first part of the section we discuss the basic command. The following subsections deal with extensions such as various methods of introducing variables to the analysis and the analysis of the residuals. Sometimes we assume that the relationship between variables is not linear but curvilinear. To estimate different forms of curvilinear relationships SPSS has the *Curve Estimation* command (see Section 18.4).

18.1 Correlation between two variables

Correlation analysis provides information about the relationship between two variables. The analysis shows both the strength of the relation and its direction (positive or negative). Is there a relationship between age and the amount spent on tennis wear? Do people who play more often spend more money on court rental? Correlation analysis answers such questions.

In this section we discuss the bivariate Pearson correlation coefficient. Correlation analysis assumes that the variables are *interval or ratio* variables. Moreover, the sample has to come from a *bivariate normal distribution*. This means that, for each value of one variable, the other variable is normally distributed, and vice versa. The correlation coefficient does not reflect every type of relationship between two variables, but only the *linear relationship*. This means that it tells you to what degree the relationship between two variables can be represented by a straight line. On the other hand, this means that if two variables are strongly related but the relationship is non-linear (e.g. a parabola or a circle), you will find a correlation coefficient of almost zero. It is therefore recommended first to create a scatterplot (see Section 6.2) with both variables, to determine whether it is worthwhile to request the Pearson correlation coefficient.

Comparable tests. In this section we discuss bivariate correlation dealing with the relationship between two variables regardless of the influence of other variables. When you want to control for the effect of a third variable, you need to apply *partial correlation* (see Section 18.2).

If the assumptions of the Pearson correlation coefficient are not met, you have to use an alternative statistic. For nominal variables you can use the *chi-square* and the *phi coefficient* (see Sections 14.3 and 14.4). If the variables are at least ordinal, you can use the *Spearman correlation coefficient* and *Kendall's tau* to determine the strength and direction of a relationship. These two measures can also be requested with Bivariate Correlations and are discussed at the end of this section under the heading 'Correlation of ordinal variables' (you can also request these two statistics with Crosstabs; see Section 14.4).

You can find the Bivariate Correlations command in the menu as follows:

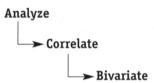

Analyze
    ↳ **Correlate**
        ↳ **Bivariate**

In the next dialogue box you specify the variables for which you want to compute the Pearson correlation coefficient. Suppose that we are interested in the relationship between the number of times a person plays tennis, the expenditure on tennis wear and the expenditure on court rental. In that case you specify the variables TimesTennis, TennisWear and CourtRental under 'Variables' (see Figure 18.1).

Besides the overview of the data used (Notes and Active Dataset), the output of Bivariate Correlations consists of a table with the correlation matrix (see Table 18.1). The diagonal of this matrix consists of ones, reflecting the correlation of a variable with itself. A correlation coefficient represents the strength of the linear relationship between two variables. A higher correlation coefficient, in absolute terms, means that the points in the scatterplot lie closer to a straight line. From Table 18.1 it appears that this applies more strongly to

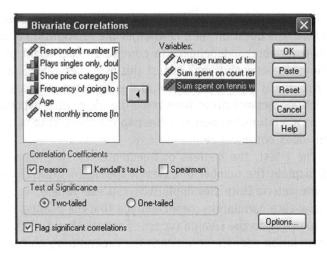

*Figure 18.1   The dialogue box of the Bivariate Correllations command,
for requesting the correlation coefficients between the variables
TimesTennis, CourtRental and TennisWear.*

the relationship between CourtRental and TimesTennis (0.864) than to the expenditures on court rental and tennis wear (0.115).

Another important property of the correlation coefficient is that, in contrast to the chi-square test for example, it also gives information on the direction of the relationship. Positive correlation means that if one of the variables increases, the other also increases. The positive correlation coefficient between TimesTennis and CourtRental indicates that, in general, people who play more often also spend more money on court rental.

Table 18.1   The output of Bivariate Correlations

Correlations

		Average number of times played (per month)	Sum spent on court rental (last year)	Sum spent on tennis wear (last year)
Average number of times played (per month)	Pearson Correlation	1	.864**	.127
	Sig. (2-tailed)		.000	.120
	N	150	150	150
Sum spent on court rental (last year)	Pearson Correlation	.864**	1	.115
	Sig. (2-tailed)	.000		.161
	N	150	150	150
Sum spent on tennis wear (last year)	Pearson Correlation	.127	.115	1
	Sig. (2-tailed)	.120	.161	
	N	150	150	150

** Correlation is significant at the 0.01 level (2-tailed).

A higher correlation coefficient means a stronger relationship between two variables. The question then is whether the relationship is also significant. Are the two variables independent (a correlation coefficient of zero) or is there a relationship between them? To test this hypothesis, SPSS performs a t-test. *The null hypothesis* H_0 for this t-test states that the correlation coefficient in the population does not differ from zero. The *alternative hypothesis* H_1 states that there is a relationship between the two variables, that is, the correlation coefficient does not equal zero.

In the t-test, the degrees of freedom equal the number of cases minus 2. SPSS displays the number of cases in the bottom line of each cell in the correlation matrix. In this example it is 150 everywhere.

Below each correlation coefficient you find the p-value, the significance level corresponding to the t-value (which is not displayed). The significance level of the correlation coefficient between the expenditures on court rental and tennis wear is 0.161. In other words, the probability of finding a correlation coefficient of at least 0.115 (in absolute terms) between CourtRental and TennisWear if there is no linear relationship between both variables in the population equals 16%. Applying a critical α of 0.05 therefore leads to acceptance of the null hypothesis: the correlation between CourtRental and TennisWear is not significant. For the correlation coefficient between CourtRental and TimesTennis, the probability that the relationship found is a matter of chance is considerably lower (p = 0.000). Therefore, this relationship is significant. To facilitate the interpretation of the results, SPSS marks all significant correlations. As indicated in the line below Table 18.1, SPSS shows two asterisks for p-values lower than 0.01. For p-values between 0.01 and 0.05 SPSS shows one asterisk.

Extensions.
The Bivariate Correlations command has various additional features. With the button Options you can request statistics and instruct SPSS how to treat missing values (see Section 18.1.1). Three other features are available in the dialogue box Bivariate Correlations and are briefly discussed below, together with an extension that is only accessible via the syntax window. Below we discuss one-tailed versus two-tailed testing, marking significant correlations, requesting a limited number of correlation coefficients (instead of the full correlation matrix) and correlation of ordinal variables.

One-tailed versus two-tailed testing – The alternative hypothesis H_1 determines whether we have to perform a one-tailed or a two-tailed t-test. If we assume that the relationship between two variables has a certain direction, we need a one-tailed test. For example, it is plausible that people who play more often spend more on court rental (positive correlation). For one-tailed testing click the option

*Table 18.2   Using the keyword WITH (only available in the syntax window)
for requesting a set of correlation coefficients*

Correlations

		Average number of times played (per month)	Age
Sum spent on court rental (last year)	Pearson Correlation	.864**	.189*
	Sig. (2-tailed)	.000	.020
	N	150	150
Sum spent on tennis wear (last year)	Pearson Correlation	.127	.163*
	Sig. (2-tailed)	.120	.047
	N	150	150

** Correlation is significant at the 0.01 level (2-tailed).

* Correlation is significant at the 0.05 level (2-tailed).

'One-tailed' under 'Test of Significance'. If you have no prior expectation regarding a positive or negative connection, you need a two-tailed test. By default, SPSS performs a two-tailed test (see the term 'Sig. (2-tailed)' in Table 18.1).

Marking significant correlations – By default, SPSS marks the significant correlation coefficients in the output (see Table 18.1). You can avoid this by deactivating the option 'Flag significant correlations' in the dialogue box Bivariate Correlations.

No full correlation matrix – In the example above, a full correlation matrix was requested. This means that all correlations between the specified variables are shown in the output. With the keyword WITH you can specify that only certain correlation coefficients have to be computed. SPSS then displays only the correlations between the variables listed before WITH and the variables listed behind WITH. You can use this keyword only when you execute the command via the syntax window. The variables before WITH form the rows of the correlation matrix and the variables behind WITH the columns (see Table 18.2). The easiest way of specifying such a command is to begin by preparing the command via the menu. Make sure that you first specify the variables that have to form the rows and only then select the variables for the columns. Next, transfer the command to the syntax window with the button Paste. Here you can type the keyword WITH at the desired location. The command is then executed by clicking the button 'Run Current' (this is the button with the arrow right).

```
CORRELATIONS
/VARIABLES= CourtRental TennisWear WITH TimesTennis Age
/PRINT= TWOTAIL NOSIG
/MISSING= PAIRWISE.
```

Correlation of ordinal variables – The Pearson correlation coefficient assumes interval or ratio variables and a bivariate normal distribution. If these assumptions are not met, the Kendall's tau or the Spearman correlation coefficient form good alternatives. Both are examples of non-parametric statistics and can be used if the variables are at least ordinal. You can request these measures in the dialogue box Bivariate Correlations under the heading 'Correlation Coefficients'. The Spearman correlation coefficient resembles the Pearson correlation coefficient, but the coefficient is computed by using the ranking of the cases (instead of the values of the cases).

Table 18.3   The Kendall's tau requested with the Bivariate Correlations command

Correlations

			Average number of times played (per month)	Sum spent on court rental (last year)	Sum spent on tennis wear (last year)
Kendall's tau_b	Average number of times played (per month)	Correlation Coefficient	1.000	.766**	.104
		Sig. (2-tailed)	.	.000	.091
		N	150	150	150
	Sum spent on court rental (last year)	Correlation Coefficient	.766**	1.000	.077
		Sig. (2-tailed)	.000	.	.184
		N	150	150	150
	Sum spent on tennis wear (last year)	Correlation Coefficient	.104	.077	1.000
		Sig. (2-tailed)	.091	.184	.
		N	150	150	150

** Correlation is significant at the 0.01 level (2-tailed).

The output of both statistics is similar to the output of Pearson correlation. Again, the requested coefficient, the significance level and the number of cases are displayed one below the other (see Table 18.3).

18.1.1 Options for statistics and missing values

With the button Options in the dialogue box Bivariate Correlations, you can request statistics and instruct SPSS how to treat missing values (see Figure 18.2).

Statistics – You can request the following two sets of statistics:

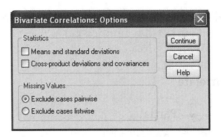

Figure 18.2   *The dialogue box of the button Options of the Bivariate Correlations command.*

- *Means and standard deviations*: the mean, the standard deviation and the number of cases for each variable;
- *Cross-product deviations and covariances*: the cross-product of the deviations is the numerator of the correlation coefficient.

Missing values – You can instruct SPSS how to treat missing values:

- *Exclude cases pairwise*: for each correlation coefficient, SPSS determines which cases can be used, that is, have valid values for both variables;
- *Exclude cases listwise*: only those cases are used that have valid values for all specified variables. In this case, therefore, all correlation coefficients are computed with the same cases.

18.2   Correlation controlled for a third variable

Bivariate correlation analysis provides information about the strength and direction of the relationship between two variables. Sometimes, however, this relationship is influenced by a third variable. For instance, Table 18.2 shows that the correlation coefficient between the number of times played (TimesTennis) and the expenditure on tennis wear (TennisWear) is not significant (r = 0.127, p = 0.120). Nevertheless, it is possible that in reality people who play more often do actually spend more money on tennis wear. In the sample, this relationship may be masked by the influence of a third variable, for example the person's income. People with higher incomes may buy more expensive tennis wear than people with lower incomes, irrespective of how often they play. To determine the true relationship between TimesTennis and TennisWear we have to control for the effect of Income. We can do this by requesting the *partial correlation coefficient* between TimesTennis and TennisWear.

You can find the Partial Correlations command in the menu as follows:

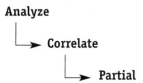

Analyze

    ⟶ **Correlate**

        ⟶ **Partial**

In the next dialogue box you specify the variables whose relationships you want to study and the variable(s) for which you want to control. In this example we are interested in the relationship between the number of times a person plays and the expenditure on tennis wear, where we control for the income effect (see Figure 18.3).

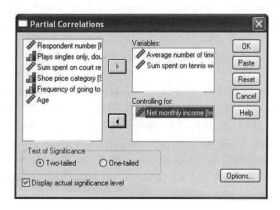

Figure 18.3   *The dialogue box of the Partial Correlations command for requesting the correlation between two variables when controlling for the effect of a third variable.*

Besides the overview of the data used (Notes and Active Dataset), the output of Partial Correlations consists of a table showing the correlation matrix (see Table 18.4). At the top of the table SPSS shows the variable(s) being controlled for, in this example only Income. Below that you find the full correlation matrix. Each cell in this matrix contains the partial correlation coefficient, the degrees of freedom for the t-test and the corresponding p-value. The bivariate correlation coefficient between TimesTennis and TennisWear was 0.127 (see Table 18.1) and has now increased to 0.2096. This correlation is significant, with a significance level of 0.010. So we do indeed find evidence that people who play more often spend significantly more money on tennis wear. The interpretation of the correlation coefficient and the t-test is the same as for bivariate correlation (see Section 18.1 for a more detailed discussion of these two subjects).

Table 18.4   The output of Partial Correlations

Correlations

Control Variables			Average number of times played (per month)	Sum spent on tennis wear (last year)
Net monthly income	Average number of times played (per month)	Correlation	1.000	.210
		Significance (2-tailed)	.	.010
		df	0	147
	Sum spent on tennis wear (last year)	Correlation	.210	1.000
		Significance (2-tailed)	.010	.
		df	147	0

Extensions.
If you want to control for the effect of more than one variable, you can specify multiple variables under 'Controlling for'. The other additional options of the Partial Correlations command are similar to those for Bivariate Correlations. In the dialogue box Partial Correlations you can specify whether you want a one-tailed or a two-tailed test (see Section 18.1) and the output will be more compact if you deactivate the option 'Display actual significance level'.

Likewise, the features available via the button Options are similar to those for Bivariate Correlations (see Section 18.1.1). The only difference is the option 'Zero-order correlations'. By checking this option you get a full (bivariate) correlation matrix that contains all specified variables, including the variables for which you control.

18.3   Regression analysis

Regression analysis is used to estimate a *linear relationship* between a dependent variable and one or more independent variables. The *dependent variable* represents the phenomenon that you want to explain and for that reason it is also called the *explained variable,* for example, the expenditure on court rental or tennis wear. The *independent variables* explain this phenomenon and for that reason they are sometimes called the *explanatory variables,* for example, the number of times a person plays tennis, or income, or age. In contrast to correlation analysis, regression analysis assumes a *causal relationship*. This means that the independent variables cause the dependent variable. For instance, the relationship between the number of times a person plays tennis and the amount spent on court rental is not arbitrary. Playing more often is the cause of paying more on court rental, so this is a causal relationship.

The regression equation

Regression analysis yields an equation that can be used to predict the dependent variable. If you know how often someone plays, you can predict how much this person pays for court rental. If there is one independent variable, the regression equation reads as follows:

$$Y = \beta_0 + \beta_1 X + e$$

In this formula Y is the dependent variable, the variable being explained, for example the amount spent on court rental. The independent variable is the explanatory variable and is indicated by X, for example the number of times a person plays tennis. The β parameters are those estimated with regression analysis and are also referred to as the *regression coefficients*. β_0 is the *intercept*. β_1 is the *slope* of the regression line. It indicates the number of units of increase in Y caused by an increase of one unit in X. The e in the equation represents the error term. This is the difference between the actual value of Y and the value of Y predicted by the model; it is therefore also called the *residual*.

Assumptions

The two most important assumptions in regression analysis involve the measurement level of the variables and the form of the relationship. As regards the measurement level, regression analysis assumes that both the dependent and the independent variables are *interval or ratio*. An exception is the use of dummy variables. A dummy is a variable with the values 1 and 0, to indicate that a certain event did or did not take place. Furthermore, regression analysis assumes that *the relationship is linear*. This means that the relationship between the dependent and the independent variables can be represented by a straight line. If this is not the case, regression analysis can still be used in some situations, namely if the equation to be estimated can be transformed into a linear one (an example of this is discussed in Section 18.3.2). Regression analysis can also be used to estimate curvilinear relationships, provided the relationship takes the form of a known mathematical function. We discuss the Curve Estimation command in Section 18.4.

Regression analysis makes a few more assumptions. It assumes that for each value of the independent variable, the dependent variable is normally distributed. The variance of the dependent variable has to be the same for each value of the independent variable (constant variance), and the residuals (the differences between the observed and predicted values of the dependent variable) should be uncorrelated.

Before you perform regression analysis, we recommend that you first examine the relationship between the variables involved, with a scatterplot or correlation analysis. The scatterplot shows whether the relationship is linear; the correlation coefficient gives an impression of the strength of the relationship between the dependent and independent variables.

The Linear Regression command

SPSS contains multiple commands for regression analysis. In this chapter we discuss only the two basic variants, Linear Regression and Curve Estimation. You can find the Linear Regression command in the menu as follows:

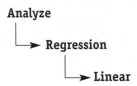

In the next dialogue box you specify how you want SPSS to perform the regression analysis. Linear Regression includes many options: witness the many input boxes and buttons. However, in the simplest case you only have to specify the dependent and the independent variables. Suppose that we want to explain the expenditure on tennis wear in terms of the income and the number of times the respondent plays. We specify the expenditure on tennis wear under 'Dependent' and income and the number of times played under 'Independent(s)' (see Figure 18.4).

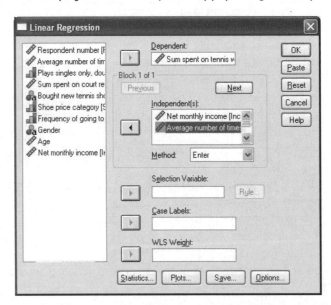

Figure 18.4   The dialogue box of the Linear Regression command. The variable TennisWear is explained by Income and TimesTennis.

Besides the overview of the data used (Notes and Active Dataset), the output of Linear Regression consists of four other elements: an overview of the variables included in the equation (Variables Entered/Removed), the overall results of the regression analysis (Model Summary), the F-test for the estimated model (ANOVA) and an overview of the estimated regression coefficients and the corresponding statistics (Coefficients).

The first part of the output summarises the fit of the model (Model Summary; see Table 18.5). The first statistic is the *multiple correlation coefficient*, simply indicated as 'R' (0.805). This coefficient can be interpreted as the simple correlation coefficient between the observed values of TennisWear and the values of TennisWear predicted with the regression equation. If the equation contains only one independent variable, the multiple correlation coefficient equals the bivariate Pearson correlation coefficient.

Table 18.5   The first part of the output of Linear Regression, with an overview of the fit statistics

Model Summary

Model	R	R Square	Adjusted R Square	Std. Error of the Estimate
1	.805[a]	.648	.644	168.664

a. Predictors: (Constant), Average number of times played (per month), Net monthly income

The square of the multiple correlation coefficient is the R^2 and indicates what proportion of the variance of the dependent variable is explained by the independent variables. R^2 is also called the *coefficient of determination*. In this example, TimesTennis and Income explain almost two-thirds of the variance of TennisWear (0.648). If all cases are exactly on the regression line, R^2 equals 1. If R^2 (almost) equals 0, this does not automatically mean that there is no relationship between the variables. It only means that no linear relationship exists.

SPSS corrects the R^2 for the number of independent variables and the number of cases, resulting in the *adjusted R^2* (Adjusted R Square).[1]

The fourth statistic, the 'Std. Error or the Estimate', is the standard error of the residuals. This is the root of the mean sum of squares of the residuals.

The second block of output contains the results of the *analysis of variance* (see Table 18.6). In this analysis, the *null hypothesis* H_0 states that all regression coefficients, with the exception of the intercept, equal zero. In other words, the R^2 of the population equals zero. The *alternative hypothesis* H_1 states that at least one regression coefficient differs from zero. In testing this

*Table 18.6   The second part of the output of Linear Regression, with the
results of the F-test*

ANOVA[b]

Model		Sum of Squares	df	Mean Square	F	Sig.
1	Regression	7711535	2	3855767.351	135.539	.000[a]
	Residual	4181799	147	28447.610		
	Total	11893333	149			

[a.] Predictors: (Constant), Average number of times played (per month), Net monthly income

[b.] Dependent Variable: Sum spent on tennis wear (last year)

hypothesis, the total variance of the dependent variable is divided into two components. One part of the variance is explained by the independent variables in the regression equation, while the other part is not explained, which is the residual. Analysis of variance compares the explained variance, which SPSS labels as 'Regression', with the non-explained variance, called 'Residual'.

The output of the analysis of variance contains the same statistics as those obtained by One-Way ANOVA. The first column displays the sums of squares (Sum of Squares) for the two components, the regression equation and the residual.

The following column contains the degrees of freedom (df). For the regression equation these equal the number of independent variables, two in this example. And for the residual it equals the number of cases minus the number of independent variables minus 1 ($150 - 2 - 1 = 147$).

The mean sum of squares is the sum of squares divided by the degrees of freedom. For the residual, the root of this value equals the 'Std. Error of the Estimate' discussed above.

The final two columns show the results of the *F-test*. The F-value is computed as the ratio of the mean sums of squares of the regression equation and the residual. In this example the F-value equals $3855767/28448 = 135.5$. SPSS also displays the significance level that corresponds to the F-value and the degrees of freedom. In this example the significance level, the p-value, is 0.000. Applying a critical α of 0.05 leads to rejection of the null hypothesis that all regression coefficients are zero. In other words, at least one regression coefficient, and the R^2 as well, significantly differs from zero.

The last part of the output describes the estimated regression equation (see Table 18.7). The first column, under B (β), contains the *regression coefficients*. Therefore, in this example the regression equation reads:

$$\textbf{Tennis Wear} = -399.93 + 0.42 \times \textbf{Income} + 12.00 \times \textbf{TimesTennis}$$

Table 18.7   The third part of the output of Linear Regression, with the regression coefficients

Coefficients[a]

Model		Unstandardized Coefficients		Standardized Coefficients	t	Sig.
		B	Std. Error	Beta		
1	(Constant)	-399.927	51.445		-7.774	.000
	Net monthly income	.421	.026	.795	16.257	.000
	Average number of times played (per month)	12.001	4.618	.127	2.599	.010

a. Dependent Variable: Sum spent on tennis wear (last year)

The signs of the regression coefficients play an important role in the interpretation of the regression equation. In the equation above, both Income and TimesTennis have a positive sign. This means that if either variable increases, the expenditure on tennis wear increases. Before you perform a regression analysis, you have to formulate hypotheses about the direction of the effects. Afterwards, you can verify whether the signs meet your expectations (see also the t-test below). In this example the signs are obvious: people with higher incomes and people who play more often spend more money on tennis wear.

A regression coefficient indicates the number of units of increase in the dependent variable caused by an increase of one unit in the independent variable. The regression coefficient does not reflect the relative importance of a variable because the magnitude of the coefficients depends on the units used for measuring the variables. For example, measuring the income in thousands of dollars (instead of just dollars) does not affect the importance of this variable, but the regression coefficient increases by a factor of 1000 (because the values of Income decrease by a factor of 1000). The regression coefficients reflect the relative importance of the variables only if all independent variables are measured in the same units.

To facilitate comparisons among the regression coefficients, SPSS also shows the coefficients that would be obtained if the variables were standardised before the regression analysis. These regression coefficients, displayed under 'Standardized Coefficients – Beta', reflect the relative importance of the independent variables.[2] They cannot represent exact importance because the beta of a variable also depends on which other variables are included in the equation (this also applies to the regression coefficients). The betas can be either positive or negative. To compare the importance of two variables, you have to use the absolute value of the beta. In that case, it does not matter whether the beta is positive or negative.

Finally, a t-test of the regression coefficients is performed. In this test, the *null hypothesis* H$_0$ states that a regression coefficient is zero. The *alternative hypothesis* H$_1$ states that a regression coefficient differs from zero. Usually we expect a coefficient to be positive, or negative, and the alternative hypothesis then states that the regression coefficient is larger (or smaller) than zero.

The t-value is the regression coefficient divided by the standard error of the regression coefficient. This standard error is found in the output under 'Std. Error' of the unstandardised coefficients (see Table 18.7). For TimesTennis the t-value is $12/4.6 = 2.6$. The degrees of freedom for the t-test equal the number of cases minus the number of independent variables minus 1. Therefore, in this example there are $150 - 2 - 1 = 147$ degrees of freedom.

The last column of the table contains the *two-tailed significance level* (the p-value) for the computed t-value. Applying a critical α of 0.05, we reject the null hypothesis that the regression coefficient equals zero, for both the two independent variables and the intercept. If you expect a positive or a negative regression coefficient (see the alternative hypothesis), you have to apply a one-tailed test and divide the displayed significance level by 2.

Extensions.

Linear Regression offers a large number of additional options. For instance, you can apply the analysis to a subset of the cases. You then have to specify a variable under 'Selection Variable' and use the button Rule to specify which group has to be included in or excluded from in the analysis. Alternatively, you could select a group of cases simply with Select Cases (see Section 10.2).

In the centre of the dialogue box of Linear Regression you find a drop-down list of labelled methods. These methods determine which independent variables are included in the analysis, and in what order. The various methods are discussed in Section 18.3.1.

Regression analysis can only be used to estimate linear relationships. Sometimes the relationship between the variables is curvilinear but the variables can be transformed in such a way that the relationship becomes linear. Subsection 18.3.2 describes an example of this. In the case of one independent variable, you can also use Curve Estimation (see Section 18.4).

The other additional options of Linear Regression can be requested with buttons. With the button Statistics you can request statistics that give a better insight into the regression equation and to what extent the assumptions are met (see Section 18.3.3). The button Plots produces charts showing the distribution of the residuals (see Section 18.3.4). With the button Save you can save residuals and predictions as variables (see Section 18.3.5). With the last button, Options, you can remove the intercept from the equation and instruct SPSS how to deal with missing values (see Section 18.3.6).

18.3.1 Methods of regression analysis

A frequent problem in regression analysis is that there are many variables that potentially influence the dependent variable and that you have to determine how many, and which, variables have to be included in the final equation. From an interpretation point of view it is preferable to explain the dependent variable by as few variables as possible. On the other hand, the aim of the analysis is to give the best possible explanation. The degree of explanation is reflected by the R^2. When more variables are added to the equation, the R^2 tends to increase. In an extreme case you obtain an equation that gives an excellent explanation, but which contains so many independent variables that the interpretation becomes very hard. In practice, you have to find a balance between the ease of explanation and the usefulness of the results.

One way of finding this balance is to include in the final equation only those variables whose regression coefficients are significant. A variant of this is not to include all variables in the equation straight away, but to include them one by one. You can then decide, before adding a variable to the equation, whether the change in the R^2 is sufficiently large to make the addition of that variable worthwhile. Yet another approach is the opposite of this: to start with an equation containing all variables and then decide which variables can be left out without strongly affecting the R^2.

Criteria – Selecting the independent variables requires a criterion to determine whether the change in the R^2 resulting from adding or removing a variable is significant. For this purpose you can use the F-test. The F-value is computed as the change in the R^2 relative to the R^2 itself[3].

SPSS has two statistics that can be used as threshold values, both for adding and removing variables from the model. Regarding adding variables:

- *The Probability-of-F-to-Enter*: the maximum acceptable significance level. If the computed significance level (probability) is lower than the entered value, the variable is added; otherwise it is not.
- *The F-to-Enter*: the minimum F-value. If the computed F-value is higher than this value, the variable is added; otherwise it is not.

Similar criteria are used for removing variables:

- The Probability-of-F-to-Remove: *the maximum acceptable significance level*. If the computed significance level (probability) is higher than the entered value, the variable is removed.
- The F-to-Remove: *the minimum F-value*. If the computed F-value is lower than this value, the variable is removed.

With the button Options (see below) in the dialogue box of Linear Regression you can specify whether SPSS has to use the significance level or the F-value as the criterion and change the default threshold values.

Methods – SPSS contains five methods that determine which independent variables are included in the equation, using the criteria discussed: Enter, Forward, Backward, Stepwise and Remove. Each of these is briefly reviewed.

1. *The Enter method.* One regression equation with all specified variables is estimated. This is the default method.

2. *The Forward method.* The variables are added to the equation one by one if they meet the criterion for entry (a maximum significance level or a minimum F-value). SPSS starts with the variable that has the largest (absolute) correlation with the dependent variable. If this variable meets the criterion for entry, a regression analysis is performed with only this variable. Next, SPSS determines which of the variables not yet included has the strongest partial correlation with the dependent variable. If this variable also meets the criterion for entry, it is included into the equation as the second variable. This process is continued until a variable no longer satisfies the criterion for entry or all variables have been included.

3. *The Backward method.* The variables are removed from the equation one by one if they meet the criterion for elimination (a maximum significance level or a minimum F-value). SPSS starts with an equation containing all independent variables. Next, it determines whether the variable that has the smallest partial correlation with the dependent variable meets the criterion for elimination. If that is the case, this variable is removed and a new equation is estimated. This process is continued until a variable no longer satisfies the criterion for elimination or all variables have been removed.

4. *The Stepwise method.* The often used Stepwise method is a combination of Forward and Backward. Adding the variables takes place in the same way as in Forward. The difference with Forward is that when variables are added, the variables already in the equation are also assessed based on the criterion for elimination, as for Backward.

In order to prevent the same variable being alternately added and removed, make sure that the 'Probability-of-F-to-Remove' is always higher than the 'Probability-of-F-to-Enter' (or the 'F-to-Remove' is lower than the 'F-to-Enter').

5. *The Remove method.* Remove can be used when you have specified the independent variables in blocks; see the buttons Previous and Next in the dialogue box of Linear Regression. All variables belonging to the same block are removed from the equation in the same step.

Selecting criteria and changing threshold values – With the button Options in the dialogue box of Linear Regression you can specify which criterion you want to apply and its threshold value (see Figure 18.5).

First you specify, under the heading 'Stepping Method Criteria', the criterion you want to apply, the *probability of F* or the *F-value*.

The two criteria can lead to different results because the degrees of freedom depend upon the number of variables in the equation. With a different number of variables the same F-value corresponds to a different significance level (and vice versa).

The second step is to specify the threshold value. The default values are shown in Figure 18.5.

*Figure 18.5   Part of the dialogue box of the button Options of the Linear
              Regression command.*

18.3.2 Regression for non-linear relationships

The regression equation represents a linear relationship between variables. The dependent variable is a weighted sum of the independent variables. The equation as shown in Section 18.3 is therefore also called a *linear additive model*. Such an equation does not contain any interaction effects between the independent variables. In this section we discuss some ways of including interaction in the model. In all examples to be discussed it is possible to transform the equation in such a way that Linear Regression can be used. Provided you have only one independent variable, you can also estimate a curvilinear relationship straight away, with Curve Estimation (see Section 18.4).

Suppose that you have a model with two variables, X_1 and X_2. The normal linear additive model then reads as follows:

$$\mathbf{Y} = \beta_0 + \beta_1 X_1 + \beta_2 X_2$$

$$\mathbf{Y} = \beta_0 + \beta_1 X_1 + \beta_2 X_2$$

One of the simplest ways to include interaction between X_1 and X_2 is by extending the model as follows:

$$\mathbf{Y} = \beta_0 + \beta_1 X_1 + \beta_2 X_2 + \beta_3 X_1 X_2$$

Again, Linear Regression can be used, by including the interaction term as a separate, third independent variable in the analysis. This variable is calculated with Compute, as follows (see Section 9.1):

$$\mathbf{X_3} = \mathbf{X_1} \times \mathbf{X_2}$$

A regression analysis is then performed with the independent variables X_1, X_2 and X_3.

Another way of including interaction in the model is to use a *multiplicative model*. The general form of a multiplicative model reads as follows:

$$Y = \beta_o \times X_1^{\beta 1} \times X_2^{\beta 2}$$

In a multiplicative model the regression coefficients indicate to what extent a one percentage change in an independent variable leads to a percentage change in the dependent variable. If the coefficient of X_1 equals -2, an increase in X_1 by 1% leads to a decrease in Y by 2%.

The multiplicative model is non-linear. For that reason, the coefficients β_o, β_1 and β_2 cannot be determined directly with Linear Regression. It is necessary first to transform the equation into a linear equation by taking the natural logarithm. The equation then becomes:

$$Ln(Y) = Ln(\beta_o) + \beta_1 \times Ln(X_1) + \beta_2 \times Ln(X_2)$$

This equation is linear and can therefore be estimated with Linear Regression. To do this, you first define three new variables with Compute, namely LnY, LnX$_1$ and LnX$_2$:

$$LnY = Ln(Y) \; Ln(X_1) = Ln(X_1) \; Ln(X_2) = Ln(X_2)$$

You can then perform linear regression with these three new variables.

18.3.3 Statistics of regression

With the button Statistics you can request statistics that give more insight into the results of the regression analysis, the variables used and the extent to which the assumptions are met (see Figure 18.6).

You can request the following statistics. Under 'Regression Coefficients' you find:

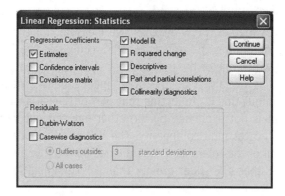

Figure 18.6   The dialogue box of the button Statistics of the Linear Regression command (the selected statistics represent the default output).

- *Estimates*: for each variable SPSS displays the regression coefficient, standard error, standardised coefficient Beta, t-value and two-tailed significance level. This is the default output (see Table 18.7).
- *Confidence intervals*: the 95% confidence intervals of each regression coefficient.
- *Covariance matrix*: two matrices, one with the bivariate correlation coefficients between the independent variables, and the other showing the variances on the diagonal and the covariances above and below the diagonal.

Additionally, you can request the following statistics:

- *Model fit*: the multiple correlation coefficient, R^2, adjusted R^2, standard error and results of the analysis of variance. This is the default output (see Table 18.5).
- *R squared change*: for each step, SPSS shows the variable added, change in the R^2, corresponding F-value and significance level. This information is relevant when using a method where variables are added or removed sequentially.
- *Descriptives*: the mean, standard deviation and number of valid cases for each variable, plus a full correlation matrix with one-tailed significance levels.
- *Part and partial correlations*: for each independent variable, SPSS computes the following three correlation coefficients with the dependent variable: zero-order, partial and part. The zero-order correlation is the normal bivariate correlation coefficient. The partial correlation reflects how much of the unexplained variance of the dependent variable is explained by the independent variable.[4] The part correlation is a measure of the increase in the R^2 if this independent variable were also added to the equation.[5] If there is no correlation between the independent variables, the part correlation is identical to the normal zero-order correlation.
- *Collinearity diagnostics*: multicollinearity refers to high correlation among the independent variables. SPSS displays two measures for this, the tolerance and the VIF. To determine the tolerance, SPSS computes the R^2 of the regression equation in which one of the independent variables is treated as the dependent variable and is explained by the other independent variables. The tolerance equals one minus this R^2, reflecting that part of the variance of an independent variable that is not explained by the other independent variables. A very low tolerance indicates multicollinearity. The VIF, the Variance Inflation Factor, is the reciprocal of the tolerance (i.e. 1 divided by the tolerance). A rule of thumb often used is that VIF values greater than 10 signal multicollinearity.

The last two options in the dialogue box Statistics deal with the residuals. You can request the Durbin–Watson test and analyse individual cases. In both cases

Table 18.8 Part of the output of the residuals analysis (button Statistics of the Linear Regression command)

Residuals Statistics[a]

	Minimum	Maximum	Mean	Std. Deviation	N
Predicted Value	242.94	1666.84	393.33	227.498	150
Residual	-317.460	406.889	.000	167.528	150
Std. Predicted Value	-.661	5.598	.000	1.000	150
Std. Residual	-1.882	2.412	.000	.993	150

[a] Dependent Variable: Sum spent on tennis wear (last year)

you also obtain a table titled 'Residuals Statistics' (see Table 18.8). This table contains several statistics for the predicted values of the dependent variable (computed with the regression equation), the residuals, the standardised predictions and the standardised residuals.

- *Durbin–Watson*: to test the correlation between successive residuals. This is referred to as serial correlation or *autocorrelation*. The Durbin–Watson test is of particular importance for time series analyses. The test statistic is between 0 and 4. A value close to 2 indicates that there is no autocorrelation. A Durbin–Watson statistic much smaller than 2 indicates positive autocorrelation; a relatively high value indicates negative autocorrelation. For the assessment you have to use a statistical table, but as a rule of thumb values less than 1 or greater than 3 signal that the assumption of independent residuals is not met. SPSS displays the Durbin–Watson statistic in the table 'Model Summary' (Table 18.5).
- *Casewise diagnostics*: produces a table, either for the outliers or for all cases, showing for each case the observed value of the dependent variable, the value predicted with the regression equation, the residual and the standardised residual. If you have specified a variable under 'Case Labels' in the dialogue box of Linear Regression, the value of this variable is also displayed. The table gives detail about the cases that are well predicted or not well predicted by the regression equation. You can request this table for: (i) *outliers outside x standard deviations* – cases with a standardised residual larger than x (you can specify a value for x) and (ii) *all cases*.

18.3.4 Graphical analysis of the residuals with Plots
The button Plots offers access to a number of charts for analysing the distribution of the residuals. In this way you can check to what extent the assumptions

made about the residuals are met by your data. The residuals have to be independent, normally distributed with a mean of zero and with a constant variance. You can request plots involving several temporarily available residuals variables (see Figure 18.7).

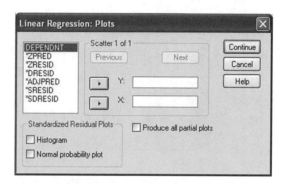

*Figure 18.7   The dialogue box of the button Plots of the Linear
                Regression command.*

Scatterplots – You can select the following seven variables to plot against one another:

- *DEPENDNT*: the dependent variable.
- *ZPRED*: the standardised predictions.
- *ZRESID*: the standardised residuals.
- *DRESID*: the residual of a case, if this case were omitted when estimating the regression equation.
- *ADJPRED*: the prediction of a case, if this case were omitted when estimating the regression equation.
- *SRESID*: Studentised residual, the residual divided by an estimate of the standard deviation for each case, which is derived from the distance between the observed values of the independent variables of that case and the means of these variables. This statistic is useful in identifying cases with an unusual combination of values for the independent variables.
- *SDRESID*: Studentised DRESID. This is the DRESID for a case divided by its corresponding standard error.

For each plot you have to select two variables. Click Next to specify another scatterplot. Figure 18.8 contains the scatterplot of the dependent variable (DEPENDNT) and the standardised predictions (ZPRED). The scatterplot shows points or the values of the variable that you specified in the dialogue box of Linear Regression under 'Case Labels' (see Figure 18.4).

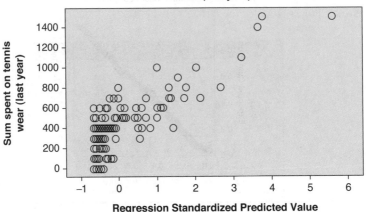

Figure 18.8   *The scatterplot of the dependent variable TennisWear and the standardized predictions (ZPRED).*

To analyse the scatterplot, the button Data Label Mode in the Chart Editor is a useful tool (see Section 6.5 for a discussion of point identification).

Charts for residuals – For the standardised residuals (the variable ZRESID in the overview above) you can request the following charts:

- *Histogram*: a histogram with a normal distribution superimposed. This chart shows for each interval the actual number of residuals and the number of residuals in the case of a perfect normal distribution.
- *Normal probability plot*: this is a scatterplot with the cumulative percentage of ZRESID on the vertical axis and on the horizontal axis the expected cumulative percentage of ZRESID if the residuals had a perfect normal distribution (see Figure 18.9). If the residuals are normally distributed, all values of ZRESID are on the diagonal. As the figure shows, the distribution of the residuals in the example matches the normal distribution rather well.

18.3.5 Saving regression variables
In Section 18.3.4 we have seen that SPSS makes a number of temporary regression variables, such as the residuals and the predictions. With Plots you can request charts of these variables. If you intend to analyse the variables at a later time or in greater detail, you can save them. The dialogue box Save, shown in Figure 18.10, gives an overview of the available regression variables.

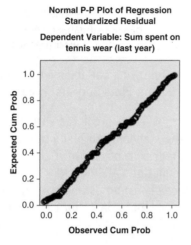

Figure 18.9 *A normal probability plot of the standardized residuals. The straight line reflects the normal distribution.*

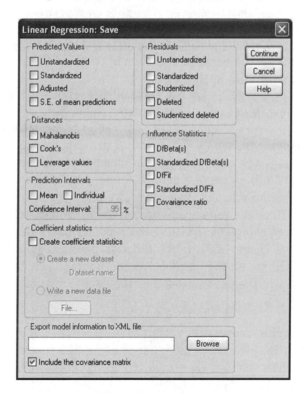

Figure 18.10 *The dialogue box of the button Save of the Linear Regression command.*

You can have these variables included in a new and opened dataset ('create a new dataset') or saved in a new file on disk ('write a new data file'). In this section we only discuss the variables mentioned under 'Predicted Values' and 'Residuals'.

Predictions – The following variables are available (the name of the variable as defined by the button Plots appears in parentheses):

- *Unstandardized*: the value predicted with the regression equation;
- *Standardized*: the standardised prediction (ZPRED);
- *Adjusted*: the prediction of a case if that case were omitted in estimating the regression equation (ADJPRED);
- *S.E. of mean predictions*: an estimate of the standard deviation of the mean value of the dependent variable for cases with the same values of the independent variables.

Residuals – The following variables are available (the name of the variable as defined by the button Plots appears in parentheses; there you can also find a description): *Unstandardized* (the difference between the observed value of the dependent variable and the prediction), *Standardized* (ZRESID), *Studentized* (SRESID), *Deleted* (DRESID) and *Studentized deleted* (SDRESID).

18.3.6 Regression options
The button Options leads to three different choices. You can specify the criteria used for the various regression methods, omit the intercept in the regression equation and specify how SPSS should treat missing values (see Figure 18.11). The first option has been discussed in Section 18.3.1. This sub-section deals with the other two.

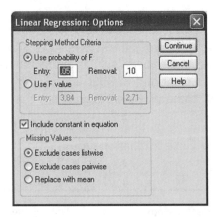

*Figure 18.11   The dialogue box of the button Options of the Linear
Regression command.*

No constant – By default, SPSS estimates a regression equation with an intercept. You get an equation without intercept, reflecting a regression line starting at the origin, by deactivating the option 'Include constant in equation'. This option requires that all variables are measured in terms of the deviation from their respective means, in order to meet the assumption that the mean of the residuals equals zero.

Missing values – SPSS has the following options for dealing with missing values:

- *Exclude cases listwise*: only those cases are used that have valid values for all dependent and independent variables.
- *Exclude cases pairwise*: for each of the correlation coefficients on which the regression analysis is based, SPSS separately determines which cases have valid values for the two variables involved.
- *Replace with mean*: missing values are replaced by the mean of the relevant variable. The regression analysis is therefore carried out with all cases.

18.4   Curvilinear regression analysis

Before you perform a correlation or regression analysis, you first need to check with a scatterplot whether the relationship between the two variables is linear. If the relationship is not linear, you can still use regression analysis, if the relationship between the dependent and the independent variable can be described in the form of a mathematical equation. In Section 18.3.2 we discussed an example of this. The drawback of that example is that you first have to define several working variables that can then be used in a linear regression analysis. With Curve Estimation you can estimate a *curvilinear relationship* directly, provided that you use only one independent variable. The command is also useful for describing the *development of a phenomenon over time,* for example, the growth trend of the number of members of an emerging tennis club.

Because many assumptions, options and output elements of Curve Estimation are similar to those of Linear Regression, the discussion in this section will be rather brief.

You can find the Curve Estimation command in the menu as follows:

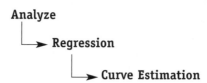

Analyze
   Regression
      Curve Estimation

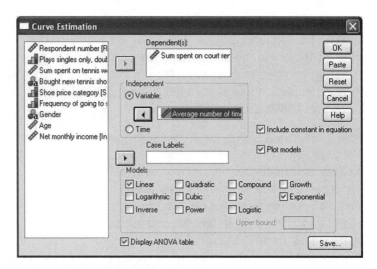

Figure 18.12   The dialogue box of the Curve Estimation command. The variable CourtRental is explained by TimesTennis with both a linear and an exponential model.

In the next dialogue box you specify the variables to be included into the regression equation and the model to be used. In this example we want to explain the expenditure on court rental by the number of times a person plays tennis. We specify the expenditure on court rental under 'Dependent(s)' and the playing frequency under 'Independent' (see Figure 18.12).

The next step is to specify the model to be estimated. In this example we estimate both a linear model and an exponential model. In the paragraph Extensions we deal with the selection of an appropriate model.

The last step is to check the option 'Display ANOVA table' to obtain more detailed information about the estimated regression equation.

Besides the overview of the data used (Notes and Active Dataset), the output of Curve Estimation consists of tables providing an overview of the estimated models (Model Description), the numbers of valid and missing cases (Case Processing Summary) and for each variable the number of positive, negative and zero values (Variable Processing Summary). Next follows for each model the results of the regression analysis in the tables Model Summary, ANOVA and Coefficients. Finally, SPSS shows a line chart showing both the predicted values and the observed values of the dependent variable (Curvefit).

The three tables with the results of the regression analysis are similar to Tables 18.5–18.7; refer to those for a description of the various statistics. The line chart Curvefit is displayed in Figure 18.13. The dependent variable is predicted with each requested model and these values are shown in a curve. Next to the statistics from the regression tables, these curve provide useful

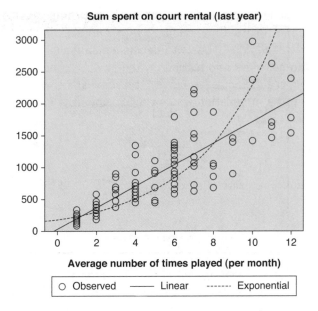

Figure 18.13   *A line chart with the observed values as well as the predictions of both estimated models (the linear and exponential model).*

information on the model fit. From the statistics (not shown) we conclude that the exponential model provides a slightly better fit than the linear model (with a slightly higher R^2). Figure 18.13 shows that for values of TimesTennis between 2 and 8 the linear model predicts higher court rental expenditures than the exponential model. Especially at higher values for TimesTennis the differences between the predictions of both models increase considerably.

Extensions.
Besides a variable from the data file, you can also use time as the independent variable. This is useful for estimating trends. In the dialogue box Curve Estimation you then have to select 'Time' (under 'Independent'). SPSS assumes that all cases are measurements made at constant intervals (e.g. always one week or one month).

You can omit the intercept from the regression equation by deactivating the option 'Include constant in equation'. The comparison plot (see Figure 18.13), which is often very useful, is not shown if you deactivate the option 'Plot models'. Finally, the button Save offers the option to save estimates as new variables in the data file.

18.4.1 Model selection
As you can see from Figure 18.12, Curve Estimation can estimate a large number of models. In practise, select an appropriate model by first creating a

scatterplot and then deciding which mathematical models are to be considered. Next, you estimate these models with Curve Estimation, and compare the results of the various models to decide which model is to be preferred.

You can get more information on the models to be estimated by pointing at a model in the dialogue box Curve Estimation and then clicking the right mouse button. In the information window SPSS shows the mathematical equation.

Notes

1 The adjusted R^2 is computed as follows (p = number of independent variables, N = number of cases):

$$R_a^2 = R^2 - \frac{p(1-R^2)}{N-p-1} = 0.648 - \frac{2(1-0.648)}{150-2-1} = 0.644$$

2 Beta is computed as follows (S_x and S_y are the standard deviations of the independent and the dependent variables, respectively):

$$\text{Beta} = \beta \frac{S_x}{S_y}$$

3 The F-value is computed as follows:

$$F = \frac{\Delta R^2(N-p-1)}{q(1-R^2)}$$

ΔR^2 = the change in R^2
N = the number of cases
p = the number of independent variables
q = the number of added variables
R^2 = the new R^2
The degrees of freedom equal q and $(N-p-1)$.
4 The partial correlation coefficient is computed as follows:

$$\text{PartialCor} = \sqrt{\frac{R_N^2 - R_0^2}{1 - R_0^2}}$$

where:
R_N^2 = the new R^2, that is, when this variable is also included in the equation.
R_0^2 = the old R^2, that is, when this variable is not included in the equation.
5 The 'part' correlation coefficient is computed as follows:

$$\text{PartCor} = \sqrt{R_N^2 - R_0^2}$$

See footnote 4 for the meaning of the symbols used.

19 Non-parametric tests

Most of the tests discussed in the preceding chapters make assumptions about the shape of the distribution of the variables. In many cases this has to be a normal distribution. Moreover, the variables often have to be interval or ratio. In practise it is not unusual that these conditions are not met. In order to test differences in such situations, we use *non-parametric tests*, also called *distribution-free tests*.

The Nonparametric Tests command in the Analyze menu leads to the following eight groups of non-parametric tests:

- the *chi-square test* for one variable, to test the observed distribution against the expected distribution (see Section 19.1);
- the *binomial test* to test the probability of a given value for a dichotomous variable (see Section 19.2);
- the *Runs test* to detect sequence effects of two values of a variable (see Section 19.3);
- the *Kolmogorov–Smirnov test for one variable* to compare the observed distribution with a theoretical distribution (see Section 19.4);
- the *Mann–Whitney test* and the *Kolmogorov–Smirnov test* to compare the means of two independent groups (see Section 19.5);
- the *Kruskal–Wallis test* and the *median test* to compare the means of two or more independent groups (see Section 19.6);
- the *Wilcoxon Signed Ranks test* and the *sign test* to compare the means of two related groups (see Section 19.7);
- the *Friedman test* to compare the means of two or more related groups (see Section 19.8).

19.1 The chi-square test

With the chi-square test you can determine whether the observed frequencies in different categories of a variable match with the expected frequencies. The chi-square test has been discussed with the Crosstabs command (see Section 14.3). However, in that situation the test was used to find out whether two variables were independent. The chi-square test performed with the Nonparametric Tests command is meant to test the distribution of one variable.

This test can be used to determine whether the various categories of a variable contain equal numbers of cases or whether a sample is representative with respect to a given characteristic (e.g. age or income). In the first case we could use the chi-square test to determine whether the sample contains (approximately) equal numbers of men and women. We can also use the test to determine whether our sample is representative. Suppose that we know how many tennis shoes were sold in each price category (cheap, medium and expensive) nationally last year. If our sample is representative with respect to the price of the tennis shoes bought, we should find the same distribution across the three price categories in the sample as nationally.

Suppose we know that equal numbers of shoes were sold in each category last year. The *null hypothesis* H_0 states that the observed distribution matches the expected distribution, that is, equal numbers of cases in each price category. The *alternative hypothesis* H_1 states that this not the case and that the number of cases per category varies.

You can find the command for the chi-square test for one variable in the menu as follows:

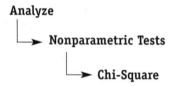

Analyze

  ↳ **Nonparametric Tests**

    ↳ **Chi-Square**

In the next dialogue box you specify the variable(s) for which a chi-square test has to be performed. In the example with the price of tennis shoes this is the variable ShoePrice (see Figure 19.1). The variables that you specify must be numeric: SPSS omits the string variables from the variables window. If you need a chi-square test for a string variable, for example Gender, you first have to transform that variable into a numeric variable with Automatic Recode (see Section 9.5).

Besides the overview of the data used (Notes and Active Dataset) the output of the chi-square test consists of a frequency table and the results of the chi-square test.

The frequency table (see Table 19.1) gives an overview of the observed (Observed N) and the expected frequencies (Expected N) for each category. The expected frequency is also called theoretical frequency. Because a total of 51 people bought new tennis shoes and equal categories were assumed, the expected frequency equals 17 for each category. The last column, Residual, contains the difference between the observed and the expected frequency.

Table 19.2 contains the results of the chi-square test: the chi-square statistic, the degrees of freedom (which equal the number of categories minus 1)

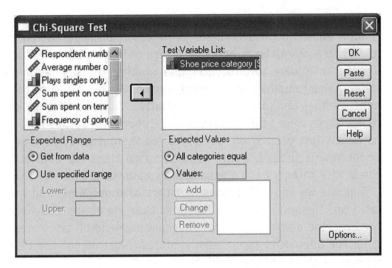

Figure 19.1 The dialogue box for performing a chi-square test for the variable ShoePrice.

and the significance level (the p-value). The significance level in this case equals 0.014. This means that if we use a critical α of 0.05, we reject the null hypothesis. In other words, not all categories of ShoePrice contain the same number of cases. The frequency table shows that the cheapest category, with shoes up to 50 dollars, contains fewer cases than the middle category, with shoes between 50 and 100 dollars.

Below Table 19.2, SPSS reports that in this case there are no categories with an expected frequency lower than 5; the minimum is 17 (refer to Section 14.3 for the assumptions of the chi-square test).

Extensions.
The chi-square test command includes three more options. For instance, the test can be performed for a limited number of categories of a variable, and you

Table 19.1 The frequency table with the numbers of cases for each category

Shoe price category

	Observed N	Expected N	Residual
Less than 50 dollar	8	17.0	-9.0
Between 50 and 100 dollar	25	17.0	8.0
More than 100 dollar	18	17.0	1.0
Total	51		

Table 19.2   The output of the chi-square test

Test Statistics

	Shoe price category
Chi-Square [a]	8.588
df	2
Asymp. Sig.	.014

[a] 0 cells (.0%) have expected frequencies less than 5. The minimum expected cell frequency is 17.0.

can specify the expected frequencies. These two options are discussed below. The dialogue box also contains the button Options to request statistics and specify how SPSS has to treat missing values. Because other non-parametric tests also have this button, these options are discussed in a separate section (Section 19.1.1).

Range of categories – Under 'Expected Range' you can specify for which categories the chi-square test has to be performed. By default, this is done for all categories ('Get from data'). Click 'Use specified range' to specify the range of values for which the test has to be performed (by entering the lowest and highest value of the range).

Expected frequencies – The null hypothesis can be specified under Expected Values. By default, SPSS tests the null hypothesis of equal frequencies for all categories. By clicking 'Values' you can specify a different null hypothesis. Enter a number in the input field next to Values and click Add, to include it in the list of expected frequencies. Click a frequency in this list to change or remove it. The order of the frequencies corresponds to the ascending order of the categories of the test variable.

The specified values represent the expected proportion of cases in each category. SPSS automatically derives the corresponding expected (theoretical) frequencies. If, in the example of the price category of tennis shoes, you know that the ratios between the three categories are 2:5:3, you can specify these three numbers. SPSS then determines how many cases each of the categories should contain, given these ratios and a sample of 51 cases.

19.1.1 Statistics and missing values with Options
With the button Options you can request statistics and specify how SPSS has to deal with missing values (see Figure 19.2).

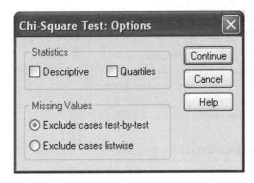

*Figure 19.2 The dialogue box of the button Options of the Nonparametric
Tests command.*

Statistics – You can request the following statistics:

- *Descriptive*: shows for each variable the number of cases, mean, standard
  deviation, minimum and maximum;
- *Quartiles*: shows for each variable the 25th percentile, 50th percentile (the
  median) and 75th percentile.

Missing values – If you perform multiple tests with one command, you can
instruct SPSS to treat missing values in either of the following ways:

- *Exclude cases test-by-test*: for each test SPSS determines which cases have
  valid values for the variables involved;
- *Exclude cases listwise*: SPSS uses only those cases that have valid values for
  all specified variables. In this case all tests are carried out with the same
  set of cases.

19.2   The binomial test

The binomial test is used to find out whether the observed data confirm that
there is a probability p for a given value of a variable (for example that a
person is male, or older than 30 years). The test distinguishes between two
categories, for example men and women, or older and younger than 30 years.
The binomial test compares the observed frequencies in the two categories
with the expected frequencies for a binomial distribution and a specified
probability.

Suppose that we have random sample, where the probabilities that a respondent is a man or a woman are equal. The *null hypothesis* H_0 then states that the probability that a respondent is male equals 50%. The *alternative hypothesis* H_1 states that this is not the case and that the probability differs from 50%.

You can find the command for the binomial test in the menu as follows:

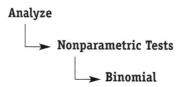

Analyze

  ↳ **Nonparametric Tests**

    ↳ **Binomial**

In the next dialogue box you specify for which variable(s) a binomial test has to be performed. The variables that you specify have to be numeric. Therefore, we have first transformed the string variable Gender into the numeric variable Sex with Automatic Recode (see Section 9.5). Following this, we have specified Sex under 'Test Variable List' (see Figure 19.3).

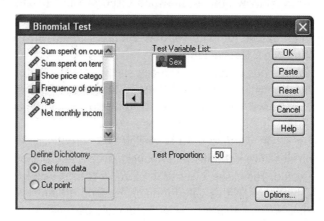

Figure 19.3 The dialogue box for performing a binomial test for the variable Sex.

Besides the overview of the data used (Notes and Active Dataset), the output of the binomial test consists of the test results (see Table 19.3). The table shows the observed frequencies for the two categories: there are 71 women and 79 men. The null hypothesis assumes a probability of 50% ('Test Prop.'). The table shows that the percentage of women does not strongly deviate from this and is 47% (see 'Observed Prop.'). Therefore, the significance level, the p-value, is high, 0.568. This means that, using a critical α of 0.05, we accept the null hypothesis that the probability of male (or female) gender is 50%.

The significance level displayed applies to two-tailed tests. If the alternative hypothesis had assumed a lower probability of interviewing a woman than

Table 19.3   The output of the binomial test

Binomial Test

		Category	N	Observed Prop.	Test Prop.	Asymp. Sig. (2-tailed)
Sex	Group 1	Female	71	.47	.50	.568[a]
	Group 2	Male	79	.53		
	Total		150	1.00		

[a] Based on Z Approximation.

a man, a one-tailed test had to be carried out. In that case you have to divide the displayed significance level by two.

Extensions.
The command for the binomial has three additional options. The test can also be carried out for variables that are not dichotomous and you can change the expected probability. Both options are discussed below. The dialogue box also contains the button Options to request statistics and instruct SPSS how to deal with missing values. This button has been discussed with the chi-square test (see Section 19.1.1).

Non-dichotomous variables – You can specify the two categories under 'Define Dichotomy'. Normally, the binomial test is carried out for dichotomous variables, variables that have only two values. In that case SPSS can automatically decide which two categories are distinguished ('Get from data'). For non-dichotomous variables a cutoff value is used to define two categories. To distinguish tennis players on age into veterans and young players click the option 'Cutpoint' and specify a value. The cases lower than or equal to this value form the first group; the cases higher than this value form the second group.

The expected probability – SPSS by default assumes that the probability of falling into the first category is 50%. By specifying a test proportion you can test a different null hypothesis. Note that, by default, SPSS performs a one-tailed test if you specify a test proportion other than 0.50.

19.3   The Runs test

The Runs test can be used to determine whether the data were collected in random order. Have people been interviewed on a strictly random basis or have groups of men and women been interviewed alternately? The Runs test distinguishes two groups, for example men and women, or high and low expenditure on tennis wear. A run is defined as a sequence of the same value of a variable, preceded by and followed by another value. Naturally, the test is only meaningful if the order of the cases in the data file has some meaning. An obvious meaning is that it is the order in which the respondents were interviewed.

Suppose we have entered the cases in the order in which they were collected and we want to know whether there are any sequence effects with respect to the age of a respondent. The *null hypothesis* H_0 states that the data file contains the observations of the variable Age in random order. The *alternative hypothesis* H_1 states that the order is not random, in which case there are two possibilities. The interviewer may have interviewed groups of people of similar age, or the interviewer has alternately interviewed older and younger respondents. In the first case the number of runs is very small, in the second case it is very large. In this situation we therefore have to carry out a two-tailed test.

You can find the command for the Runs test in the menu as follows:

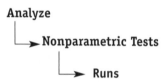

Analyze
    Nonparametric Tests
        Runs

In the next dialogue box you specify the variable(s) for which a Runs test has to be performed. The specified variables have to be numeric. In this example you specify Age as test variable (see Figure 19.4). As you can see in the block under 'Cutpoint', SPSS by default distinguishes two groups based on the median of the variable.

Besides the overview of the data used (Notes and Active Dataset), the output of the Runs test consists of the test results (see Table 19.4). The test value, the median of Age, is 30. There are 70 persons younger than 30 years,

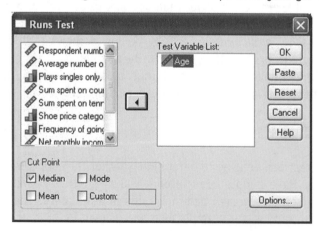

Figure 19.4   The dialogue box for performing a Runs test for the variable Age.

Table 19.4   The output of the Runs test

Runs Test

	Age
Test Value[a]	30
Cases < Test Value	70
Cases >= Test Value	80
Total Cases	150
Number of Runs	81
Z	.878
Asymp. Sig. (2-tailed)	.380

a. Median

while 80 persons are 30 years or over. The number of runs, that is, groups of cases with the same value, is 81. The computed Z-value is 0.878, which corresponds to a two-tailed significance level (p-value) of 0.380. If we use a critical α of 0.05, we will not reject the null hypothesis. In other words, there is no reason to assume that with respect to age the respondents were not interviewed in random order.

Extensions.
The command for the Runs test offers two additional options. You can specify in four different ways how SPSS should distinguish between the two groups (see below). The dialogue box also contains the button Options to request statistics and instruct SPSS how to deal with missing values. This button has been discussed with the chi-square test (see Section 19.1.1).

Specifying the grouping – 'Cut Point' lists four possible cutoff values to define two groups, namely on the basis of the median of the test variable, the mean, the mode or a value that you can specify yourself (Custom).

The first group of cases is always formed by the cases lower than the cut point and the second group by those equal to or higher than the cut point.

19.4   The Kolmogorov–Smirnov test

The Kolmogorov–Smirnov test is used to determine whether the observed distribution matches a given theoretical distribution. Examples of theoretical distributions are a normal, a uniform or a Poisson distribution. Ordinal measurement of the variable is sufficient. Many tests, like the t-test or analysis of variance, assume that the sample is from a normally distributed population. If you have doubts about this, you can use the Kolmogorov–Smirnov test to determine whether the sample data match the normal distribution (or some other theoretical distribution). The Kolmogorov–Smirnov test can also be used to test whether two samples were taken from the same population or from populations with the same distribution (see Section 19.5).

Suppose we want to determine whether the observed values of the expenditure on tennis wear are normally distributed. The *null hypothesis* H_0 states that this is the case, and the *alternative hypothesis* H_1 states that the observed distribution differs from this. The Kolmogorov–Smirnov test in fact compares the observed cumulative relative frequency with that according to the theoretical distribution.

You can find the command for the Kolmogorov–Smirnov test in the menu as follows:

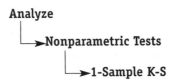

Analyze

  ↳**Nonparametric Tests**

    ↳**1-Sample K-S**

In the next dialogue box you specify the variable(s) for which a Kolmogorov–Smirnov test has to be performed. These variables have to be numeric. In this example we specify TennisWear as test variable (see Figure 19.5). As you can see in the block under 'Test Distribution', SPSS by default tests the observed distribution against the normal distribution.

Besides the overview of the data used (Notes and Active Dataset), the output of the Kolmogorov–Smirnov test consists of the test results (see Table 19.5). As noted in the footnote of the table, SPSS compares the observed distribution with the normal distribution. To determine the cumulative distribution of the normal

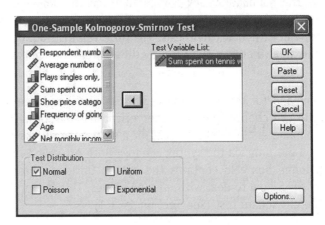

Figure 19.5 The dialogue box for performing a Kolmogorov–Smirnov test for the variable TennisWear.

Table 19.5   The output of the Kolmogorov–Smirnov test

One-Sample Kolmogorov-Smirnov Test

		Sum spent on tennis wear (last year)
N		150
Normal Parameters [a,b]	Mean	393.33
	Std. Deviation	282.526
Most Extreme Differences	Absolute	.123
	Positive	.123
	Negative	-.082
Kolmogorov-Smirnov Z		1.504
Asymp. Sig. (2-tailed)		.022

a. Test distribution is Normal.

b. Calculated from data.

distribution SPSS needs a mean and standard deviation. These parameters are derived from the sample. In other words, the observed distribution is compared with a normal distribution with the sample mean (393.3) and the sample standard deviation (282.5).

The lower part of the table contains the results of the Kolmogorov– Smirnov test. First, SPSS displays the most extreme differences between the normal distribution and the observed cumulative relative frequency. The largest absolute difference is known as the Kolmogorov–Smirnov D. In the final two lines SPSS displays the Kolmogorov–Smirnov Z-value and its two-tailed significance level (the p-value). In this example the significance level is so low (0.022) that we have to reject the null hypothesis. The observed distribution of the expenditure on tennis wear therefore significantly differs from the normal distribution.

Extensions.

The command for the Kolmogorov–Smirnov test has three additional options. First, you can choose from four theoretical distributions. You can also specify which parameters SPSS should use for a distribution; this cannot be done via the menu but only via the syntax window. Both extensions are discussed below. The dialogue box also contains the button Options to request statistics and instruct SPSS how to deal with missing values. This button has been discussed with the chi-square test (see Section 19.1.1).

Theoretical distributions – Under 'Test Distribution' you find the four theoretical distributions against which you can test the observed distribution:

- *Normal distribution*;
- *Uniform distribution* (a distribution where each value has the same probability of occurrence);
- *Poisson distribution*;
- *Exponential distribution*.

Parameters for the distribution – Each distribution has one or more parameters (see below). By default, SPSS derives these parameters from the sample data. However, you can also specify the parameters. This cannot be done via the menu: you will have to use the syntax window. The easiest way is first to prepare the command via the menu. Then you copy the command to the syntax window with Paste. The command contains the name of the distribution in parentheses. The desired parameters come before the closing parenthesis. The parameters have to be separated from the name of the distribution and from each other by commas. You can execute the command by clicking 'Run Current' (the button with the arrow right). For each distribution you can specify the following parameters:

- *Normal distribution*: the mean and the standard deviation, in that order;
- *Uniform distribution*: the minimum and the maximum, in that order;
- *Poisson distribution*: the mean;
- *Exponential distribution*: the mean.

19.5   Tests for two independent groups

In this section we discuss tests that are used to determine whether the averages of two independent samples equal each other. If they are equal, we assume that both samples are from the same population. For instance, you can determine whether the mean age of people who play only singles equals that of the doubles players, and whether, on average, men spend the same amount of money on tennis wear as women. For this purpose SPSS offers the following four tests: Mann–Whitney, Kolmogorov–Smirnov, Moses extreme reactions and the Wald–Wolfowitz runs. In this section we only discuss the first two tests, the Mann–Whitney test (also called Wilcoxon test) in Section 19.5.1 and the Kolmogorov–Smirnov test in 19.5.2.

Comparison with the t-test – The Mann–Whitney test and the Kolmogorov–Smirnov test are non-parametric tests that are often used when the assumptions of the t-test are not met. This applies in particular to the requirement of the t-test that the variable is an interval or ratio variable and the population normally distributed. If the assumptions of the t-test are met, that test is preferred because the t-test is better at detecting actual differences between groups. The reason is that the t-test uses more information, for example the observed values instead of the ranking of the observations.

Mann–Whitney or Kolmogorov–Smirnov? – Both the Mann–Whitney test and the Kolmogorov–Smirnov test are used to determine whether two samples were taken from the same population. The literature shows a slight preference for the Mann–Whitney test for large samples[1] and the Kolmogorov–Smirnov test for very small samples. Another difference is that a two-tailed Kolmogorov–Smirnov test is also sensitive to differences in dispersion and skewness (see Section 19.5.2).

19.5.1 The Mann–Whitney or Wilcoxon test

With the Mann–Whitney test, or the similar Wilcoxon test, you can test whether two independent samples were taken from populations with the same distribution. What this is actually testing is whether the two groups have the same median. The test can answer questions like: do men, on average, spend the same amount of money on tennis wear as women? Do people who bought expensive tennis shoes play equally often as people who bought cheap shoes? The Mann–Whitney test is often used instead of the t-test (see above). For the Mann–Whitney test, ordinal variables are sufficient.

Suppose that we want to determine whether people who play only singles play equally often as people who play only doubles. The *null hypothesis* H_0 then states that the number of times played per month is the same for singles players and doubles players. The *alternative hypothesis* H_1 states that the two groups do not play equally often.

You can find the command for the Mann–Whitney test in the menu as follows:

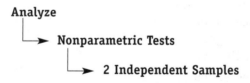

Analyze

  ⮑ **Nonparametric Tests**

    ⮑ **2 Independent Samples**

In the next dialogue box you specify the variable(s) for which a Mann–Whitney test has to be performed, and the grouping. In our example TimesTennis is the test variable and SingleDouble is the grouping variable (see Figure 19.6). Both the test variable and the grouping variable have to be numeric. Where necessary, you can transform a string variable into a numeric variable with Automatic Recode (see Section 9.5).

The grouping mentioned next to SingleDouble is specified with the button Define Groups. Code 1 refers to singles players, code 2 to doubles players.

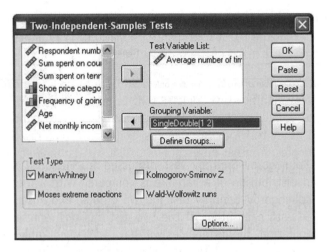

Figure 19.6   The dialogue box for performing a Mann–Whitney test for the variable TimesTennis.

Besides the overview of the data used (Notes and Active Dataset), the output of the Mann–Whitney test consists of rank information and the test results.

In executing the Mann–Whitney test, SPSS first determines the ranking of the cases on the basis of the number of times a person plays. Table 19.6 shows, for each group, the number of cases, the mean rank and the sum of the ranks.

The second part of the output contains the test results, with the Mann–Whitney U (414.5) and the Wilcoxon W (667.5) (see Table 19.7). The W is the sum of the ranks of the smallest group. Because the sample size is larger than 30, the standard normal distribution is used instead of the exact probability. The Z-value of -1.45 corresponds to a two-tailed significance level (p-value) of 0.147. In other words, if we use a critical α of 0.05 we will not reject the null hypothesis. It therefore appears that, although the mean ranking number for the doubles players (37.86) is higher than that of the singles players (30.34), the difference is not so large that we can conclude that the playing frequency of doubles players is significantly higher than that of singles players.

Extensions.
The dialogue box contains the button Options to request statistics and instruct SPSS how to deal with missing values. This button has been discussed with the chi-square test (see Section 19.1.1).

19.5.2 The Kolmogorov–Smirnov test for two groups
The Kolmogorov–Smirnov test for two groups is used to test whether two samples are from the same population. For example, you can determine whether the expenditure on court rental is the same for men as for women. This test is a variant

Table 19.6   The overview of the observed ranking

Ranks

	Plays singles only,	N	Mean Rank	Sum of Ranks
Average number of times played (per month)	Singles only	22	30.34	667.50
	Doubles only	48	37.86	1817.50
	Total	70		

of the Kolmogorov–Smirnov test discussed in Section 19.4. In that test the observed distribution of a variable is compared with a theoretical distribution. In the Kolmogorov–Smirnov test for two groups, two observed distributions are compared with each other. If the two distributions represent samples from the same population, the differences will have to be negligibly small.

Suppose we want to determine whether the expenditure on court rental is the same for men as for women. The *null hypothesis* H_0 then states that there are no differences in the expenditures on court rental between men and women. The *alternative hypothesis* H_1 states that the expenditures of the two groups are different. The Kolmogorov–Smirnov test compares the cumulative relative frequency of the two groups. A *two-tailed test* leads to the rejection of the null hypothesis if the distributions are different. The cause may be differences in mean (central tendency), dispersion or skewness. A *one-tailed test* aims to find out whether the expenditure on court rental of men is significantly higher than that of women (or the other way round). In that case the Kolmogorov–Smirnov test is comparable with the Mann–Whitney test. For both tests, ordinal variables are sufficient.

You can find the command for the Kolmogorov–Smirnov test for two groups in the menu as follows:

Table 19.7   The output of the Mann–Whitney and Wilcoxon test

Test Statistics[a]

	Average number of times played (per month)
Mann-Whitney U	414.500
Wilcoxon W	667.500
Z	-1.451
Asymp. Sig. (2-tailed)	.147

a. Grouping Variable: Plays singles only, doubles only or both

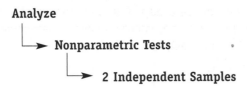

Analyze
 └──➤ **Nonparametric Tests**
         └──➤ **2 Independent Samples**

In the next dialogue box you specify the variable(s) for which a Kolmogorov–Smirnov test has to be performed and the grouping. This is the same dialogue box as for the Mann–Whitney test (see Section 19.5.1). In the block 'Test Type', check 'Kolomogorov-Smirnov Z' (and deselect Mann-Whitney, if you do not wish to perform that test).

The output of the Kolmogorov–Smirnov test for two groups is similar to that of the Kolmogorov–Smirnov test for one group, both in presentation and in interpretation (see Section 19.4, and Table 19.5 in particular).

Extensions.
The dialogue box contains the button Options to request statistics and instruct SPSS how to deal with missing values. This button has been discussed with the chi-square test (see Section 19.1.1).

19.6   Tests for two or more independent groups

Both the Kruskal–Wallis test and the median test are used to determine whether the distributions of two or more independent samples are equal. With these tests you can determine, for example, whether the amounts spent on tennis wear differ between people who play only singles, only doubles, or both. The Kruskal–Wallis test is discussed in Section 19.6.1 and the median test in 19.6.2.

Comparison with analysis of variance – The Kruskal–Wallis test and the median test are non-parametric tests that are often used when the assumptions of analysis of variance are not met. This applies in particular to the requirement of analysis of variance that the variable is an interval or ratio variable and the population normally distributed. If the assumptions of analysis of variance are met, that test is preferred because analysis of variance is better at detecting actual differences between groups. The reason is that analysis of variance uses more information, for example the observed values instead of the ranking of the observations.

Kruskal–Wallis test or median test? – In both tests the observed values are replaced by new values. The Kruskal–Wallis test uses the ranks; the median test is based on whether a case lies above or below the overall median. Because the Kruskal–Wallis test uses more information, it is more powerful than the median test. The median test can be used if the exact values of a number of extreme cases are unknown. In that case it is not possible to determine a ranking as required by the Kruskal–Wallis test, but it is known whether a case lies above or below the median.

19.6.1 The Kruskal–Wallis test

The Kruskal–Wallis test is an extension of the Mann–Whitney test, in the sense that the latter test compares two groups whereas the Kruskal–Wallis test compares two or more groups. It tests whether the different samples were taken from the same population. Just as the Mann–Whitney test is a good alternative for the t-test, the Kruskal–Wallis test forms a good alternative for analysis of variance (see above). For the Kruskal–Wallis test a variable has to be at least ordinal.

Suppose we distinguish three groups of tennis players on the basis of the type of play they practise (only singles, only doubles and both). With the Kruskal–Wallis test we can answer the question whether the three groups spend equal amounts of money on tennis wear. The *null hypothesis* H_0 then states that the median of the amount spent on tennis wear is the same for the three groups. The *alternative hypothesis* H_1 states that the median is not the same for all three groups.

You can find the command for the Kruskal–Wallis test in the menu as follows:

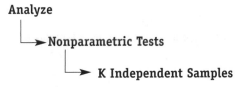

Analyze

  ➤ **Nonparametric Tests**

    ➤ **K Independent Samples**

In the next dialogue box you specify the variable(s) for which a Kruskal–Wallis test has to be performed and the grouping. In this example we specify TennisWear as test variable and SingleDouble as grouping variable. Both the test variable and the grouping variable have to be numeric; if necessary you can transform a string variable into a numeric variable with Automatic Recode (see Section 9.5).

You can specify the grouping with the button Define Range. In the next dialogue box you specify a minimum and a maximum. Figure 19.7 shows the dialogue box after all data have been specified.

Besides the overview of the data used (Notes and Active Dataset), the output of the Kruskal–Wallis test consists of rank information and the test results. Just as for the Mann–Whitney test, the cases are ranked in ascending order and for each group SPSS shows the number of cases and the mean ranks (see Table 19.8).

On the basis of the ranks, SPSS computes the value of the Kruskal–Wallis H. Because the distribution of H is influenced by ties, cases with the same rank,

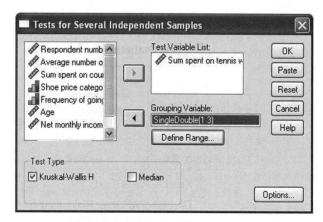

Figure 19.7   The dialogue box for performing a Kruskal–Wallis test for the variable TennisWear.

SPSS controls for this effect. The H statistic approximately follows a chi-square distribution and in the output it is therefore indicated as 'Chi-Square' (see Table 19.9). The degrees of freedom equal the number of groups minus 1, so in this case there are 2.

Table 19.8   The overview of the mean ranks

Ranks

	Plays singles only,	N	Mean Rank
Sum spent on tennis wear (last year)	Singles only	22	74.45
	Doubles only	48	80.64
	Singles and doubles	80	72.71
	Total	150	

The significance level, displayed in the last line of the table, is so high (0.597) that we do not reject the null hypothesis. In other words, we have no reason to assume that the medians of the amounts spent on tennis wear by the three groups differ significantly.

Extensions.
The dialogue box contains the button Options to request statistics and instruct SPSS how to deal with missing values. This button has been discussed with the chi-square test (see Section 19.1.1).

19.6.2 The median test
The median test is used to determine whether two or more independent samples were taken from the same population. The median test assumes that a variable

Table 19.9 The output of the Kruskal–Wallis test

Test Statistics[a,b]

	Sum spent on tennis wear (last year)
Chi-Square	1.031
df	2
Asymp. Sig.	.597

[a.] Kruskal Wallis Test

[b.] Grouping Variable: Plays singles only, doubles only or both

is at least ordinal. For each case it is determined whether it lies above or below the overall median. Next, a chi-square test is carried out with these data.

Suppose we distinguish three groups of tennis players on the basis of the type of play they practise (only singles, only doubles, and both). With the median test we can answer the question whether the respondents in the three groups have the same age. The *null hypothesis* H_0 then states that the median ages in the three groups are the same. The *alternative hypothesis* H_1 states that the medians are not equal for all three groups.

You can find the command for the median test in the menu as follows:

Analyze

 └▸ **Nonparametric Tests**

  └▸ **K Independent Samples**

In the next dialogue box you specify the variable(s) for which a median test has to be performed and the grouping. This is the same dialogue box as for the Kruskal–Wallis test (see Section 19.6.1). In the block 'Test Type', check 'Median' (and deselect Kruskal–Wallis, if you do not want that test).

Besides the overview of the data used (Notes and Active Dataset), the output of the median test consists of a crosstable and the test results. For each category, the crosstable shows how many persons score higher than, or lower than the median (see Table 19.10). For instance, there are nine respondents who play only singles and who are above the median age. In the table of test results (Table 19.11), you see that the median age is 30 years. Therefore, 39 respondents are aged 30 or below and play both singles and doubles.

*Table 19.10   The crosstable with the number of cases above and below
the median for each category*

Frequencies

		Plays singles only, doubles only or both		
		Singles only	Doubles only	Singles and doubles
Age	> Median	9	21	41
	<= Median	13	27	39

Next, a chi-square test is performed on the crosstable. In this case, the computed chi-square equals 1.104. The degrees of freedom equal the number of groups minus 1 (that is, 2). The significance level, displayed in the last line of the table, is so high (0.576) that we may assume that no real differences in median age exist among the three groups distinguished.

Extensions.
You can also use the median test to test whether the medians for the different groups equal a specified value (see below). The dialogue box contains the button Options to request statistics and instruct SPSS how to deal with missing values. This button has been discussed with the chi-square test (see Section 19.1.1).

Testing group medians against a specified value – In the median test, the null hypothesis states that the medians of the different groups are equal. In executing the test, SPSS compares each case with the median of the entire sample.

Table 19.11   The output of the median test

Test Statistics[b]

	Age
N	150
Median	30.00
Chi-Square	1.104[a]
df	2
Asymp. Sig.	.576

a. 0 cells (.0%) have expected frequencies less than 5. The minimum expected cell frequency is 10.4.

b. Grouping Variable: Plays singles only, doubles only or both

Instead of the overall median you can also specify a value. This cannot be done via the menu: you will have to use the syntax window. The easiest way is first to prepare the command via the menu. Then you copy the command to the syntax window with Paste. In the command, immediately following the word Median, you have to specify a value in parentheses. The command can then be executed by clicking 'Run Current' (the button with the arrow right).

19.7   Tests for two related groups

In Section 19.5 we discussed two tests (Mann–Whitney and Kolmogorov–Smirnov) that are used to compare two groups. The assumption then is that the two groups form two independent samples. In this section we discuss non-parametric tests that are used if the two groups are related to each other. This is the case if, for example, you have interviewed couples who play tennis, or if you are dealing with measurements before and after. For this purpose SPSS has the following three tests: the Wilcoxon Signed Ranks test, the sign test and the McNemar test. In this section we discuss the first two tests, the Wilcoxon Signed Ranks test in Section 19.7.1 and the sign test in Section 19.7.2.

Comparison with the paired t-test – The Wilcoxon Signed Ranks test and the sign test are non-parametric tests that are often used when the assumptions of the paired t-test are not met. This applies in particular to the requirements of the t-test that the variable is an interval or ratio variable and that the population is normally distributed. If the assumptions of the paired t-test are met, that test is preferred because the paired t-test is better at detecting actual differences between groups. The reason is that the t-test uses more information, for example the observed values instead of the ranking of the observations.

The Wilcoxon Signed Ranks test or the sign test? – Both the Wilcoxon Signed Ranks test and the sign test determine which of the two elements in a pair scores higher. In addition, the Wilcoxon Signed Ranks test also uses the magnitude of the difference. Does a husband spend a little more on court rental than his wife or is the difference considerable? Where the sign test only includes information about the sign of the difference (positive or negative), the Wilcoxon Signed Ranks test also uses the ranking of the differences. This means that the Wilcoxon Signed Ranks test uses more information than the sign test and is therefore better at detecting actual differences. If, however, you have no information on the magnitude of the difference within a pair, you have to use the sign test.

19.7.1 The Wilcoxon Signed Ranks test
The Wilcoxon Signed Ranks test is used to determine whether two related samples (two variables) have the same median and distribution. The variables have

to be ordinal at least. Suppose that we have asked couples who play tennis about the number of times per month each of them plays. The Wilcoxon Signed Ranks test can then answer the question whether husbands and wives play equally often. The test is often used instead of the paired t-test (see above).

In this example the *null hypothesis* H_0 states that there is no difference between husbands and wives with regard to the number of times per month they play. The *alternative hypothesis* H_1 states that the two groups do not play equally often.

You can find the command for the Wilcoxon Signed Ranks test in the menu as follows:

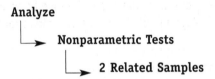

Analyze

⌐➤ **Nonparametric Tests**

⌐➤ **2 Related Samples**

In the next dialogue box you specify which variables form a pair. The variable HusbandTennis represents the number of times the husband plays tennis and WifeTennis indicates how often the wife plays tennis. If you click these variables in the variables window, SPSS includes them in the block 'Current Selections' (at the lower left in the dialogue box). When both variables have been included here, click the button with the arrow right. SPSS then moves the pair of variables to the 'Test Pair(s) List' (see Figure 19.8).

Besides the overview of the data used (Notes and Active Dataset), the output of the Wilcoxon Signed Ranks test consists of an overview of the differences in ranks and the test results. The Wilcoxon Signed Ranks test first determines the

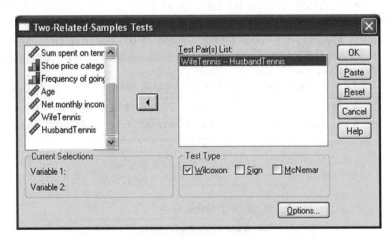

Figure 19.8 The dialogue box for performing a Wilcoxon Signed Ranks test.

difference between each pair and then ranks the absolute differences. Based on these ranks SPSS computes a Z-value. Table 19.12 gives an overview of the differences. For 33 couples the husband plays less often than his wife, while for 84 couples the opposite is true. In the other 33 cases husband and wife responded they played equally often (the ties).

The Wilcoxon Signed Ranks test not only determines who plays more often, but also considers the magnitude of the difference between husband and wife. This is reflected in the ranks of the differences. The mean of these numbers is 36.14 if the wife plays more often than her husband. In the opposite situation, husbands who play more often than their wives, the mean rank is 67.98.

In other words, it turns out that not only do husbands play more often than their wives (84 against 33 couples), but also that the difference between husband and wife is larger if the husband plays more often (see the mean rank of 67.98 versus 36.14).

Table 19.12   The overview of the differences in rank

Ranks

		N	Mean Rank	Sum of Ranks
HusbandTennis - WifeTennis	Negative Ranks	33[a]	36.14	1192.50
	Positive Ranks	84[b]	67.98	5710.50
	Ties	33[c]		
	Total	150		

[a.] HusbandTennis < WifeTennis

[b.] HusbandTennis > WifeTennis

[c.] HusbandTennis = WifeTennis

Table 19.13 contains the result of the Wilcoxon Signed Ranks test. In this computation, SPSS controls for ties, cases with the same rank. The Z-value is rather high, -6.233, which is not surprising after the above conclusion. The two-tailed significance level (the p-value) is so low that it is clear that we have to reject the null hypothesis that husbands and wives play equally often.

Table 19.13   The output of the Wilcoxon Signed Ranks test

Test Statistics[b]

	Husband Tennis - WifeTennis
Z	-6.233[a]
Asymp. Sig. (2-tailed)	.000

[a.] Based on negative ranks.

[b.] Wilcoxon Signed Ranks Test

Extensions.
The dialogue box contains the button Options to request statistics and instruct SPSS how to deal with missing values. This button has been discussed with the chi-square test (see Section 19.1.1).

19.7.2 The sign test

The sign test is used to determine whether two related samples (two variables) have the same median. The variables have to be at least ordinal.

To illustrate the sign test we use the same example as in Section 19.7.1. We have asked couples about the number of times per month that each of them plays and we use the sign test to find the answer to the question whether husbands and wives play equally often. In this example, the *null hypothesis* H_0 states that there is no difference between husbands and wives with regard to the median of the number of times per month they play. The *alternative hypothesis* H_1 states that the two groups do not play equally often.

Another application of the sign test is to compare the median in the sample with some other value (e.g. the median found in a national survey). Before you carry out the sign test, you first have to compute a new variable whose value for all cases equals the value against which the median in the sample has to be tested (with Compute; see Section 9.1).

You can find the command for the sign test in the menu as follows:

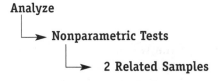

Analyze
└──▶ **Nonparametric Tests**
     └──▶ **2 Related Samples**

In the next dialogue box you specify which variables form a pair (in this case HusbandTennis and WifeTennis). This is the same dialogue box as the one used for the Wilcoxon Signed Ranks test (see Section 19.7.1). In the block 'Test Type' check 'Sign' (and deselect Wilcoxon, if you do not want that test).

Besides the overview of the data used (Notes and Active Dataset), the output of the sign test consists of a frequency table of the differences and the test results. The frequency table of the differences between husbands and wives contains the same information as that of the Wilcoxon Signed Ranks test. In 33 couples the husband plays less often than the wife, the opposite applies to 84 couples and in another 33 couples both play equally often (see Table 19.14).

Table 19.15 contains the result of the sign test. Owing to the large number of cases, SPSS computes the Z-value (for 25 differences or less, the binomial

Table 19.14 The frequency table of the differences between husbands and wives

Frequencies

		N
HusbandTennis	Negative Differences [a]	33
- WifeTennis	Positive Differences [b]	84
	Ties [c]	33
	Total	150

[a]. HusbandTennis < WifeTennis

[b]. HusbandTennis > WifeTennis

[c]. HusbandTennis = WifeTennis

Table 19.15 The output of the sign test

Test Statistics[a]

	Husband Tennis - WifeTennis
Z	-4.623
Asymp. Sig. (2-tailed)	.000

[a]. Sign Test

distribution is used). The Z-value of −4.623 has a two-tailed significance level (p-value) of 0.000. This means that we reject the null hypothesis of equal medians for the two groups (husbands and wives).

Extensions. The dialogue box contains the button Options to request statistics and instruct SPSS how to deal with missing values. This button has been discussed with the chi-square test (see Section 19.1.1).

19.8 Tests for two or more related groups

The Wilcoxon Signed Ranks test and sign test discussed in Section 19.7 are used if two related groups are compared. Sometimes we have more than two groups, for example when we ask people about their opinions on several products. If we use an ordinal scale, for example a five-point scale, the Friedman test is appropriate for determining whether the median score is the same for all products. If the variable is dichotomous, for example if we ask people whether they know a product or brand, Cochran's Q test can be used. Finally, Kendall's W measures the extent of agreement among a number of respondents. In this section we discuss only the Friedman test.

19.8.1 The Friedman test

The Friedman test is used to determine whether the medians of a number of related samples equal each other. Suppose we have asked people to rate four tennis halls. How do they rate the playing characteristics of the court? How are the changing rooms? Each respondent assigns a mark between 1 and 10 to each tennis hall. We can then use the Friedman test to determine whether the median score is the same for each tennis hall. The *null hypothesis* H_0 states that the medians for all halls are equal, while the *alternative hypothesis* H_1 states that this is not the case.

You can find the command for the Friedman test in the menu as follows:

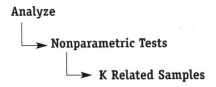

Analyze

⌞➤ **Nonparametric Tests**

⌞➤ **K Related Samples**

In the next dialogue box you specify which variables have to be tested. In this case Hall1, Hall2, Hall3 and Hall4 are specified as test variables (see Figure 19.9).

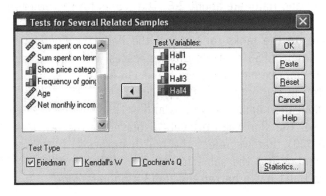

Figure 19.9   The dialogue box for performing a Friedman test.

Besides the overview of the data used ('Notes'), the output of the Friedman test consists of an overview of the mean ranks and the test results. For each respondent the Friedman test determines the ranking of the four halls and then computes the sum of the ranks for each hall. The first part of the output of the Friedman test is an overview of the mean ranks of the tennis halls (see Table 19.16). If the medians are equal for all four halls, the mean rank for each hall equals 2.5 (because the ranks run from 1 to 4). It turns out that, indeed, the means

Table 19.16   The overview of the mean rank for each tennis hall

Ranks

	Mean Rank
Hall1	2.86
Hall2	2.52
Hall3	2.13
Hall4	2.50

Table 19.17   The output of the Friedman test

Test Statistics[a]

N	150
Chi-Square	27.560
df	3
Asymp. Sig.	.000

a. Friedman Test

for Hall2 and Hall4 are about 2.5. The scores for the other two halls are clearly higher (Hall1: 2.86) and lower (Hall3: 2.13).

Based on the ranks for each of the halls the Friedman statistic F is computed, where SPSS controls for ties, cases with the same rank. The Friedman statistic approximately matches the chi-square distribution and is therefore indicated in the output as 'Chi-Square' (see Table 19.17). The degrees of freedom equal the number of groups minus 1, so there are 3 degrees of freedom in this case. The significance level, displayed in the last line of the table, is so low (0.000) that we reject the null hypothesis. In other words, the median judgement is not the same for all four halls. In particular, it seems that on average Hall1 has a better and Hall3 a poorer score.

Extensions.
The dialogue box contains the button Statistics to request statistics. These statistics are the same as those discussed with the chi-square test in Section 19.1.1.

Note

1 S. Siegel and N.J. Castellan Jr., *Nonparametric Statistics*, McGraw-Hill, 1988, p. 151.

20   Customising SPSS

In many instances SPSS applies default settings, perhaps without your being aware of it. With most analyses you can use buttons like Options and Statistics to diverge from SPSS's default settings. In many other situations SPSS also applies default settings that can be changed. In this chapter we deal with the features that enable you to customise the package.

It is often practical just to start off using the default settings. If, after some time, you notice that you are repeating certain operations quite often (like changing the number of decimals, for example), we recommend that you consider whether you can avoid this by changing a default setting. Changing default settings used to be rather difficult, but in the most recent versions of SPSS it is straightforward. As a result, there is no reason to postpone customising default settings until it saves you a lot of time. If you can gain from it, even in a session of a few hours, it is certainly worthwhile.

This chapter divides the various ways of customising default settings into three groups. Section 20.1 discusses the wide range of options for customising the operations of SPSS with *Edit > Options*. Customising the toolbars is the topic of Section 20.2 and changing the menus of Section 20.3.

This chapter does not pretend to be comprehensive. We want to demonstrate the options offered by SPSS for customising the software. In specific situations, you can use this chapter to locate quickly where in SPSS you can find the option to change a default setting.

20.1   Changing the functions of SPSS

You can change default settings that influence the operations of SPSS by choosing in the menu:

The next dialogue box has a number of tabs in which you can change the values of a large number of default settings (see Figure 20.1). Below we briefly discuss the following tabs:

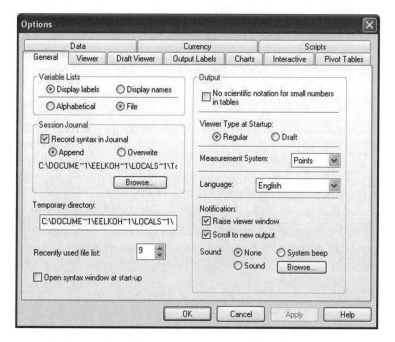

Figure 20.1   The dialogue box for changing the default settings of SPSS.

- *General*: settings like the measurement unit and the way variables are presented in dialogue boxes;
- *Viewer*: how the various output elements (objects) are shown;
- *Output Labels*: how variables and values are displayed in the output (as descriptions, or names and codes);
- *Charts*: e.g. the use of templates, colours, borders and grid lines in charts;
- *Pivot Tables*: the default layout of tables;
- *Data*: e.g. the number of decimals for new variables and date variables;
- *Currency*: specifying currency formats.

General. In the tab General can you change the following properties, among other things:

- the display of *variables in dialogue boxes*: as labels or as names, and in alphabetical order or in the order in which they occur in the data file;
- the use of the *journal file,* which keeps track of all executed SPSS commands;
- the *number of recently used files* displayed in the File menu;
- whether a *syntax window* should automatically be opened upon starting up SPSS;

- the *measurement system* used by SPSS: points, inches or centimetres;
- the *language*: SPSS can use several languages in the output;
- *output notification*: among other things, whether the Viewer should automatically be displayed with the most recent output.

Output window – Viewer. In the tab Viewer you can, among other things, change the following properties:

- the *initial display of output elements*: for each element (log, warning, Notes, title, table, chart and text) you can specify whether it should be shown or hidden in the output, and its justification (left, centred, right);
- *title properties*: font, font size and style (bold, italics, and so on);
- *text output page*: width (in number of characters) and length (in number of lines);
- *text output properties*: font, font size and style (bold, italics, and so on).

Output Labels. In the tab Output Labels you can specify for variables and values whether SPSS should display labels or names (codes) in the output. You can also specify that SPSS should show both; in other words, both the code and the value label, and both the variable name and the variable label.

Charts. In the tab Charts you can, among other things, change the following properties:

- *templates for charts*: a useful option when you often want to create charts with the same layout;
- *font* for new charts;
- *colours*: if you use coloured charts, select the option 'Cycle through colors only', if you always print the charts in black and white, we recommend 'Cycle through patterns only'. In the latter case, SPSS uses different fill patterns and marker symbols instead of colours to distinguish variables or groups;
- *ratio width to height of chart* ('Chart Aspect Ratio'). You can specify an aspect ratio for width relative to height (between 0.1 and 10; specify 1 for square charts);
- a *frame*: a box surrounding only the chart itself (Inner frame) and/or surrounding the entire chart including descriptions and titles (Outer frame);
- *grid lines*: a grid line is a horizontal or vertical line in the chart that makes it easier to read the values on the vertical or the horizontal axis. Horizontal grid lines are added with 'Scale axis', vertical grid lines with 'Category axis'.

Pivot Tables. In the tab you can specify, among other things, the default 'Table Look' (see also Section 6.7) and the table editing mode, which can vary from editing all tables in the Viewer to each table in a separate window.

Display and calculation of variables – Data. In the tab Data you can change the following properties:

- *when calculations are performed*: without delay ('immediately') or only when the variables are needed in an analysis ('before used'). Postponing calculating can save time in situations where a number of computations have to be performed on a very large number of cases;
- display format: number of *positions* (width) and number of *decimals* for new numeric variables;
- *date variables*: how SPSS should deal with two-digit year data.

Currency. In the tab Currency you can create five different currency display formats (from CCA to CCE). For each format you can specify a prefix (for example the dollar, pound or euro sign) and a suffix. This can be done both for all values as well as for negative values. You can also specify a decimal sign (period or comma).

20.2   Customising the toolbar

Customising the toolbar is a very useful option if you use certain SPSS commands often. Although the most recently executed analyses can be recalled with Dialog Recall, you can speed up work with SPSS still further by including a customised button in the toolbar for those commands that you use very often.

You can customise the toolbar by selecting from the menu:

View

└──▶ **Toolbars**

The next dialogue box is displayed in Figure 20.2. In this dialogue box you can specify which toolbar is displayed in which SPSS window (see under 'Document type'). You can create customised toolbars with the button New Toolbar (see below). In the example of Figure 20.2 a new toolbar with the name 'My toolbar' has been made. Toolbars can be deleted with Delete and changed with Customize.

Creating a new toolbar. After you have clicked New Toolbar, a dialogue box appears in which you specify the name of the new toolbar and the SPSS windows

Figure 20.2   The dialogue box for changing the toolbar (View > Toolbars).

in which the toolbar will be used (e.g. the Data Editor, the Viewer and the Syntax Editor). You can specify the content of the toolbar by clicking Customize (see below).

Changing the toolbar. With Customize you can specify the content of the toolbar. You can add new buttons, change button positions and remove buttons.

New buttons are added as follows: the dialogue box contains all SPSS menus and the corresponding commands. An empty space between buttons is called 'Separator'. In front of each command you find an icon that you can drag to the toolbar (in the lower half of the dialogue box). You can also create customised commands with New Tool. You can *remove buttons* by dragging them out of the toolbar. You can change the *order of the buttons* by dragging them within the toolbar.

With Edit Tool you can create customised icons, with Properties you specify the windows for which a toolbar will be used and with Clear Toolbar you remove all buttons from the toolbar.

20.3   Changing the menus

Changing the menus is useful when you often use the same SPSS commands that are located in different menus, or commands that require selections from multiple menu levels. Note that it is often easier to create buttons for this purpose.

You can change the menus by selecting from the menu:

Utilities

Menu Editor

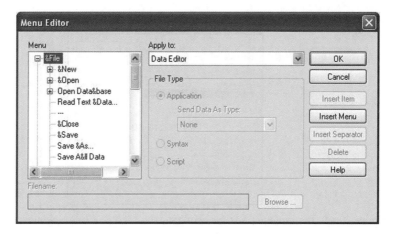

Figure 20.3   The dialogue box for changing the menus (Utilities > Menu Editor).

The next dialogue box is displayed in Figure 20.3. In this dialogue box you can specify for each menu which commands should be included and in what order. As you can see, the menus are displayed in the form of a hierarchy, where the highest level contains the commands found in the menu line on the screen, the next lower level the commands listed in the various menus, and the level below that the commands from the submenus. The & symbol precedes the underscored letter that you can use to select the command with one keystroke.

Under 'Apply to' you can specify the SPSS window in which the modified menu will be used (e.g. the Data Editor or the Viewer). Use Insert Menu to add a new menu at the highest level, Insert Item to add elements at lower levels and Insert Separator to add a separating line. With Delete you can remove a menu or a menu item.

Index